First World War
and Army of Occupation
War Diary
France, Belgium and Germany

34 DIVISION
103 Infantry Brigade
Northumberland Fusiliers
9th and 24th Battalion
4 January 1916 - 31 July 1917

WO95/2466/2

The Naval & Military Press Ltd
www.nmarchive.com
Published in association with The National Archives

Published by

The Naval & Military Press Ltd

Unit 10 Ridgewood Industrial Park,

Uckfield, East Sussex,

TN22 5QE England

Tel: +44 (0) 1825 749494

www.naval-military-press.com

www.nmarchive.com

This diary has been reprinted in facsimile from the original. Any imperfections are inevitably reproduced and the quality may fall short of modern type and cartographic standards.

© **Crown Copyright**
Images reproduced by permission of The National Archives, London, England, 2015.

Contents

Document type	Place/Title	Date From	Date To
Heading	WO95/2466/3 9 Bn Northumberland Fusiliers 1917 Aug-1918 May Catalogue Saps April		
War Diary	Camp	01/08/1917	03/08/1917
War Diary	Billets	04/08/1917	10/08/1917
War Diary	Camp	11/08/1917	15/08/1917
War Diary	Trenches	16/08/1917	21/08/1917
War Diary	Bouvincourt	22/08/1917	26/08/1917
War Diary	Trenches	27/08/1917	31/08/1917
Miscellaneous	To Officer C/O R.I.S. 3G	31/08/1917	31/08/1917
Operation(al) Order(s)	Relief Orders No. 1	28/08/1917	28/08/1917
Heading	9th Bn Northd Fusiliers War Diary Volume XXI September 1917 Vol 23		
War Diary	Trenches	01/09/1917	01/09/1917
War Diary	Reserve	02/09/1917	04/09/1917
War Diary	Trenches	05/09/1917	17/09/1917
War Diary	Billets	18/09/1917	24/09/1917
War Diary	Trenches	25/09/1917	28/09/1917
War Diary	Billets	29/09/1917	30/09/1917
Miscellaneous	To O i/c R.F.S.B. Base	11/09/1917	11/09/1917
Miscellaneous	To O i/c R.F.S.B Base	13/09/1917	13/09/1917
Miscellaneous	Relief Orders No. 2 9th Bn. Northumberland Fusiliers	01/09/1917	01/09/1917
Operation(al) Order(s)	Relief Order No. 4		
Heading	Casualties 9th (Northd Hussars) Bn The Northd Fus Appendix "C"		
Miscellaneous	To O i/c. R.F.S.B Base	16/09/1917	16/09/1917
Miscellaneous	To Officer i/c Regular Infantry Section 3S	17/09/1917	17/09/1917
Miscellaneous	To O i/c. R.F.S.B.	09/09/1917	09/09/1917
Miscellaneous	Appendices To War Diary For December 1917		
War Diary	Billets	01/10/1917	13/10/1917
War Diary	Trenches	14/10/1917	16/10/1917
War Diary	Billets	17/10/1917	31/10/1917
Miscellaneous	To O i/c R.F.S.B. Base	01/10/1917	01/10/1917
Miscellaneous	Special Order of The Day By Field Marshal Sir Douglas Haig	19/10/1917	19/10/1917
Heading	9th Bn Northd Fusiliers. War Diary Volume XXIII November 1917		
Heading	War Diary 9th (Northd Hussars) Bn. Northumberland Fusiliers November 1917		
War Diary	Trenches	01/11/1917	12/11/1917
War Diary	Billets	13/11/1917	17/11/1917
War Diary	Camp	18/11/1917	24/11/1917
War Diary	Trenches	24/11/1917	30/11/1917
Map	Sketch Map Showing Posts in Trench System Held By.		
Miscellaneous	Heninel Trench Map		
Heading	9th. Bn Northd Fus War Diary Nov. 1917 Appendix-B		
Operation(al) Order(s)	Operation Order No. 1 Appendix D	23/11/1917	23/11/1917
Miscellaneous	War Diary		
Map	Guemappe		
Heading	9th (N.H) Bn Northd Fusiliers War Diary Nov. 1917 Appendix E2		

Miscellaneous	War Diary Nov 1917 Pursuit Scheme Appendix E	20/11/1917	20/11/1917
Map	Guemappe		
Miscellaneous	Guemappe		
Operation(al) Order(s)	Operation Order No. 2 Appendix G	29/11/1917	29/11/1917
Map	Cambrai		
Map			
Heading	War Diary 9th Bn Northd Fus. Appendix. F.		
Heading	War Diary 9th Bn Northd Fus. Appendix F		
Heading	9th Bn Northd Fusiliers. War Diary Volume XXIV December 1917 Vol 28		
War Diary	Trenches	01/12/1917	07/12/1917
War Diary	Camp.	08/12/1917	17/12/1917
War Diary	Camp & Trenches	18/12/1917	18/12/1917
War Diary	Trenches	19/12/1917	22/12/1917
War Diary	Billets	23/12/1917	25/12/1917
War Diary	Billets & Trenches	26/12/1917	26/12/1917
War Diary	Trenches	27/12/1917	30/12/1917
War Diary	Camp	31/12/1917	31/12/1917
Map	Appendix A		
Operation(al) Order(s)	Operation Order No. 3	02/12/1917	02/12/1917
Operation(al) Order(s)	Operation Order 1	10/12/1917	10/12/1917
Miscellaneous	War Diary		
Operation(al) Order(s)	Operation Order No 2	11/12/1917	11/12/1917
Miscellaneous	War Diary		
Operation(al) Order(s)	9th Northumberland Hussars Battn Northumberland Fusiliers Operation Orders No 6	13/12/1917	13/12/1917
Miscellaneous	War Diary		
Operation(al) Order(s)	Operation Order No. 7. 9th. (Northumberland Hussars) Battn. Northumberland Fusiliers.	17/12/1917	17/12/1917
Operation(al) Order(s)	Operation Orders No. 8 9th (Northd Hussars.) Bttn Northumberland Fusiliers.	21/12/1917	21/12/1917
Operation(al) Order(s)	Operation Orders No. 9 9th (Northd Hussars) Battn. Northumberland Fusiliers.	25/12/1917	25/12/1917
Operation(al) Order(s)	Operation Orders No. 10 9th (Northd Hussars) Battn Northumberland Fus.	29/12/1917	29/12/1917
Operation(al) Order(s)	9th (N.H) Bn Northd Fusiliers Operation Order No. 4	06/12/1917	06/12/1917
Operation(al) Order(s)	Operation Order No. 5	06/12/1917	06/12/1917
Operation(al) Order(s)	26th. (S) Bn. Northumberland Fusiliers. Operation Order No. 116	03/12/1917	03/12/1917
Operation(al) Order(s)	103rd Infantry Brigade. Operation Order No. 159	03/12/1917	03/12/1917
Heading	War Diary 9th (Northd Hussars) Battalion Northd Fusiliers. January 1918 Vol 29		
War Diary	Camp	01/01/1918	02/01/1918
War Diary	Camp & Trenches	03/01/1918	03/01/1918
War Diary	Trenches	04/01/1918	07/01/1918
War Diary	Billets	08/01/1918	10/01/1918
War Diary	Trenches	11/01/1918	15/01/1918
War Diary	Camp	16/01/1918	19/01/1918
War Diary	Trenches	20/01/1918	23/01/1918
War Diary	Billets	24/01/1918	25/01/1918
War Diary	Camp	26/01/1918	31/01/1918
Miscellaneous			
Miscellaneous	Appendices To War Diary For January 1918		
Map	A		
Operation(al) Order(s)	Operation Orders No. 11 9th (Northd Hussars) Battn Northumberland Fusiliers	02/01/1918	02/01/1918

Miscellaneous	Special Order of The Day By Field-Marshal Sir Douglas Haig	01/01/1918	01/01/1918
Miscellaneous	Special Order of The Day by Major General G.L. Nicholson, C.N.G., Commanding, 34th Division.	01/01/1918	01/01/1918
Miscellaneous	War Diary		
Miscellaneous			
Miscellaneous	103B/3/228.G.	17/01/1918	17/01/1918
Miscellaneous	Special Order of The Day By Field-Marshal Sir Douglas Haig	05/01/1918	05/01/1918
Operation(al) Order(s)	Operation Orders No. 12 9th (Northumberland Hussars) Battn Northumberland Fus.	06/01/1918	06/01/1918
Operation(al) Order(s)	Operation Orders No 13 9th (Northumberland Hussars) Bn. Northumberland Fusiliers.	10/01/1918	10/01/1918
Operation(al) Order(s)	Operation Orders No. 14 9th (Northumberland Hussars) Battn Northumberland Fusiliers.	14/01/1918	14/01/1918
Operation(al) Order(s)	Operation Orders No 15. 9th (Northumberland Hussars) Bn. Northumberland Fusiliers.	18/01/1918	18/01/1918
Operation(al) Order(s)	Operation Orders No 16. 9th (Northumberland Hussars) Bn. Northumberland Fusiliers.	22/01/1918	22/01/1918
Miscellaneous	War Diary		
Operation(al) Order(s)	Operation Orders No 17. 9th (Northumberland Hussars) Bn. Northumberland Fusiliers.	24/01/1918	24/01/1918
Miscellaneous	Special Order of The Day By Field-Marshal Sir Douglas Haig	30/01/1918	30/01/1918
Operation(al) Order(s)	Operation Orders No 18. 9th (Northumberland Hussars) Battn. Northumberland Fusiliers.		
Miscellaneous	War Diary		
Operation(al) Order(s)	Operation Orders No 17	26/02/1918	26/02/1918
Miscellaneous	War Diary		
Heading	War Diary February 1918. 9th (N.H) Bn. Northumberland Fusiliers Vol 30		
War Diary	Camp	01/02/1918	09/02/1918
War Diary	Bn Hdqrs C.G Coys of Buneville A & B Cop Transt Monts. En. Ternois	10/02/1918	26/02/1918
War Diary	Bn Hdqrs C.G Coys of Buneville A & B Cop Transt Monts. En. Ternois to Barly	27/02/1918	27/02/1918
War Diary	Barly No 2 Camp Blairville	28/02/1918	28/02/1918
Miscellaneous			
Operation(al) Order(s)	Movement Order No 1 9th (Northd Hussars) Battn Northumberland Fusiliers.	07/02/1918	07/02/1918
Miscellaneous	War Diary		
Operation(al) Order(s)	Movement Order No. 2. 9th (Northd Hussars) Battn. Northumberland Fusiliers	08/02/1918	08/02/1918
Miscellaneous	War Diary		
Operation(al) Order(s)	Operation Orders No 17. 9th (Northumberland Hussars) Battn. Northumberland Fusiliers.	26/02/1918	26/02/1918
Miscellaneous			
Operation(al) Order(s)	Operation Order No 17. 9th (Northumberland Hussars) Battn. Northumberland Fusiliers.		
Map	Roclincourt		
Miscellaneous			
Miscellaneous	Glossary		
Miscellaneous	9th (N.H) Bn. Northumberland Fusiliers. War Diary March 1918 Appendices Attached		
War Diary	Blairville	01/03/1918	07/03/1918
War Diary	In The Line	07/03/1918	12/03/1918

War Diary	Trenches	12/03/1918	31/03/1918
Miscellaneous			
Heading	34th Division. 103rd Infantry Brigade. War Diary 9th Battalion The Northumberland Fusiliers March 1918 Report on Operations 21st-22nd March 1918 attached		
Operation(al) Order(s)	Operation Orders. No. 19 9th (Northumberland Hussars) Battn. Northumberland Fusiliers.	02/03/1918	02/03/1918
Miscellaneous	Retained		
Miscellaneous	9th. (Northd Hussars) Battn Northd Fusiliers Report on Operations Round St. Leger March 21st. And 22nd. 1918 Appendix II	21/03/1918	21/03/1918
Miscellaneous	B. 26 C 8.3 Shown Presumally & rzad T 26.C.8.3		
Miscellaneous		02/04/1918	02/04/1918
Miscellaneous	Instructions For Recounaisaner Parties Appendix A	03/03/1918	03/03/1918
Map	Appendix C1		
Heading	9th. Bn Northd Fus War Diary March 1918 Appendices C1 C2 C3 Sketch Maps		
Diagram etc	Appendix C2		
Diagram etc	Appendix C3		
Heading	Appendix "D" precedes war Diary.		
Miscellaneous	34th Div. No. A/222 Appendix E/F/G	29/03/1918	29/03/1918
Miscellaneous	Special Order Of The Day by Major General C.L. Nicholson, C.B., C.M.G., Commanding, 34th Division. Appendix F	03/04/1918	03/04/1918
Miscellaneous	Special Order of The Day by Lt Col. 9th (NH) Battn. Northd Fusiliers Appendix G	05/04/1918	05/04/1918
Operation(al) Order(s)	103rd Infantry Brigade Order No. 187	10/03/1918	10/03/1918
Operation(al) Order(s)	103rd Infantry Brigade Order No. 188	18/03/1918	18/03/1918
Miscellaneous	To accompany 103rd Infantry Brigade Order No. 188. Table "A"		
Miscellaneous	March Table to accompany O.O. 190		
Miscellaneous	March Table To accompany 103rd Inf Brigades O. Order 191		
Miscellaneous	March Table To accompany O. O 192		
Miscellaneous	Special Order of The Day By Field-Marshal Sir Douglas Haig Appendix H	23/03/1918	23/03/1918
Miscellaneous	Special Order of The Day By Field-Marshal Sir Douglas Haig	23/03/1918	23/03/1918
Miscellaneous	Special Order of The Day By Field-Marshal Sir Douglas Haig	24/03/1918	24/03/1918
Miscellaneous	Special Order of The Day By Field-Marshal Sir Douglas Haig	25/03/1918	25/03/1918
Miscellaneous	Special Order of The Day By Field-Marshal Sir Douglas Haig	27/03/1918	27/03/1918
Miscellaneous	Special Order of The Day By Field-Marshal Sir Douglas Haig	28/03/1918	28/03/1918
Miscellaneous	Special Order of The Day By Field-Marshal Sir Douglas Haig	29/03/1918	29/03/1918
Miscellaneous	Special Order of The Day By Field-Marshal Sir Douglas Haig	30/03/1918	30/03/1918
Miscellaneous	Special Order of The Day By Field-Marshal Sir Douglas Haig	31/03/1918	31/03/1918
Operation(al) Order(s)	Operation Orders No 20 9th (Northumberland Hussars) Bn Northumberland Fusiliers.	06/03/1918	06/03/1918
Operation(al) Order(s)	Operation Orders No 21 9th (Northumberland Hussars) Battn. Northumberland Fusiliers.	19/03/1918	19/03/1918

Type	Description	Date From	Date To
Miscellaneous	War Diary		
Operation(al) Order(s)	Operation Orders No 22. 9th (Northumberland Hussars) Battn Northumberland Fusiliers.		
Miscellaneous	War Diary		
Operation(al) Order(s)	Operation Orders No 22	18/03/1918	18/03/1918
Operation(al) Order(s)	Operation Order No. 23		
Operation(al) Order(s)	Operation Orders No 24. 9th (Northumberland Hussars) Bn. Northumberland Fusiliers.	26/03/1918	26/03/1918
Operation(al) Order(s)	Movement Order No 25		
Operation(al) Order(s)	Operation Order No 25A		
Miscellaneous	Memorandum.	29/03/1918	29/03/1918
Map	British Trenches revised from information received to 17.2.18		
Map			
Heading	9th Bn Northd Fus War Diary March 1918. Appendix B		
Operation(al) Order(s)	Operation Orders No 26 9th (Northumberland Hussars) Battn Northumberland Fusiliers	30/03/1918	30/03/1918
Miscellaneous	War Diary		
Operation(al) Order(s)	Operation Orders No 27 9th (Northumberland Hussars) Battn. Northumberland Fusiliers.	31/03/1918	31/03/1918
Miscellaneous	War Diary		
Miscellaneous	Battle of The Somme. 1918. Attack on Third Army, March 21st, 1918. Notes by Lt. Col. W.A. Vignoles, D.S.O.		
Miscellaneous	Battle of The Somme. 1918. Attack on Third Army, March 21st. 1918	21/03/1918	21/03/1918
Miscellaneous	Fighting on March 22nd. 1918	22/03/1918	22/03/1918
Miscellaneous	Marginal Notes by Lt.-Col. W.A. Vignoles. Third Army Chapters	21/03/1918	21/03/1918
Miscellaneous	Chapter W.A.V./4 (continued) Section II The Battle of March 21st & 22nd 1918. St Leger.	21/03/1918	21/03/1918
Miscellaneous	To O i/c R.F.S.B Base	10/09/1917	10/09/1917
Map	Enemys Attack		
Heading	103rd Brigade. 34th Division. War Diary 9th Battalion Northumberland Fusiliers April 1918		
War Diary	In Trenches Near Armentieres	01/04/1918	08/04/1918
War Diary	Trenches Armentieres	09/04/1918	21/04/1918
War Diary	Boeschepe	21/04/1918	21/04/1918
War Diary	St Jan Ter Biezen	22/04/1918	26/04/1918
War Diary	Brandhoek Line	27/04/1918	27/04/1918
War Diary	St Jan Ter Biezen	28/04/1918	29/04/1918
War Diary	Oost Cappel	30/04/1918	30/04/1918
Miscellaneous	9th Bn. Northumberland. Fusiliers	03/05/1918	03/05/1918
Miscellaneous	Report On The Fighting in Which The 9th Bn Northd Fus. Appendix A	30/04/1918	30/04/1918
Miscellaneous	103rd Inf. Bde. & c. Appendix G	01/05/1918	01/05/1918
Miscellaneous	Special Order of The Day by Major General C.L. Nicholson, C.B., C.M.G., Commanding 34th Division.	22/04/1918	22/04/1918
Miscellaneous	34th Div. No. A/222	22/04/1918	22/04/1918
Miscellaneous	Extract From "The Nation"-27th April 1918.	27/04/1918	27/04/1918
Miscellaneous	Special Order Of The Day By Field-Marshal Sir Douglas Haig	30/04/1918	30/04/1918
Operation(al) Order(s)	Operation Orders No 27 Appendix H	31/03/1918	31/03/1918
Miscellaneous	Retained		
Operation(al) Order(s)	Operation Orders No 28 9th (Northd Hussars) Battn Northumberland Fusiliers	06/04/1918	06/04/1918

Miscellaneous	War Diary		
Miscellaneous	Operation Orders	11/04/1918	11/04/1918
Miscellaneous	OC. C.D.C. 1	16/04/1918	16/04/1918
Miscellaneous	Operation Orders. 9th (N.H.) N.F		
Operation(al) Order(s)	Operation Order No 30 9th (N.H.) Battn Northumberland Fusiliers.	25/04/1918	25/04/1918
Operation(al) Order(s)	Operation Order No 31 9th (N.H.) Bn Northumberland Fusiliers.		
Operation(al) Order(s)	Operation Order 32	27/04/1918	27/04/1918
Operation(al) Order(s)	Operation Order No 32. 9th (Northd Hussars) Bn Northumberland Fusiliers.		
Miscellaneous	103rd 34th Brigade. Division Corps.	02/04/1918	02/04/1918
Miscellaneous	103rd 34th Brigade. Division. April 2nd 1918	02/04/1918	02/04/1918
Miscellaneous	103rd Brigade. 34th Division. Corps	02/04/1918	02/04/1918
Miscellaneous	War Diary Appendix "C" May 1918	02/04/1918	02/04/1918
Heading	9th (Northd Hussars) Bn Northd. Fusiliers. War Diary May 1918 Appendices Vol 33		
Heading	34th Division. 103rd Infantry Brigade. Maps To Accompany War Diary 9th Battalion Northumberland Fusiliers April 1918		
Map	Map. A.		
Heading	9th Northd Fus. War Diary May 1918 Appendix A		
Heading	War Diary 9th Bn Northd Fus. April 1918 Appendices B.C.D.E.F Maps Cover No 3		
Map	Bois Grenier		
Miscellaneous	Glossary.		
Map	Belgium And Part Of France		
Map	Trenches Corrected To 24-9-17		
Miscellaneous			
Miscellaneous	Glossary		
Map	Belgium And Part Of France		
Miscellaneous	28 S W Appendix II		
Map	Belgium And Part Of France.		
Miscellaneous	Belgium And Part Of France.		
Miscellaneous	27 S.E. Appendix E		
Miscellaneous	Belgium		
Map	Belgium.		
Map	Appendix F		
War Diary	Cost Cappell	01/05/1918	16/05/1918
War Diary	Bournonville.	22/05/1918	22/05/1918
War Diary	Lalacque	26/05/1918	26/05/1918
War Diary	Lalacque Camp	27/05/1918	31/05/1918
Miscellaneous			
Operation(al) Order(s)	Operation Orders No 32. 9th (Northd Hussars) Bn Northumberland Fusiliers. Appendix B		
Miscellaneous	Routine Orders by Major General C.L. Nicholson, C.B., C.M.G., Commanding, 34th Division.	04/05/1918	04/05/1918
Operation(al) Order(s)	Operation Orders No 33 9th (Northd Hussars) Battn Northumberland Fusiliers.	01/05/1918	01/05/1918
Operation(al) Order(s)	Operation Orders No 34. 9th (Northd Hussars) Battn Northumberland Fusiliers	04/05/1918	04/05/1918
Operation(al) Order(s)	9th (Northd. Hussars) Bn. Northd. Fusiliers. Operation Order No 36	12/05/1918	12/05/1918
Operation(al) Order(s)	9th (Northd. Hussars) Battn Northd Fusiliers. Operation Order No 37	12/05/1918	12/05/1918

Operation(al) Order(s)	9th (Northd Hussars) Bn. Northd. Fusiliers. Operation Order No 38	15/05/1918	15/05/1918
Miscellaneous	Retired		
Operation(al) Order(s)	Operation Orders No 39 9th (Northumberland Hussars) Bn Northumberland Fusiliers.	25/05/1918	25/05/1918
Miscellaneous	War Diary		
Miscellaneous	102nd Infantry Brigade Provisional Defence Scheme Left Sub-Sector 34th Divisional Front.	03/05/1918	03/05/1918
Miscellaneous	VIII Corps G. 5697	03/05/1918	03/05/1918
Miscellaneous			
Heading	WO95/2466/4 24 Bn Northumberland Fusiliers 1916 Jan-1917 July		
Heading	34th Division 103rd Infy Bde 24th Bn North'd Fus. Jan 1916-Jly 1917. Amalgameted With 27 Bn		
Miscellaneous	24th Northumb Fus:		
Heading	Operation Orders Appendix 'B'		
Heading	24th Northumb. Fus Vol 1 Jan 16 To Jly 17		
War Diary	Sutton Veny	04/01/1916	11/01/1916
War Diary	Southampton	11/01/1916	12/01/1916
War Diary	Havre	12/01/1916	18/01/1916
War Diary	Esquerdes	17/01/1916	22/01/1916
War Diary	Esquerdes Le Romarin	23/01/1916	23/01/1916
War Diary	Le Romarin	24/01/1916	06/02/1916
War Diary	Vieux Berquin	07/02/1916	07/02/1916
War Diary	Erquinghem	08/02/1916	13/02/1916
War Diary	Armentiers	14/02/1916	29/02/1916
Heading	24 North Fus Vol 3		
War Diary	Armentieres	01/03/1916	10/04/1916
War Diary	Neuf Berquin.	11/04/1916	11/04/1916
War Diary	Nor Becque	12/04/1916	12/04/1916
War Diary	Wardrecques	13/04/1916	13/04/1916
War Diary	Moulle	14/04/1916	04/05/1916
War Diary	St Gratien	05/05/1916	05/05/1916
War Diary	Franvillers	06/05/1916	09/05/1916
War Diary	Dernancourt	10/05/1916	21/05/1916
War Diary	Bresle	22/05/1916	31/05/1916
Heading	24th (S) Bn. Northd. Fus. (1st Tyneside Irish) War Diary For The Month Of June 1916. XXXIV		
War Diary	Bresle	01/06/1916	02/06/1916
War Diary	Franvillers	03/06/1916	04/06/1916
War Diary	Franvillers And Dernancourt	05/06/1916	09/06/1916
War Diary	Franvillers	10/06/1916	28/06/1916
War Diary	Dernancourt	29/06/1916	30/06/1916
Heading	103rd Bde. 34th Div. War Diary Brigade temporarily transferred to 37th Division 6th July-Rejoined 34th Division. 22nd August. 24th Battalion Northumberland Fusiliers (1st Tyneside Irish) July 1916		
Heading	103rd Brigade. 37th Division. 34th Division from 22nd August 1/24th Battalion Northumberland Fusiliers August 1916		
War Diary	Field	01/08/1916	14/08/1916
War Diary	Gouy-Servins	15/08/1916	15/08/1916
War Diary	Divion	16/08/1916	23/08/1916
War Diary	Neuf Berquin	24/08/1916	26/08/1916
War Diary	Cardonette	27/08/1916	27/08/1916
War Diary	Lavieville	28/08/1916	28/08/1916

War Diary	Bois Noir	29/08/1916	31/08/1916
Miscellaneous	34th Div. No. CH/290	18/08/1916	18/08/1916
Map	Belgium And Part Of France		
Miscellaneous	Belgium & Part Of France Sheet 29		
War Diary	Contalmaison	01/09/1916	09/09/1916
War Diary	Albert	10/09/1916	12/09/1916
War Diary	Lavieville	13/09/1916	15/09/1916
War Diary	Contalmaison	16/09/1916	17/09/1916
War Diary	Becourt	18/09/1916	18/09/1916
War Diary	Franvillers	19/09/1916	20/09/1916
War Diary	Bouchon	21/09/1916	23/09/1916
War Diary	Estaires	23/09/1916	23/09/1916
War Diary	Armentieres	24/09/1916	28/09/1916
War Diary	Epinette (Sector)	29/09/1916	30/09/1916
War Diary	Armentieres	01/10/1916	11/10/1916
War Diary	Epinette (Armentieres)	11/10/1916	16/10/1916
War Diary	Armentieres	17/10/1916	22/10/1916
War Diary	Epinette L.S. Sector	23/10/1916	31/10/1916
War Diary	Armentieres	01/11/1916	02/11/1916
War Diary	Epinette (Sector)	03/11/1916	09/11/1916
War Diary	Armentieres	10/11/1916	14/11/1916
War Diary	Epinette	15/11/1916	26/11/1916
War Diary	Fort Rompu	27/11/1916	30/11/1916
Heading	War Diary of 24th Bn Northumberland Fusiliers, (1st Bn Tyneside Irish) Volume XII		
War Diary	Fort Rompu	01/12/1916	10/12/1916
War Diary	Rue Du Bois Sector	11/12/1916	16/12/1916
War Diary	Rue Marle	17/12/1916	23/12/1916
War Diary	Fort Rompu	24/12/1916	28/12/1916
War Diary	Bois Grenier Sector.	29/12/1916	30/12/1916
War Diary	Bois Grenier	01/01/1917	10/01/1917
War Diary	Fort Rompu	10/01/1917	15/01/1917
War Diary	Rue Marle	16/01/1917	19/01/1917
War Diary	Chappelle d'Armentieres	20/01/1917	27/01/1917
War Diary	Armentieres	27/01/1917	27/01/1917
War Diary	Berthen	28/01/1917	28/01/1917
War Diary	Wallon Cappel	29/01/1917	29/01/1917
War Diary	Tatinghem	30/01/1917	31/01/1917
Heading	24th Northd. Fus. Vol 14 War Diaries. Vol XIV. February 1917		
War Diary	Tatinghem	01/02/1917	18/02/1917
War Diary	Wardrecques	19/02/1917	19/02/1917
War Diary	Thiennes	20/02/1917	20/02/1917
War Diary	Rely	21/02/1917	21/02/1917
War Diary	Valhuon	22/02/1917	22/02/1917
War Diary	Chelers	23/02/1917	24/02/1917
War Diary	Bethonsart	25/02/1917	28/02/1917
Heading	24th (S) Battn Northumberland Fusiliers War Diary for March 1917 Volume No. XV. Vol 15		
War Diary	Bethonsart	01/03/1917	02/03/1917
War Diary	Ecoivres	03/03/1917	07/03/1917
War Diary	Arras	08/03/1917	08/03/1917
War Diary	Trenches	08/03/1917	14/03/1917
War Diary	Arras	14/03/1917	19/03/1917
War Diary	Ecoivres	20/03/1917	31/03/1917

Heading	24th. (S) Btn. Northumberland Fusiliers. (1st Tyneside Irish) War Diary Volume XVI For April 1917		
War Diary	Arras	01/04/1917	03/04/1917
War Diary	Rollincourt	04/04/1917	05/04/1917
War Diary	Arras	06/04/1917	08/04/1917
War Diary	Line	09/04/1917	14/04/1917
War Diary	Abbaye-De-Neuville	14/04/1917	14/04/1917
War Diary	B-Aux-C	15/04/1917	21/04/1917
War Diary	Arras	22/04/1917	22/04/1917
War Diary	Blangy	23/04/1917	24/04/1917
War Diary	Oppy-Line	24/04/1917	29/04/1917
War Diary	Arras	30/04/1917	30/04/1917
Heading	War Diary For May 1917. Volume XVII 24th (S). Bn Northumberland Fusiliers (1st Tyneside Irish)		
War Diary	Grand Rullecourt.	01/05/1917	07/05/1917
War Diary	Boquemaison	08/05/1917	08/05/1917
War Diary	Montrelet	26/05/1917	28/05/1917
War Diary	St. Nicholas	29/05/1917	31/05/1917
Heading	24th (S). Battn. Northumberland Fusiliers. War Diary for June. 1917 Volume XVIII		
War Diary	Front Line Trenches	21/06/1917	21/06/1917
War Diary	St. Nicholas Camp	22/06/1917	22/06/1917
War Diary	Maizieres	30/06/1917	30/06/1917
War Diary	Gavrelle	01/06/1917	01/06/1917
War Diary	Sunken Road infront of Arras	02/06/1917	04/06/1917
War Diary	Railway Cutting Infront of Arras	04/06/1917	08/06/1917
War Diary	Front Line Trenches	09/06/1917	11/06/1917
War Diary	St. Nicholas Camp.	18/06/1917	18/06/1917
Heading	24th Battn Northd Fusiliers. War Diary Volume XIX July 1917. Vol		
War Diary	Maizieres	01/07/1917	05/07/1917
War Diary	Peronne	06/07/1917	10/07/1917
War Diary	Hancourt	17/07/1917	17/07/1917
War Diary	Vendelles	19/07/1917	20/07/1917
War Diary	Vadencourt	26/07/1917	26/07/1917
War Diary	Front Line	30/07/1917	31/07/1917

WO 95 2466/3

9 BN NORTHUMBERLAND
FUSILIERS
1917 AUG - 1916 MAY *

* CATALOGUE SAYS APRIL

WAR DIARY / INTELLIGENCE SUMMARY

Army Form C. 2118

Place	Date	Hour	Summary of Events and Information	Remarks and references to Appendices
France	Aug 1st		Day devoted to cleaning of equipment, kit & clothing	
France	2nd		Orders received that the Battalion was being transferred from 52nd Brigade, 17th Divn. to 103rd Brigade, 34th Divn. Farewell orders by L.O.C. 17th Divn. read as follows:- "On the occasion of the transfer of the 9th Inf Bn. to another Division, the General Officer Commanding wishes to place on record his appreciation of the fine work done by this Battalion throughout the last two years' service in France. All ranks of the Battalion have shown the finest fighting spirit, and have worthily upheld the traditions of the famous Regiment to which the Battalion belongs. The L.O.C. much regrets that the exigencies of the service make it necessary for the Northumberland Fusiliers to leave his command, and he is glad to take the opportunity of thanking the officers, N.C.O.s & men for their unvaried good work in the past & wishes them all success in their new formation." (Sd) W.H. Protheroe Lt Col, A.A. & Q.M.G. 17th Divn	
France	3rd		Battalion marched from St Nicholas camp, having stayed out by four different bands from units of 17th Divn. to ARRAS where they entrained. Buses left at 9.55 am and proceeded via BAPAUME and PERONNE (first line 11 and ST QUENTIN) to BOUVINCOURT (Sheet 62° S.E.) where Battalion billeted. The following telegram was received. "All ranks very much regret your departure and wish you all the very best of luck". From The Lincolns.	

21

WAR DIARY
or
INTELLIGENCE SUMMARY

Army Form C. 2118

9th Northumberland Fusiliers

Place	Date 1915	Hour	Summary of Events and Information	Remarks and references to Appendices
Billets	Aug 5th	5 P	The billet required a lot of work on them and time was spent in this. Also fatigue parties were supplied by the Battalion.	Acts
Billets	6th		The Battalion was included in Field Marching Order, by Infantry Brigade. Commanding 103rd Infantry Brigade. The undermentioned officers having joined the Battalion on 28th & 31st July were taken on strength shown as follows: Lt O.S. Newman — A Lt J.M. Hay — A Lt A.H. Ancell — A 2Lt Astarium — B Lt T. Fletcher — C 2Lt BCT Almon — C Lt W. Hurton — D	Acts
Billets	7th		Fatigue parties of 3 officers and 200 men were supplied for work under R.E.'s. Remainder engaged in Musketry Platoon training.	Acts
Billets	8th		The Divisional Commander inspected the Battalion in fighting order at 10.30 am. Baths were allotted to all companies during the afternoon. "B" "C" companies fired a practice on range in Q.14 (and 63 c S.E.) was booked to C Coy. Lt O'Willaman honours & Awards. Lt W.S. Bell has been awarded the Military Cross for gallantry.	Acts

WAR DIARY or INTELLIGENCE SUMMARY

Army Form C. 2118

9th B. Northumberland Fusiliers

Place	Date 1917	Hour	Summary of Events and Information	Remarks and references to Appendices
Buttle	9th		Working parties of 8 Officers and 480 other ranks were outfitted for work under R.E's.	A.W.
Bices	10th		The following were published for information:- "Lt. Gen. Beauvoir authorize Major O.R. Osborne D.S.O. Hants to wear the badge of Lieut. Colonel Without official intimation in London Gazette." "2/Lt. Heintraub to be R.B. Locke." "2/Lt. R.W. Steelworth." vice Lieut. Colonel to London Gazette.	A.W.
Camp	11th to 15th		Battalion Travelled at 7.0p.m. marched to VADENCOURT, to relieve 21st Batt. Northumberland Fusiliers in Brigade Reserve (R.17 A.4. Sheet 62° S.E) In camp at VADENCOURT. Fatigue parties were provided both day & night for work on front line of posts and on Intermediate Line (Maj. that NAVROY.) Brig. Gen. H.E. Eason D.S.O. Resumed command of the Brigade on 10th inst. Battalion Travelled at 9p.m. on 15th inst, Proceeded to relieve 24/27th Btn. in front line of sector L.31.D.67 L.30.A.79 (Ref. sheet NAVROY EDITION 1)	A.W. A.W.
Trenches	16th		This sector of the line proved to be very quiet and during the night we established complete control of No Man's Land by means of strong patrols. Casualties 1 O.R. wounded	W.R.

WAR DIARY
or
INTELLIGENCE SUMMARY

(Erase heading not required.)

9th Bn Northumberland Fusiliers

Army Form C. 2118

Place	Date	Hour	Summary of Events and Information	Remarks and references to Appendices
Fonches	17th		A very quiet day was spent. A strong patrol reconnoitred the enemy trenches to see if they were occupied. Patrol found that the enemy line was strongly held and withdrew having 4 O.R. wounded	W.R.
Fonches	18th		A very quiet day. Patrols at night rifle grenaded the enemy trenches causing much heavy trench mortar barrage Casualties 7 OR	W.R.
Fonches	19th		Patrols at night again rifle grenaded the enemy trenches Casualties :- Nil	W.R.
Fonches	20th		Patrols at night found "NOMANSLAND" clear of the enemy while the day had been very quiet. Casualties Nil	W.R.
Fonches	21st		We were relieved during the night by the LUCKNOW CAVALRY BDE the relief passing off without incident. Relief was completed about 12 midnight. On relief the Companies marched to BOUVINCOURT where we went into billets	W.R.

WAR DIARY
or
INTELLIGENCE SUMMARY

(Erase heading not required.)

Army Form C. 2118

9th Bn Northumberland Fus

Place	Date	Hour	Summary of Events and Information	Remarks and references to Appendices
BOUVINCOURT	22nd		The morning was spent resting and cleaning up clothing, equipment etc. In the evening training was carried out in views of Operations to be carried out at a later date	WR.
BOUVINCOURT	23rd		Day was devoted to training	WR.
BOUVINCOURT	24–25th		Training as above	WR.
BOUVINCOURT	26th		From 9am the Bn was in readiness to move by bus at half an hours notice being part of the Divisional Front. At 7pm the Bn embussed for JEANCOURT and from there marched to the Intermediate line in L22C Central for a hot meal was prepared. At 10pm the Bn moved forward to a point of assembly in G.17.d preparatory to an attack on the enemy trench system that 5 squad.	WR.
Jencher	27th		Bn was ready at point of assembly at 3am (Zerohour) and the barrage commenced. The Companies started to advance but as	

Army Form C. 2118

WAR DIARY
or
INTELLIGENCE SUMMARY
(Erase heading not required.)

9th Northumberland Fusiliers

Place	Date	Hour	Summary of Events and Information	Remarks and references to Appendices
Fauches	27th	Contd	B on the left had not got into position. They halted and were finally withdrawn to dugouts in L.22.C. Casualties 1 O.R. wounded. Remained at duty.	W.P.R.
Fauches	28th		At night the Bn. moved forward and relieved the 106th Royal Scots in the trenches in G.1.B & D which they had captured from the enemy early in the morning of the 26th. There was considerable enemy shelling and 14 casualties were suffered. Capt R. HORAN was wounded, 1 O.R. killed and 12 O.R. wounded. Relief was complete at 5.25 a.m. 29th.	W.P.R.
Fauches	29th		The day was moderately quiet and we had no casualties. The trenches had been very badly knocked about by shell fire and there was no wire in front of the trenches.	W.P.R.
Fauches	30th		The day was moderately quiet and we suffered no casualties.	W.P.R.

WAR DIARY
or
INTELLIGENCE SUMMARY

(Erase heading not required.)

Army Form C. 2118

9th Bn Northumberland Fusiliers

Place	Date	Hour	Summary of Events and Information	Remarks and references to Appendices
Trenches	31st		This day was not quite so quiet as the two previous days. Casualties 2 O.R. wounded.	WR

3-9-17
In the Field

D.R. Turnbull
Lieut Col
Comdg 9th Northd Fus

To Officer i/c
R.I.'s 3 G.

Herewith Casualty Report No 160. Please.

Appendix B

Regt No	Rank & Name	Coy	Date	Casualty
201079	Pte Hunnam J	A	28.8.17	Wounded
	Capt R Horan		29.8.17	"
5801	Sgt Wilson P	A	"	"
14705	L/Cpl Ord J	A	"	"
48523	Pte Rootham A.E.	A	"	"
23742	" Dougall A	A	"	"
18/1454	" Hanson H	A	"	"
29869	L/Cpl Clarkson J	B	"	"
24032	Pte Connell J	B	"	"
41241	" Stringer P	B	"	"
12930	" Bond R	B	"	"
24076	" Eshelby J	B	"	Killed
4328	" Burford L	B	"	"
1601	" Robinson J.R.	B	"	Wounded
200567	" Davies J	C	"	"
28360	" McLaughlin M	D	"	"
44602	" Riley H	D	"	"
48520	" Robertson W	A	31.8.17	"
16622	" Scott R.T.	C		

C R Osborne Lieut & QM
for O.C. 9th North'd Fus

Copy No 1

Relief Orders No 1

1. The Battalion will relieve the 6th Royal Scots and a small portion of the 10th Lincolns on northern end between G.1.D.65.30 and G.1.B.60.19.

   'A' and 'D' Coys will relieve front line and the boundary between these Companies will be G.1.D.65.70.

   'B' Coy will be in support and will occupy POND TRENCH.

   'C' Coy will be in reserve in QUARRY in L.5.D.

   Battalion Headquarters will be established at L.11.D.3.7.

II. Companies will leave in the following order. A. D. B and C Companies H.Q. leaving at 9. pm. Companies at 10 minutes interval. Guides will be met at Cross Roads at L.11.B.4.1

III. Relief will be reported complete using the code OLIVER TWIST.

IV. An enemy counter attack is expected on this portion of the front. It is suggested that saps in the form of T pieces be pushed out at vantage points and manned by Lewis Gun teams. These should be so sited that the whole front can be swept.

V. It is reported that the enemy has dug

a post at the NORTH corner of RUBY WOOD. Its estimated garrison is 40 men. It is supposed that he is endeavouring to construct a redoubt with QUENNEMONT TRENCH. This must be prevented. A reconnaissance of this point should be made at the earliest possible moment.

VI. Each Company will collect 10 petrol tins. These will be carried full with the Coys.

VII. Wiring will be carried out under Company arrangements.

W. Robertson
Captain & Adjutant
9th Northd. Fus.

28.8.17

Copy No. 1   War Diary
"   " 2   2nd in Command
"   " 3   A Coy
"   " 4   B Coy
"   " 5   C Coy
"   " 6   D Coy

9ᵀᴴ Bᴺ NORTHᴰ FUSILIERS
WAR DIARY
VOLUME XXI
SEPTEMBER 1917

Army Form C. 2118

WAR DIARY
or
INTELLIGENCE SUMMARY

(Erase heading not required.)

Ojt (S) Bn Northumberland Fusiliers

Instructions regarding War Diaries and Intelligence Summaries are contained in F. S. Regs., Part II. and the Staff Manual respectively. Title Pages will be prepared in manuscript.

Place	Date	Hour	Summary of Events and Information	Remarks and references to Appendices
TRENCHES	Sept 1st		A moderately quiet day was spent. During the night the Bn was relieved by the 25th Bn North'd Fus relief being reported complete at 2.25 am. Casualties:- Nil. Bn came into Bde Reserve	WR.
RESERVE	2nd		A working party of 2 companies was supplied for work on FERRET TRENCH a new support trenches being dug in G1 B&B. Casualties 1 OR killed 1 OR wounded	WR.
RESERVE	3rd		A similar working party was found. Casualties Nil	WR.
RESERVE	4th		Working parties found as for the 3rd. Casualties Nil.	WR.
trenches	5th		The Bn moved into the line and relieved the 25th Bn North'd Fus A quiet relief was carried out and relief was complete by 2.30 am	WR.

WAR DIARY
or
INTELLIGENCE SUMMARY
(Erase heading not required.)

9th (S) Bn Northumberland Fusiliers

Army Form C. 2118.

Place	Date	Hour	Summary of Events and Information	Remarks and references to Appendices
Trenches	6th		A quiet day was spent in the trenches. Casualties Nil	WAR.
Trenches	7th		There was a fair amount of shelling during the day. Casualties 1 OR wounded	WAR.
Trenches	8th		Enemy shelled our trenches frequently during the day and unfortunately sustained several casualties. Casualties 2 OR Killed 5 OR wounded	WAR.
Trenches	9th		The 102nd July Bn carried out an attack at 12.15am on RAILWAY TRENCH and (WOOD) TRENCH from G.7.3.75.50 and G.13.3.85.80 (Sheet 1/10000 GUILLEMONT FARM map) At the same time the 27th & North 7ng assaulted TRIANGLE TRENCH from A.15.D.15.02 to about A.25.D.30.10. All objectives were captured and considerable number of prisoners taken. This Bn sector came in for a considerable amount of shelling and we sustained 9 casualties - LIEUT S. ADAMS wounded, 1 OR Killed 7 OR wounded. Unfortunately 2/Lt S. ADAMS died of his wounds on reaching the dressing station at TEMPLEUX	WAR. WAR. WAR.

Army Form C. 2118.

WAR DIARY
or
~~INTELLIGENCE SUMMARY~~

(Erase heading not required.) 9th (S) Bn Northumberland Fusiliers

Instructions regarding War Diaries and Intelligence Summaries are contained in F. S. Regs., Part II. and the Staff Manual respectively. Title pages will be prepared in manuscript.

Place	Date	Hour	Summary of Events and Information	Remarks and references to Appendices
Fenches	10th	1PM	October the enemy counter attacked on the trenches captured by the 27th Bn Northd Fus this am after a very heavy preliminary bombardment and succeeded in gaining the trenches back suffering a considerable number of casualties in doing so. There was a considerable amount of shelling on this Bn front during the day. Casualties 6 O.R. wounded	WR
Fenches	11th		At 3am the 103rd Infy Bde carried out a further attack on WOOD TRENCH after a heavy bombardment and succeeded again in capturing their objective. There was a considerable amount of shelling during the day. Casualties 1 OR. killed 4 OR. wounded	WR
Fenches	12th	At 2.30am	the enemy carried out an attack on A Coy sector after a heavy bombardment. He succeeded in reaching our parapet but was driven off by machine gun and rifle fire. A wire of congratulation was received from the Corps and Divisional Commander. Casualties 2Lt A.S. NEWMAN and 8 O.R. wounded	WR
Fenches	13th		The enemy intermittently shelled our trenches during the day. Casualties 1 OR. Killed 1 O.R. Died of wounds 2 OR wounded	WR

WAR DIARY
or
INTELLIGENCE SUMMARY

(Erase heading not required.) 9t(S)Bn N'ttd Fus

Instructions regarding War Diaries and Intelligence Summaries are contained in F. S. Regs., Part II. and the Staff Manual respectively. Title pages will be prepared in manuscript.

Place	Date	Hour	Summary of Events and Information	Remarks and references to Appendices
Trenches	14.4.17		In the evening the Bn was relieved by the 24/27th Bn N'ttd Fus relief being reported complete at 11.20pm. This had been the quietest day during the tour. The Bn became Bn in Brigade Reserve and was distributed in L10 & 13. Casualties 1 OR killed 1 OR wounded.	WR
Trenches	15th/17th		Battalion HQ. were situated at L.10.d.4.5. in Brigade Reserve, Working parties. Working parties finished each night. Casualties 3 OR killed 3 OR wounded	W.P.
Trenches	17th		On night 17/18th the Battalion was relieved by 21st Batt Northd Fus moved back to billets at BERNES.	W.P.
Billets	18th 19th 20th		At BERNES. A message of congratulation from the Brand Commander was sent forwarding of the action of the Bn during operations just carried out.	W.P.
Billets	24th		On night 24th/25th the Battalion moved up to the 150 Bdg Brigade Reserve Sector on the left support sector.	W.P.
Trenches	25th & 26th		The Batt was in support for this period providing working parties mostly. On its front line tours the line to the 5th Bn Royal Fusiliers kept its march back billets and BERNES. Casualties 1 OR wounded	W.P.

Army Form C. 2118.

WAR DIARY
or
INTELLIGENCE SUMMARY
(Erase heading not required.)

Instructions regarding War Diaries and Intelligence Summaries are contained in F. S. Regs., Part II. and the Staff Manual respectively. Title pages will be prepared in manuscript.

Place	Date	Hour	Summary of Events and Information	Remarks and references to Appendices
Ribble	30/9	5 pm	Batt. entrained at 12.15am & proceeded by train to PERONNE	Off
Ribble	30/9	30'	Batt. detrained at PERONNE FLAMICOURT, detrained at BORDEAUX at MONT and marched from there to BLAIRVILLE arriving the 2/10.16. The Battn. drew from ammunition the 2/10.16 to the Batt. in the Northumberland Stables (North Haven) the Northumberland Stables	Off
				Off

A.R. Osborne
Lieut-Col
Comdg 9th (Notts & Derby) Bn. The Watts Fus

1-10-17

A5834 Wt. W4973/M687 750,000 8/16 D. D. & L. Ltd. Forms/C.2118/13.

To O i/c R.I.P.3.
Base

Herewith casualty "164
Report No 164 please.

Regd No.	Rank & Name	Coy	Date	Casualty.
25/220	L/C Florentine. L.	B	10.9.14	Wounded.
13157	Pte Spencer. G.	C	do	do.
12807	" Cummings.	A	do	do.
44613	" Shaw. A.	A	do	do.
39496	" Brown. L.	A	do	do.
22717	L/c Potter. J.	A	do	do.

for O.C. 9th (S) Bn North'd Fusiliers
Lt. R.G.W.

In the Field
11.9.14.

20/6 L.i.S.3
Base
165.

Herewith Casualty report No 165 phase.

Regd No.	Rank & Name	Co	Date	Casualty
5214	Pte Lampard S.	A	11.9.17	Wounded
18690	· Weatherly G.	A	do	do
13111	· Hara J.	A	do	Killed
39/331	· Binns A.	A	do	Wounded
Lieut	A.S. Newman	A	12.9.17	do
1387?	L/C Colton A.	A	do	do
39036	Pte Dempsey L.	A	do	do
1659	· Finnigan J.	A	do	do
19297	· Middleton T.W.	A	do	do
18620	· Smith A.L.	A	do	do
44580	· Dawson E.E.	A	do	do
48544	· Wood C.	A	do	do
13237	· Bradbury H.	C	do	do

For O.C. 9 North'd Fusiliers

In the Field
13.9.17

SECRET | RELIEF ORDERS No 2 | Copy. No 1

Ref. Map.
1/10000
GUILLEMONT
FARM.

9th BN. NORTHUMBERLAND FUSILIERS

1. The Battalion will be relieved by 25th Bn. Northd. Fus: in the right subsector tonight.

2. 'C' Coy 25th Bn. Northd Fus: will relieve 'A' Coy
   'D' Coy 25th Bn. Northd Fus: will relieve 'C' Coy
   These 2 Coys will leave Battn. H.Qrs at 8.30 pm.
   'A' Coy 25th Bn. Northd Fus: will relieve 'D' Coy and
   'B' Coy 25th Bn. Northd Fus: will relieve 'B' Coy.
   These two Coys will leave Battalion H.Qrs at 9.45 pm.

3. On relief Battalion H.Qrs remain as at present. A and B Coys on relief will move to vicinity of Battn. H.Qrs. D Coy to QUARRY in L.10.A and C Coy to SUNKEN ROAD in L.11.A. Each Coy will send 1 Officer and 1 N.C.O. to take over accommodation, defence schemes, trench stores &c during the afternoon.

4. Defence schemes, aeroplane photographs, maps shewing dispositions, work in progress, trench stores, ammunition and reserve rations will be handed over on relief and receipts forwarded to Battn. H.Qrs by 9 am on the 2nd inst.

5. Each Coy will detail 3 guides to report to Battn. H.Qrs at 8.15 pm.

6. All empty petrol tins will be brought out and dumped at Battn. H.Qrs en route. D Coy will bring out Cup Attachments. Box Periscopes will be handed over.

7. Completion of relief will be wired to Battalion H.Qrs. using the code 'SNATCHER'.

ACKNOWLEDGE.

Copy. No 1 War Diary
       2   2nd in Command
      3-6 Companies
       7   25th Bn. Northd Fus:
       8   24/27 Bn. Northd Fus:

W.A. Robertson
Captain & Adjutant
9th Northd. Fus:

1st Sept. 1917.

SECRET.   Copy No 2

RELIEF ORDER No 4.

1. The Battalion will be relieved in the A2 Sector tonight.
   'A' & 'D' Coys will be relieved by the Lucknow Battn:
   'B' & 'C' Coys will be relieved by the 'C' Coy 25th Bn: Northd. Fus:

2. An advance party of 1 Officer, 1 N.C.O and 1 guide per platoon of 'C' Coy 25th Bn: Northd. Fus: will report during the afternoon and will take over stores from both 'B' & 'C' Coys. Defence schemes and details of work in progress and proposed will be handed over and the receipts in duplicate forwarded to this office on completion of relief.

3. O.C. 'C' Coy will detail 2 Officers, 3 N.C.Os, and 24 men to remain behind for patrolling of B.1 Sector. They will report to O.C. 26th Bn Northd. Fus. at 7 pm. who has arranged for their accommodation.

4. 'A' and 'D' Coys will each detail 1 guide per platoon to report to Battalion H.Q. at 7.30 pm. to guide in platoons of the Lucknow Bn: The Lucknow Bn: will arrive in platoons at 200 yards distance but will have been "told off" to garrison the posts. O.C. 'A' and 'D' Coys will have guides ready at Coy H.Q. to take detachments to their respective posts.
   All trench stores, reserve rations, defence schemes, details of work being done and work proposed, light signals etc. and duplicate receipts forwarded to this office as early as possible.

5. 'A' and 'D' Coys will send out no patrols tonight and all patrolling will be undertaken by the Lucknow Battn:

6. Completion of relief will be reported by wire using the code VANITY FAIR.

7. On relief Companies will march to BOUVINCOURT making a halt at O.5.c.20.05 where two cookers will be with tea. Breakfast will be ready on arrival at BOUVINCOURT.

8. Transport
   1 limber for 'B' and 'C' Coys will report at 10 pm to convey Lewis guns, mess kit, camp kettles, our own petrol tins etc. Company Commanders' horses will be there at same time.
   1 limber each will report to 'A' and 'D' Coys H.Q. at 12 midnight for petrol tins, Lewis guns etc. Company Commanders' horses will be there at same time.
   Mess Cart will report at Battn: H.Q. at 9 pm. H.Q. Officers' horses at 11 pm.

   ACKNOWLEDGE.
                                                                W.F. Robertson
   Copy No 1 Records   Capt. & Adjt.
        "   2 War Diary   4/6 Bn Northd. Fus:
        "   3 9th in Command
        "   4 O.C. A Coy
        "   5   " B "
        "   6   " C "
        "   7   " D "
        "   8 Transport Officer.

Casualties

9th (North'd Hussars) B'n The North'd Fus:

Appendix "C"

To O.C. R.I.B.
Base.

ORDERLY ROOM 16 SEP 1917 No. 785 8TH (SERVICE) BATT. NORTH'N FUSILIERS

Herewith Casualty
Report to 16.0 please.

Regtl No.	Rank	Name	[ ]	[ ]	Casualty
????	Pte	O'Brien J.	–	D Coy	Killed
421	Cpl	Glew W.	–	A do	Died of Wounds
23754	Pte	Colledge H.	–	A do	Wounded
8005	Sgt	Draper J.	–	A do	do
29/178	Pte	Stringer R.	–	A do	Killed
34104	Pte	Sunderland R.	–	A do	Wounded

To O.C. 8th Batt N.F.
G. McLeod
Lieut ?

K.O. 17

To Officer i/c
Regular Infantry Section 3 S
Casualty Report No 161 please

Regt No	Rank + Name	Coy	Date	Casualty
6090	Pte Williams J	B	31.8.17	Wounded
30/869	" Collins H	B	"	-Do-
29/450	LC Greenwood ?	A	2.9.17	Killed
17971	Pte Anthony H	B	"	Wounded

O.C. R.I.S.B.

Herewith Casualty
Report No: 162 please.

Regtl No	Rank	Name	Co	Date	Casualty
45188	Pte	Parks J.	B	9.9.17	Wounded
35904	"	Major J.	B	do	do
45403	L/Cpl	Cohen S.	B	do	Killed
31809	Pte	Little W.H.	B	do	do
23577	"	Cliss S.E.	B	do	Wounded
40168	"	Towle C.	B	do	do
24241	"	Smith P.	B	do	do
24/1398	"	Ashburner A.	B	do	do
44245	"	Foster A.E.	B	do	do

Lt. & Mr
for O.C. 10th Bn North'd Fus:

L. McEued
O.O.N.

APPENDICES TO WAR DIARY FOR DECEMBER 1917

'A' Sketch Map shewing Posts.

'B' Operation Orders
        No. 3 of 2.12.17
        No. 4 of 6.12.17
        No. 5 of 6.12.17
        No. 1 of 10.12.17
        No. 2 of 11.12.17
        No. 6 of 13.12.17
        No. 7 of 17.12.17
        No. 8 of 21.12.17
        No. 9 of 25.12.17
        No. 10 of 29.12.17

'C' Special Orders of the Day

'D' Brigade Letter S.C. 19/42 calling for rolls of men who have been awarded decorations.

'E' Congratulatory letters.

'F' Instructions for the carrying out of a raid on enemy trenches.

WAR DIARY
or
INTELLIGENCE SUMMARY

9th (Northumberland Hussars) Bn Northumberland Fus

Army Form C. 2118.

Vol 26

Place	Date	Hour	Summary of Events and Information	Remarks and references to Appendices
Billets	Oct 1st		At BLAIRVILLE. The day was devoted to Interior Economy.	WW3
Billets	2nd		At BLAIRVILLE. Lt.Col. A. Bryant D.S.O. assumed command of the Battalion from to-day. The draft from 14th Northumberland Fusiliers paraded & carried out training in Arm drill & Rotun drill.	WW3
Billets	3rd		At BLAIRVILLE. Training was carried on during the day. The battalion was inspected on parade by the Divisional Commander.	WW3
Billets	4th		At BLAIRVILLE. Training was carried out in accordance with programme during the day. W/M Portmore R.T.O. G.3 & Lt. G. Osmond Lieutenant	WW3
Billets	5th		At BLAIRVILLE. Training programme continuing during the day. Major R. Osborne having proceeded for a Senior Officers School Aldershot in accordance with orders received from Army late	WW3

23°

WAR DIARY
or
INTELLIGENCE SUMMARY.

(Erase heading not required.) 9th (Northumberland Hussars) Bn Northumberland Fus.

Army Form C. 2118.

Place	Date	Hour	Summary of Events and Information	Remarks and references to Appendices
Billets	Oct 6th	—	At BLAIRVILLE. Training as per programme. War canned out during the day.	WD.
Billets	7th	—	At BLAIRVILLE. The Battalion paraded for Church Parade	WD.
Billets	8th	—	The Battalion paraded at 5.15 pm & marched to BEAUMETZ and entrained there at 7.30 pm for PROVEN. The Battalion detrained at PROVEN and marched to PUTNEY CAMP.	WD.
Billets	9th 10th 11th	—	PROVEN. The Battalion carried out training in "the Attack" according to programme.	WD.
Billets	12th	—	PROVEN. The Battalion moved by train from PROVEN STATION about 3.30pm & arrived at BOESINGHE where it detrained about 4.30pm; whence they marched to bivouacs at STRAY FARM.	WD.
Billets	13th	—	STRAY FARM. The Battalion left STRAY FARM about 4pm to relieve 18 Battn The Rifle Brigade. B & C Company in front line attached to the 25th Bde Northumberland Fus 2 and No 2 Company in EAGLE TRENCH. A quiet relief was carried out and relief was complete at 7.30pm.	WD.

Army Form C. 2118.

WAR DIARY
or
INTELLIGENCE SUMMARY.
(Erase heading not required.) 9th (Northumberland Fusiliers) Bn Northumberland Fus."

Instructions regarding War Diaries and Intelligence Summaries are contained in F. S. Regs., Part II. and the Staff Manual respectively. Title pages will be prepared in manuscript.

Place	Date	Hour	Summary of Events and Information	Remarks and references to Appendices
Trenches	Oct 14th		No 1 Company returned from Front Line, where they had been exposed to somewhat shelling during the day & the previous night, to EAGLE TRENCH. Casualties 1 O.R. Killed, 2 O.R. Wounded	JWSA
Trenches	15th		EAGLE TRENCH. From midnight of 14th inst until about 4am of the 15th inst the enemy heavily shelled EAGLE TRENCH with gas shell, in consequence we sustained rather severe casualties from this cause. Casualties:- Capt TANFIELD, Lieut J. PEARSON, and 2nd Lieuts. A WILSON, T.T. COOK, and 36 Other Ranks. At dusk No 2 Company moved forward to TRAGIQUE FARM.	JWSA
Trenches	16th		The Battalion was relieved by 20th Batt Northumberland Fus: and bivouacked at STRAY FARM, for the night. Whilst in TRAGIQUE FARM the enemy bombarded shelled No 2 Company. Casualties. 1 O.R. Killed. 6 O.R. Wounded. Lt E.S. HOPE wh. also wounded, but remained at duty.	JWSA

Army Form C. 2118.

WAR DIARY
or
INTELLIGENCE SUMMARY.

(Erase heading not required.) 9th Northumberland (Hussars) B: Northumberland Fus~

Instructions regarding War Diaries and Intelligence Summaries are contained in F. S. Regs., Part II. and the Staff Manual respectively. Title pages will be prepared in manuscript.

Place	Date	Hour	Summary of Events and Information	Remarks and references to Appendices
Billets	Oct 17th		STRAY FARM. About 9am. the enemy shelled STRAY FARM and unfortunately a shell struck Battalion Headquarters, the inmates of which were killed instantaneously. Casualties { Lt. Col. A. Bryant D.S.O. Capt. J. W. F. Robertson. Killed { Lt. R. Radham (Intelligence Officer) Capt. F.C. Davies R.A.M.C. (att?) At 11 a.m. the Battalion moved off in charge of Capt Brady and arrived at BOESINGHE at 12.30 p.m. The Battalion entrained at 3 p.m. for CARDOUEN CAMP where they arrived at 6 p.m.	W.S.
Billets	18th		CARDOUEN CAMP. The day was devoted to Interior Economy.	W.S.
Billets	19th		CARDOUEN CAMP. The day was devoted to training & Interior Economy	W.S.

Army Form C. 2118.

WAR DIARY
or
INTELLIGENCE SUMMARY.
(Erase heading not required.) 5th N. Northumberland Fusiliers 149th Northumberland Inf.

Place	Date	Hour	Summary of Events and Information	Remarks and references to Appendices
Billets	Oct 19th (cont)		CARDOUEN CAMP. Major J. S. Allen M.C. assumed command of the Battalion from today. Capt. I. G. C. Purdy assumed 2nd in command of the Battalion from today. 2nd Lt. W. Austin was appointed Acting Adjutant from today. The following promotions took place in the Battalion :— Temp. 2nd Lt. and A/Capt. R Attwood to be Temp. Lt. Temp. 2nd Lieut. J. Pearson to be Temp. Lt. Temp. Lt. J. McF. Craven to be Temp. Capt.	NWA
Billets	20th		CARDOUEN CAMP. The day was devoted to training. The division Gas Officer carried out an inspection of the anti-gas appliances of the Battalion.	NWA
Billets	21st		The Battalion paraded at 10.15 am & marched via ELVERDINGHE to SOULT CAMP arriving at the Camp at 12.30 pm.	NWA
Billets	22nd		SOULT CAMP. Training was carried out during the morning. The Battalion supplied carrying parties in the night of the 21st/22nd.	NWA

A5834 Wt. W4973/M687 750,000 8/16 D.D.&L. Ltd. Forms/C.2118/13.

WAR DIARY
or
INTELLIGENCE SUMMARY.

Army Form C. 2118.

9th N/Mander and Newsury Bn Northumberland Fus

Place	Date	Hour	Summary of Events and Information	Remarks and references to Appendices
Billets	Oct. 22nd (cont)		SOULT CAMP. and in the night of the 22nd inst, carrying up to the front line under the 209th Field Coy R.E. + wire parties sustained the following casualties:— 2 O.R. Killed 2 O.R. Wounded 1 O.R. Wounded (Remained at duty) 2nd Lieut. G.M.L. Logie having been before a medical board on the 26th Sept 1917 + certified unfit for General Service was accordingly struck off the strength of the Battalion from that date.	M.W.A. M.W.A.
Billets	23rd		SOULT CAMP. The Battalion paraded at 10 a.m. and marched to BOESINGHE. Then entrained there at midday + proceeded to PROVAN where they detrained + marched to PUTNEY CAMP arriving at 4 p.m.	M.W.A.
Billets	24th		PUTNEY CAMP. The day was devoted to parades, inspections of kit + equipment + general cleaning up of same.	M.W.A.

Army Form C. 2118.

WAR DIARY
or
INTELLIGENCE SUMMARY.
(Erase heading not required.) 9th (Northumberland Fusrs) 1st Northumberland Fus.

Place	Date	Hour	Summary of Events and Information	Remarks and references to Appendices
	Oct.			
Billets	25th 26th		PUTNEY CAMP. The usual parades & training in Platoon & Company drill, Musketry, Physical drill & Bayonet fighting were carried out. Companies were in ranges - the Battalion was practiced in "The Mask".	Nil.
Billets	27th & 28th		PUTNEY CAMP. The Battalion paraded at 3pm and marched to HOUPOUTRE station and entrained there for BOISLEUX AU MONT arriving there & detraining at 5am. on the 28th inst. The Battalion marched from the station at BOISLEUX AU MONT to Camp at DURHAM LINES where they took over from the 6th Battn Black Watch at 10.30am.	Nil.
Billets	29th 30th		DURHAM LINES. Training as per programme was carried out. During there days the men were lectured by their officers on Trench Warfare tactics.	Nil.
Billets	31st		DURHAM LINES. The Battalion paraded at 8.30am and marched by companies to the HINDENBURG LINE immediately South of HENINEL where they relieved the 6th Battn Gordon Highlanders. (Sgts S15SW)	Nil.

A3834 Wt. W4973/M687 750,000 8/16 D. D. & L. Ltd. Forms/C.2118/13.

Army Form C. 2118.

WAR DIARY
or
INTELLIGENCE SUMMARY.

(Erase heading not required.) 9th Bn (Northumberland Huzzars) 1st Mtd Bde

Instructions regarding War Diaries and Intelligence Summaries are contained in F. S. Regs., Part II. and the Staff Manual respectively. Title pages will be prepared in manuscript.

Place	Date	Hour	Summary of Events and Information	Remarks and references to Appendices
	Oct		Support battalion of the Right Brigade. A quiet relief was carried out, relief being complete at 1 p.m.	Illis.

[signature]
Major
Commanding 9th (Northumberland Huzzars) Bn
Northumberland Fus.

Base

1st North Canadian
Report No 167 Phase

Reg No	Rank & Name	Bn	Cas Casualty
235610	Pt Reid E.G.	D Coy	wounded

Captain Ashmore
O.C.... Royal ...

In the field
1st October 1917

SPECIAL ORDER OF THE DAY
By
FIELD-MARSHAL SIR DOUGLAS HAIG,
K.T., G.C.B., G.C.V.O., K.C.I.E.,
Commander-in-Chief, British Armies in France.

The following telegrams are published for the information of all ranks:—

To THE FIELD MARSHAL COMMANDING-IN-CHIEF, BRITISH ARMIES IN FRANCE, FROM CHIEF OF THE IMPERIAL GENERAL STAFF, WAR OFFICE.

16-10-17.

Following from Prime Minister for Sir Douglas Haig, begins, The War Cabinet desire to congratulate you and the troops under your Command upon the achievements of the British Armies in Flanders in the great battle which has been raging since July 31st. Starting from positions in which every advantage rested with the enemy, and hampered and delayed from time to time by most unfavourable weather, you and your men have nevertheless continuously driven the enemy back with such skill, courage and pertinacity as have commanded the grateful admiration of the peoples of the British Empire and filled the enemy with alarm.

I am personally glad to be the means of transmitting this message to you and to your gallant troops, and desire to take this opportunity of renewing my assurance of confidence in your leadership and in the devotion of those whom you command. Ends.

FROM THE FIELD MARSHAL COMMANDING-IN-CHIEF, BRITISH ARMIES IN FRANCE, TO CHIEF OF THE IMPERIAL GENERAL STAFF, WAR OFFICE.

17-10-17.

Please convey the following in reply to the message from the Prime Minister transmitted by you yesterday.

The British Armies in France are proud to have won the congratulations of the War Cabinet and the generous appreciation conveyed in your message of the efforts made and the results achieved in Flanders since the 31st July. All ranks are determined to achieve victory and feel confident of doing so. I beg to thank you for your expression of confidence in myself and in the great Imperial Army in France which I have the honour to command.

D. Haig. F.M.

General Headquarters,
19th October, 1917.

Commander-in-Chief,
British Armies in France.

PRINTED IN FRANCE BY ARMY PRINTING AND STATIONERY SERVICES   PRESS A 10/17

WAR DIARY

9TH Bn NORTHD FUSILIERS.

VOLUME XXIII

NOVEMBER

1917

WAR DIARY –

9th [9/Northd Hussairs] Bn.

Northumberland Fusiliers –
November 1917

Appendices –

A. Sketch map showing posts.

B. Map of trench system.

C. Special orders of the day.

D. Operation Order No 1. 23-11-17

E1. Instructions in case of enemy retirement. –
E2. Map to illustrate above.

F. Enemy order of battle on III Army front 24-11-17

G. Operation order No 2. 27-11-17

WAR DIARY
or
INTELLIGENCE SUMMARY

(Erase heading not required.) 9th (Northumberland Fusiliers) Bn Northumberland Fus.

Army Form C. 2118

Place	Date	Hour	Summary of Events and Information	Remarks and references to Appendices
Trenches	12, 2, 3rd, 13th	Nil	HINDENBURG SUPPORT (Sheet 1/20,000 France 51B SW) about N35c. The Battalion supervised a working party in front line carrying ranking parties to mend the trenches where required. Casualties — nil	Nil
Trenches	4th	4.15	The Battalion moved forward into the front line relieving the 25th Bn Northumberland Fusiliers in the Left Subsector. A quiet relief was carried out, relief was complete by noon. Casualties. nil	Nil
Trenches	5th (to 7th)		Three quiet days were spent in the trenches. There was some trench mortaring by the enemy. Casualties. 2nd Lt E.S. Hope M.C. wounded.	Nil
Trenches	8th		The Battalion was relieved by the 25th Bn Northumberland Fus. A quiet relief was carried out, relief was complete by 12 noon. On completion of relief the Battalion marched back into Brigade Support. Casualties — Nil.	Nil

Army Form C. 2118

WAR DIARY
or
INTELLIGENCE SUMMARY
(Erase heading not required.) J.G. W. Mackland Maj/ 8o N'thumberland Fus

Instructions regarding War Diaries and Intelligence Summaries are contained in F.S. Regs., Part II. and the Staff Manual respectively. Title Pages will be prepared in manuscript.

Place	Date	Hour	Summary of Events and Information	Remarks and references to Appendices
Trenches	Nov 9th 10th 11th		Three quiet days were spent. Working parties & carrying parties were employed. Casualties NIL.	N/A
Trenches	12th		The Battalion was relieved by the 11th Batt. Suffolk Regt. Against relief was carried out & relief was complete at 2pm. On completion of relief the Battalion marched back into Divisional Reserve at NORTHUMBERLAND LINES (Sheet 51 f. 15 S.W.) M22t central. 20,000 The Battalion marched back by Companies & arrived in camp at about 5pm. Casualties NIL.	N/A
Billets	13th		NORTHUMBERLAND LINES. The day was devoted to Interior Economy. Kit inspections were carried out & the men were bathed. Major J.N. Ridley joined the Battalion and assumed the duties of 2nd in Command from to-days date.	N/A
Billets	14th 15th 16th 17th		NORTHUMBERLAND LINES. The mornings were devoted to Physical Drill & Musketry Training. Specialists returned to their Platoons. Wapons etc for the Attack. The afternoons were given to Company, and various parties for fatigues with N.E. Coys and various areas. Casualties NIL.	N/A

1875 Wt. W593/326 1,000,000 4/15 J.B.C. & A. A.D.S.S./Forms/C. 2118.

WAR DIARY
or
INTELLIGENCE SUMMARY

(Erase heading not required.) 9th (Northumberland Hussars) Bn Northumberland Fus.

Army Form C. 2118

Place	Date Nov.	Hour	Summary of Events and Information	Remarks and references to Appendices
Camp.	18th		NORTHUMBERLAND LINES. The Battalion paraded at 9.30am for Church Parade	
"	19th		Specialist training as usual were carried out during the day. Night operations were carried out at 4.30pm. The practice was to fall in on the alarm being sounded.	
"	20th		The day was spent interviewing & the wounded prisoners were carried out. It was in the course of the morning by Brd Lieut Turnpin that if CAMBRAI it was thought probable that the enemy might evacuate front of the line he now holds between BULLECOURT & the River SCARPE, accordingly the Battalion (from 6.30pm to 10pm) was instructed to move Kit an hour's notice to a pre-arranged rendezvous.	
"	21st		Parades of running in were made. A tactical scheme was carried out during the morning.	
"	22nd		The usual programme of training was carried out.	
"	23rd		Major W.A. VIGNOLES D.S.O. 10th Bn. The Lincolnshire Regt. arrived & took over command of the Battalion. Major J.S. ALLEN M.C. assumed the duties of 2nd in command of the Battalion. During the day parades & training were carried out as usual - Information were to the effect of movements & apparent of the enemy & counter-attacks were produced by the Patrols.	
"	24th		The Battalion paraded in fighting order at 9am ennobled by Companies via MERCATEL - THENIN & HINDENBURG Line to the Left Sub Sector where it relieved the 10th Bn. The Lincolnshire Regt in the front line. The relief was were were fallen by 6pm in the night.	See O.O. No 1 APPENDIX D.

WAR DIARY or INTELLIGENCE SUMMARY

Army Form C. 2118

(Erase heading not required.)

Instructions regarding War Diaries and Intelligence Summaries are contained in F.S. Regs., Part II. and the Staff Manual respectively. Title Pages will be prepared in manuscript.

Place	Date Nov.	Hour	Summary of Events and Information	Remarks and references to Appendices
TRENCHES	24th (cont)		A Coy in Centre, D Coy in the Left. C Coy which was in reserve in MALLARD TRENCH. The enemy was quiet near us. He opened fire at 2 p.m. Against our men working in the trenches. Owing to the superior alertness of our sentries & the vigilance of the Officers & N.C.O.s the enemy had to be driven to hand to hand combat with the enemy constantly, accordingly during the night, he was thoroughly cleared from NO MANS LAND. Bid 4 Officers were sent out from the trenches. Our patrols were thoroughly cleared of no man's land to the enemy wire. Patrols brought up to 10 (time; to time; where wire was found & marked. At dep. he movingly filled in Lewis Gunners safe in enemy patrols as well as machine rifle grenades. Time was taken in hand to hand combat with the enemy who were found to be very strong numerically but not in strength. Casualties 2 O.R. wounded. 1 O.R. wounded but remained at duty.	For sketch of trenches & posts see Appendix A. M.A. For general Map see Appendix B
TRENCHES	25th		Against day was spent in the lines. At 9 a.m. the enemy in retaliation, opened Trench Mortar fire on our front line rifles in H.Q. Trench. Our reply was immediately delivered by machine and artillery. Our artillery scoring direct hits. Whilst Mcquality at once ok the Bombing Trench M. fire gave a good account of our 2 O.R. killed, 1 O.R. wounded. Later in the day (in part moonlight) quite a number of hostile patrols were observed. Several parties were observed by our Lewis gunners, we were careful complete control of NO MAN'S LAND	M.A.
TRENCHES	26		Against day was open in the trenches. Our artillery & T.M.'s as usual, entered the enemy trenches, wire and from 10 AM. till 4 P.M. at intervals during the night. This retaliation was very feeble & with the exception of two others to put T.M.'s which fell on the front line & support. The Centre Coy nothing happened. Casualties 1 O.R. Wounded. The enemy patrols was active during the night time each Coy front. The enemy was not however in NO MAN'S LAND & we were nimble after & detected the order & trenches at various points from Avenue to NO MAN'S LAND. He did not replied to our fire except in isolated instances.	M.A.

† Owing to our successful attacks on Nov. 20 & at Coast towards CAMBRAI and on TUNNEL TRENCH
U.7 - U.14 - U.20 - U.21. Sheet 51.B.SW/20,000 scale.

WAR DIARY or INTELLIGENCE SUMMARY

Army Form C. 2118

(Erase heading not required.) 97 No Man's Land from the No Man's Land trenches

Instructions regarding War Diaries and Intelligence Summaries are contained in F. S. Regs., Part II. and the Staff Manual respectively. Title Pages will be prepared in manuscript.

Place	Date	Hour	Summary of Events and Information	Remarks and references to Appendices
TRENCHES	27th	—	Another quiet day. No shots. Our artillery was active during the day. At intervals [illegible] up personal attention which the enemy replied. Got into no-man's-land from the exit Coy 3 mt. The enemy wire was extensively [illegible] on afternoon by our patrols from NO MAN'S LAND & at our point were held. Traversing [illegible] and [illegible] on our wire. The enemy strained our our patrols and made [illegible] attempts to get through his wire returned with [illegible], but in each occasion he was sported by O.G. fire from our posts. [illegible] man was made as well as advice of Rifle Granades. [illegible] 2nd Lt. C L STEPHENSON was wounded by a rifle granade and died later in the evening of his wounds.	W.I.D.
TRENCHES	28th	—	At 2.30 am the Bn. H.Q. was relieved by the 25th Bn's North'd Fus. The relief was quiet. Our own wire completed by 10 A.M. A Coy in the Bn's H.Q. moved in Brigade Support with A Coy in THE ROOKERY, B Coy in CONGREVE TRENCH, C Coy in EGRET TRENCH, D Coy in EGRET LOOP & Bn. Headquarters AT THE NEST. Lt. PIGGOTT assumed the Bn. Cdrs took over command. D Coy working carrying parties was supplied during the night.	see O.O. No 2 Appendix G W.I.D
TRENCHES	29th	—	A quiet day was spent in the trenches with no further works of night. Working & carrying parties were supplied for R.E.'s & Trench Mortars.	
TRENCHES	30th	—	Another very quiet day was experienced. During the afternoon the Bombers remounted this exception [illegible] on the Russian in an effort to blow up the [illegible] TUNNEL TRENCH. In this even he was repulsed. At the same time he carried out a short T.M. bombardment on our front line trenches. Our artillery & T.M.'s all calibres retaliated & silenced the enemy.	C

Appendix C. gives special orders of the day issued by G. H.Q. mostly referring to other sectors.

Appendix E (1+2) gives instructions for pursuit (with map) issued the enemy retire to Broxant Quéant Line. E.

Appendix F gives Enemy order of Battle on 3rd Army front on 24th 11-17.

[signature] Lt Col
Commdg.

WAR DIARY
INTELLIGENCE SUMMARY
(Erase heading not required.)

Army Form C. 2118.

NOVEMBER 1917.

Place	Date	Hour	Summary of Events and Information	Remarks and references to Appendices

Strength of Battalion at beginning of month — 42 Officers   1/54 O.R.
  "   "   "   "   end of month   — 38 Officers   741 O.R.

Casualties

Killed	Wounded	Evacuations	Commissions	Transfers
3	4	58	5	3

Drafts   week ending 9". — 36
           "   "   16". — 8
           "   "   23" — 8
           "   "   30" — 8
                          Total 60

Officers

Joined
Lieut. E.W. Guy 1/11
  "   H.P. Hargett 1/11
Major Hon. J.R. Ridley 12/11
Lieut. Col. W.A. Vignoles DSO 22/11
Lieut. G.B.L. Piggott 28/11

Killed
Lieut. G.L. Stevenson 28/11

Wounded
Lieut. D'B. Hope M.C.
  6th transfer to R.F.C.
2nd Lieut. C.H. Perritt 1/11
   "   H.S. Miller 1/11
   "   G.R. Terry 1/11
   "   G. Massie 1/11

Evacuated
Lieut. B.C. Adamson 2/11
Transfer to Dragoon Guards
Lieut. A. Harrison 5/17

Decorations:
No. 4112/8 Pte. C. Rossington — Military Medal — 11th Nov 1917.

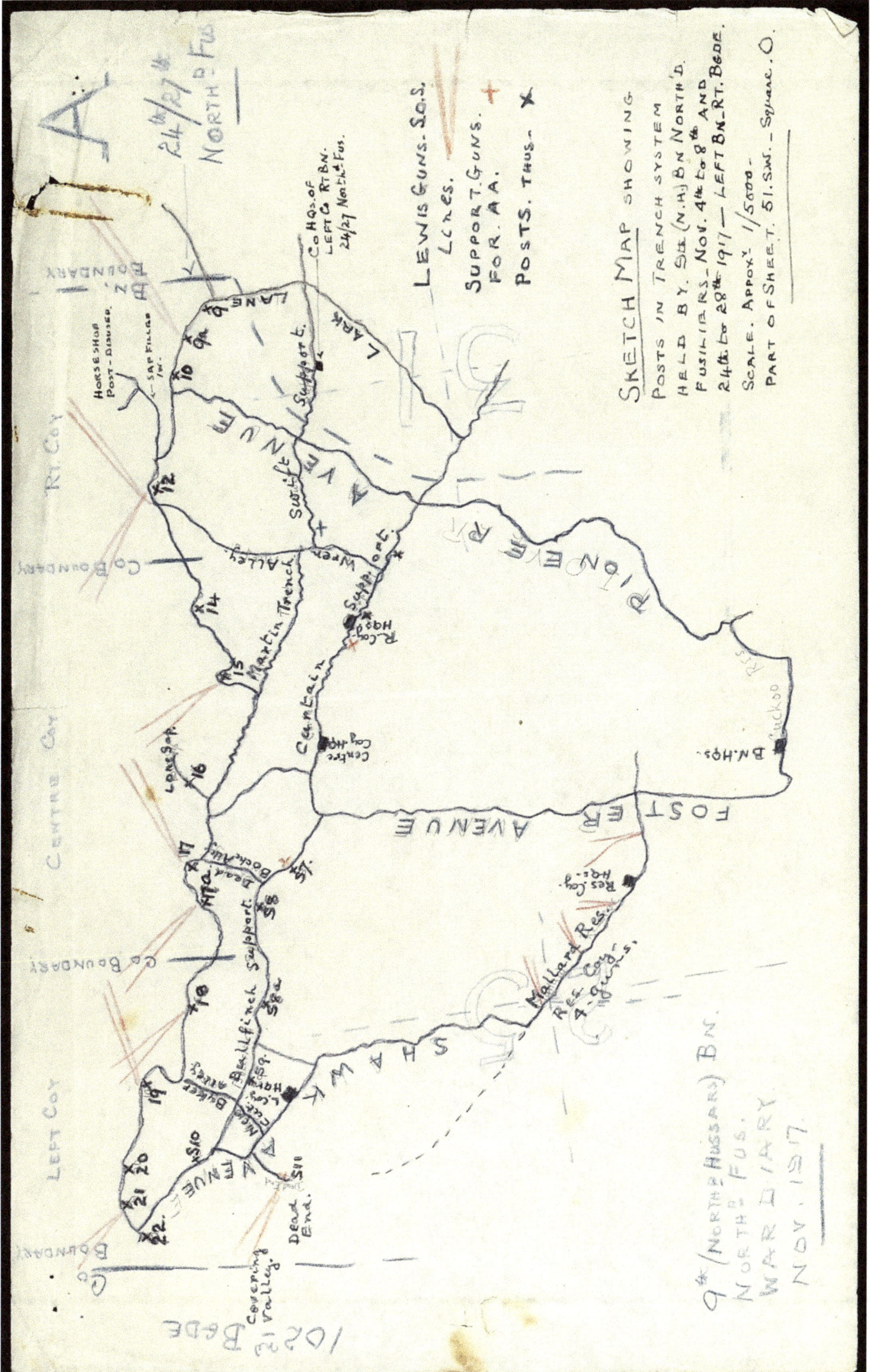

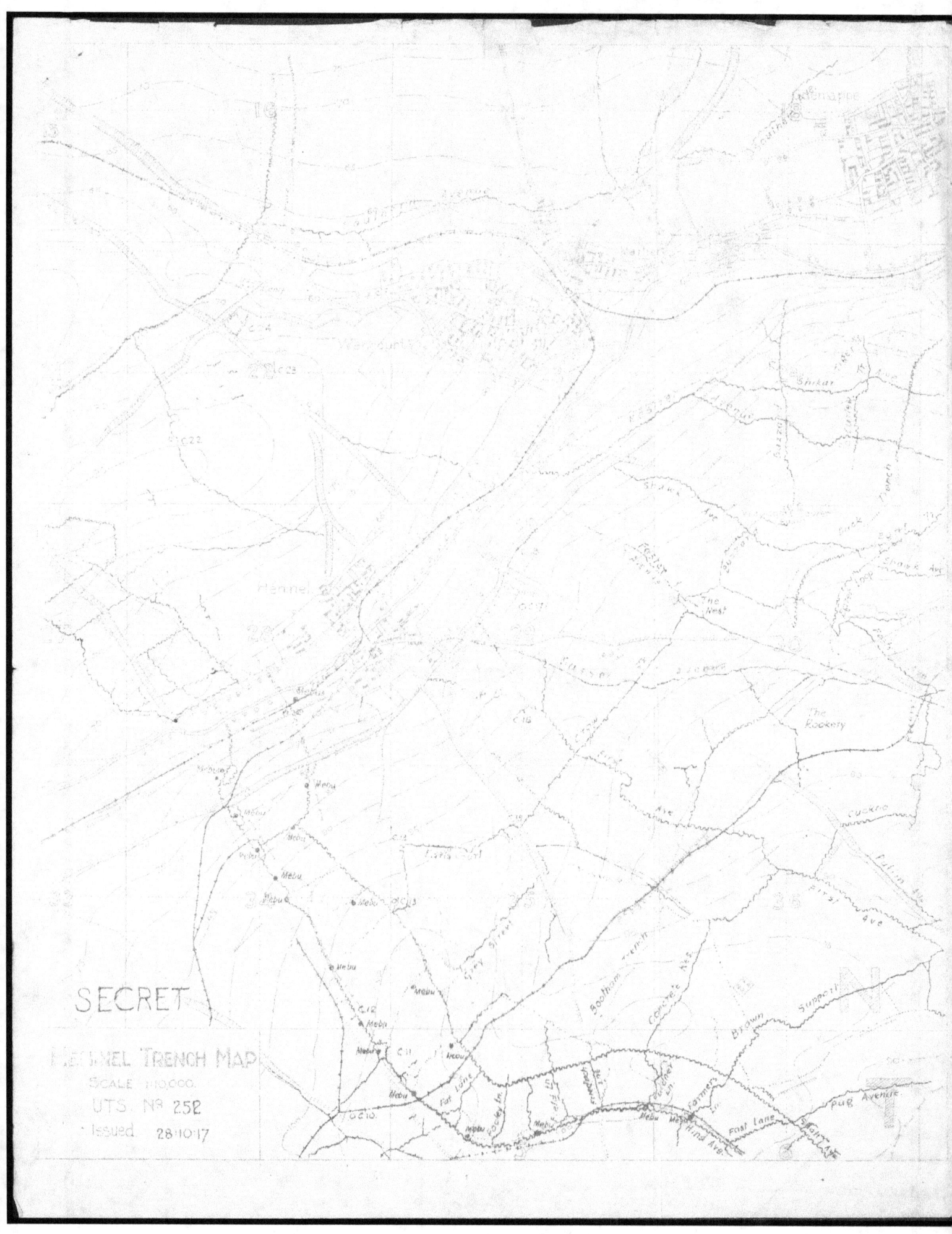

9th Bn North'd Fus
WAR DIARY
Nov. 1917

APPENDIX B

9th Bn North'n Fus
WAR DIARY
Nov. 1917

APPENDIX _ B

SECRET. WAR DIARY Nov. 1917   APPENDIX II

Operation Order No 1.   Copy No. 7

1. Move. The 9th (Northd. Hussars) Bn. Northd. Fusiliers will relieve the 10th Lincolns (101st Brigade) in the left subsector tomorrow Nov. 24th. Boundaries, LARK LANE and Post 9 inclusive to left Brigade Boundary W.26.a.45.60.

2. Advance Parties. As detailed proceeded to the line this morning — The Provost Sergt. 3 Regtl. Police & 1 N.C.O. per Coy to take over stores & 1 Cook per Coy will proceed this afternoon. One days rations for the Bn. will be taken up by transport, & dumped at Bn. HQs. The Police will act as guard over these.

3. Disposition. The Companies will be disposed in the line, Right Forward Coy. B, Centre A. Left D. & MALLARD RESERVE C Coy.
These Coys will take over the Coy. sectors as they are at present held by 10th Lincolns.

4. Order of move. Companies will move from Camp in the order D, A, B, C & Bn. HQs, and march with intervals of 200 yds between platoons.
Leading platoon to move off at 8.0. AM. They will leave CRUCIFIX at 10.0 AM. & to be clear of cross roads N.34.a.7.7 by 10.15 AM.

5. Route. Through MERCATEL, — NEUVILLE VITASSE, thence along road through N.20.a.9.0. N.26 central — St MARTIN SUR COJEUL to CRUCIFIX in N.33.d.30.95, thence via HINDENBURG LINE, CONCRETE RESERVE, and CUCKOO RESERVE.

6. Guides. One per platoon will meet Companies as follows: —
RIGHT COMPANY at Junction CUCKOO RES & PIONEER AVENUE
Other COMPANIES at Battalion Headquarters.

7. Stores. Aeroplane Photographs, trench maps, ammunition, grenades, lights, reserve water, Defence Schemes, Intelligence, and details of work in hand & proposed will be taken over together with Trench Stores. Receipts to reach Bn HQs by 12.0 noon 25th inst.

8. Special Trench Stores. Comprising Grenades, S.A.A. S.O.S. Rockets, wire cutters Rations & water are to be taken over separately, & a separate receipt sent to Bn. H.Qs. by 12.0 noon 25th inst.

9. Transport. Two limbered wagons for the Coys, & one for HQs will leave the camp at 7.45 AM. to be at the CRUCIFIX at 9.45 AM. with Lewis Guns & Magazines & Signalling Equipment.

10. Completion of Relief. Will be notified by sending the code word "PHOEBE" to Bn H.Qs.

W. Sutton
2/Lt & Adjutant
9th (Northd. Hussars) Bn. Northd. Fusiliers

23:11:1917.

Copies No 1 to 4. Coys
" 5. QM.
6. T.O
7. War Diary
8. File
9. C.O.

SECRET.

War Diary.

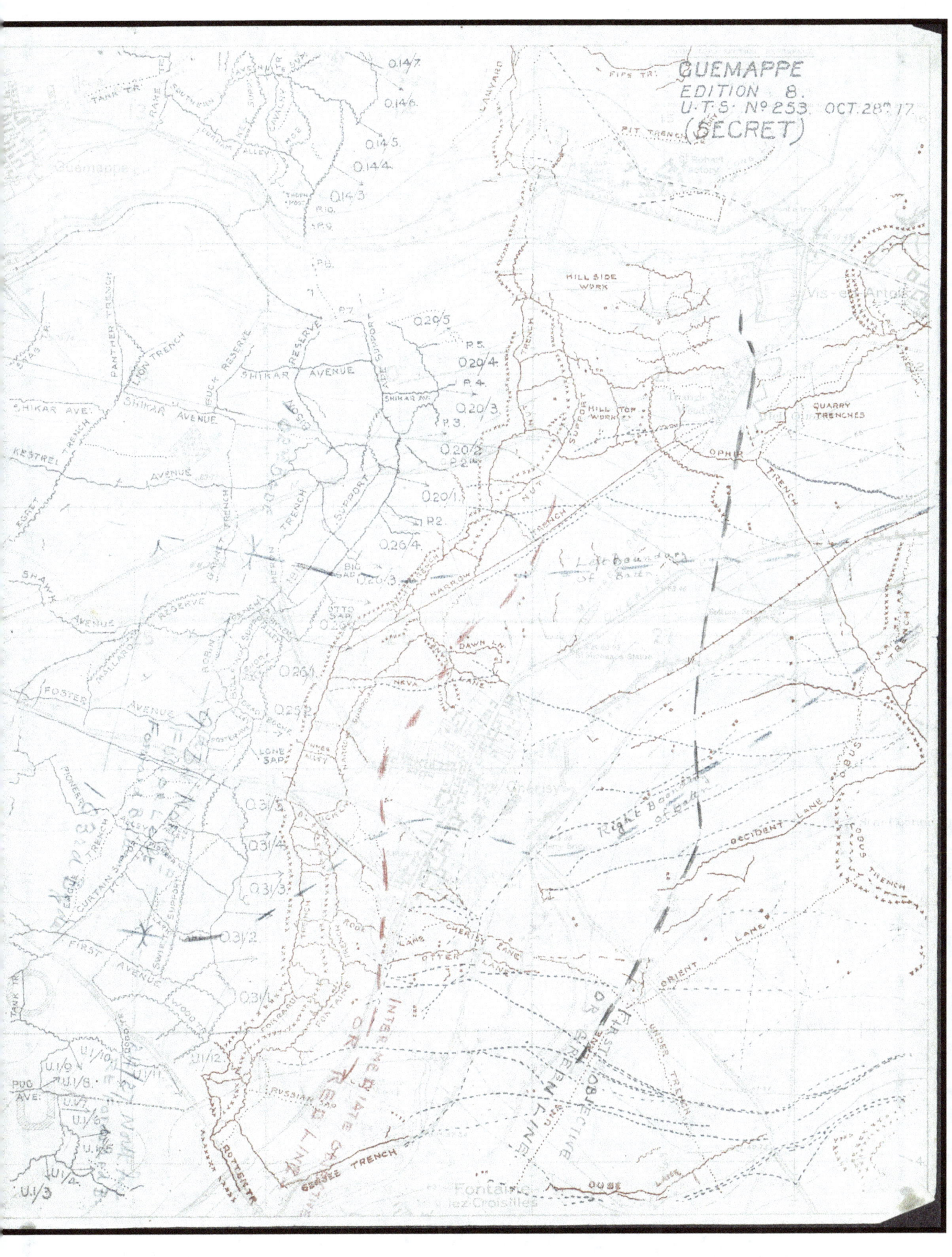

9th (N.H.) Bn. North'd **APPENDIX. E2**
Fusiliers
WAR DIARY
Nov. 1917

9th (N.H.) Bn. North'd
Fusiliers
WAR DIARY
Nov. 1917

9th (N.H.) Bn. Northd. Fusiliers

War Diary
Nov. 1917

Appendix E2

SECRET   WAR DIARY Nov 1917   APPENDIX "E"
PURSUIT SCHEME

1. The following instructions are issued in order that no time may be lost in following up the enemy should he withdraw voluntarily to the QUEANT – DROCOURT LINE.

2. In such operations the enemy will be retiring over prepared ground under cover of guns firing from positions behind his main defences, therefore the process of following him up will necessarily be deliberate, but touch with him must be maintained.

3. By day, careful observation, and by night, active patrolling are the means by which information can be gained as to a withdrawl.
   Any indications of a withdrawl either actual or suspected are to be reported at once, and flanking Companies informed.

4. The advance of our troops will be made by "Bounds" to successive objectives and each "Bound" will be preceded and covered by advanced detachments.

5. If the Battalion is in the line and the enemy withdraws, voluntarily or because his flank is threatened, officers patrols will push at once to the RED LINE, which is the present enemy front system.
   When this is reported clear & on receipt of orders from Battalion H.Q., Companies will move forward.
   Their distribution will be the same as in our front line, B. Coy. on the right, A Coy in the centre, & D. Coy on the left.
   The Coy in MALLARD will move to our present front line system on receipt of orders from Battn. H.Q.

6. The RED LINE when occupied will be at once consolidated, O.C. Coys taking advantage of tactical points. Defended localities will be made sufficient for one platoon. These should be mutually supporting. Constant touch must be established with flanks. All action taken & progress made must be reported at once to Battn. H.Q. Our present front line will continue to be the MAIN LINE of defence until either the RED LINE is consolidated, or our patrols are firmly established on the GREEN LINE

7. When the RED LINE is occupied & consolidation in progress, patrols will be pushed forward as follows:-
   RIGHT COY. to CHERRY BRIDGE (through CHERISSY) to secure the crossing of the R. SENSEE at this point.
   CENTRE COY. through CHERISSY to secure the crossing at O.27.c.3.9. where a new bridge is to be built.
   LEFT COY. to junction of SUNKEN ROADS at O.27.c.3.2.
   Touch must be established between these patrols, when in position; & touch will be established with Right Battn. at CHERRY BRIDGE and CHERRY CHURCH (O.32.c.4.7).
   Touch will also be established with Left Brigade by our left patrol. All progress made to be reported to Bn. H.Q.

8. During this phase, Bn. H.Q. will remain at O.25.c.05.45.

9. As soon as patrols are in these positions the Battalion will be prepared to move to the GREEN LINE, but will not do so until ordered.

FOR MAP see E.2.

20.11.1917.

W. Hutton
2/Lieut & a/Adjutant
9th (N.H.) Bn. R. Scottish Fusiliers

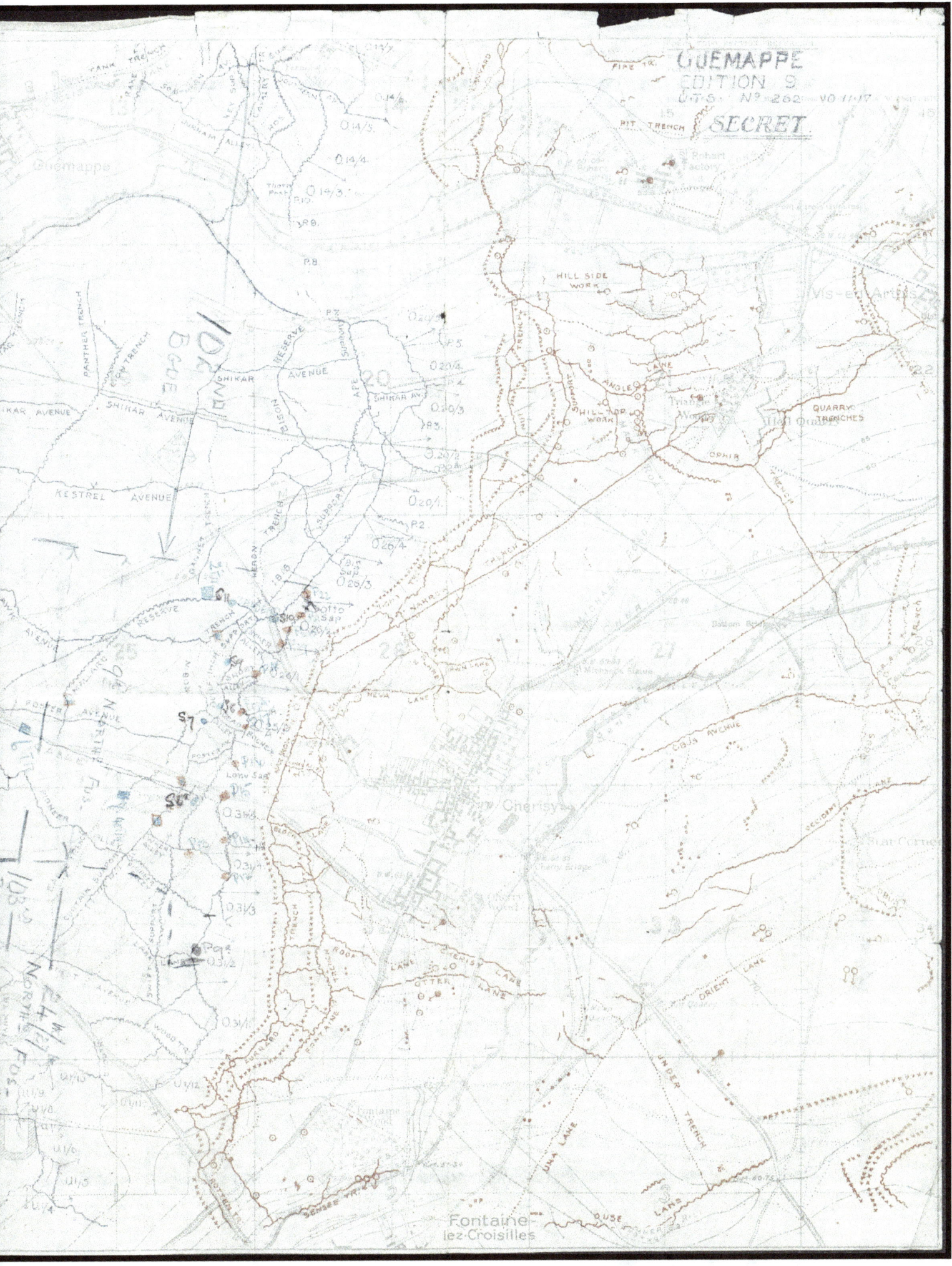

GUEMAPPE

GUEMAPPE

SECRET. WAR DIARY APPENDIX G
27.11.17.

Operation Order No 2

1. Relief.
The 25th Bn. North'd Fusiliers will relieve the 9th (N.H.) Bn. North'd Fus. in the left subsector tomorrow.

2. Guides.
Guides will be provided at the rate of one per post for front line companies, & one per platoon for Coy in MALLARD RESERVE.

Guides for right Coy will be at junction of PIONEER & CURTAIN at 8.0 A.M.

Guides for centre & left Coys will be at respective Coy. H.Qs. at 8.0 A.M.

Guides for Coy in MALLARD RESERVE will be at junction MALLARD & FOSTER AV. at 8.15 A.M.

3. Order of Relief.
Relieving Battalion will come in as follows:-
Right Coy – Left Coy – Centre Coy – Reserve Coy.

4. Stores.
All trench stores, aeroplane photographs, Defence schemes, Programme of work & work proposed etc, will be handed over on relief & receipts obtained.

All permanent stores, bombs, rifle grenades, preserve waters etc will be handed over separately & receipts obtained.

One Officer, one N.C.O. & two O.R. per Coy & one N.C.O. from Bn. H.Qs. will proceed to take over stores etc from the positions they are going to.

These N.C.O's will take over before the 25th Bn. North'd Fus. moves tomorrow.

Duplicates of stores taken over will be sent in to the Orderly Room by 6.0 p.m. tomorrow.

5. Distribution. The relief Coys will proceed as follows:—
"B" Coy. CONCRETE RESERVE — "D" Coy to EGRET LOOP. "A" Coy THE ROOKERY & CUCKOO RESERVE "C" Coy, one platoon THE NEST, two platoons EGRET TRENCH & one platoon CUCKOO COURT.

One Officer or Senior N.C.O. per Coy will proceed today to reconnoitre these areas. Special attention will be paid to defence scheme & programme of work so that continuity is observed.

6. Coys will report their arrival in their new areas by using the code-word SOUTH SHIELDS.

7. Rations. Coys will carry out the unexpended portion of the day's rations.
Rations for the 29th will be brought up to Bn. Hqrs. & distributed to Coys tonight. These will be handed over on relief. If relieving Coys are weaker than ours, difference of rations will be carried out by our Coys.
Rations will be taken over by Coys in their new areas.

W. Sutton Lieut.
a/adjt
for Lieut Col
Comdg. 9th (N.H.) Bn. North'd Fusiliers

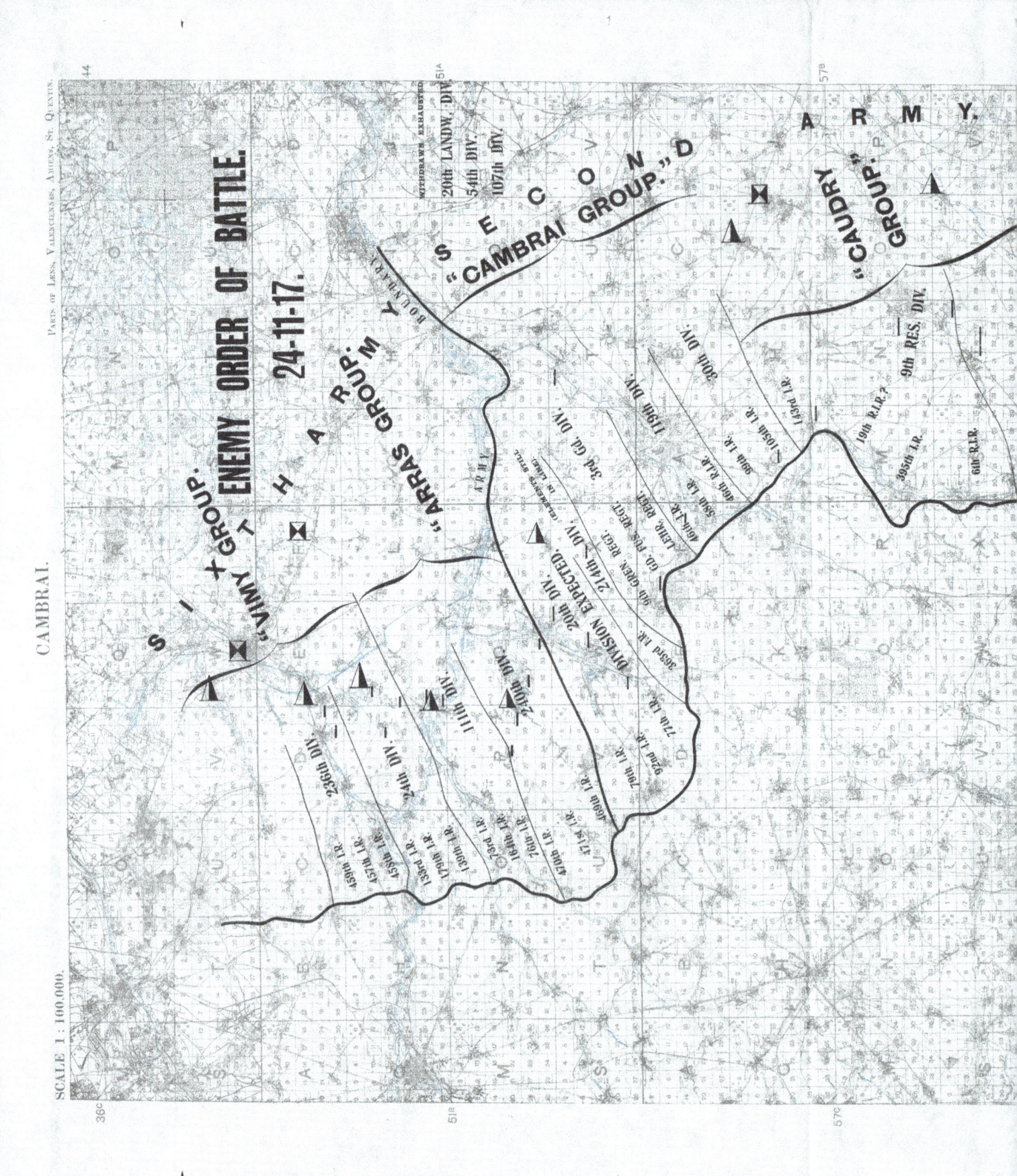

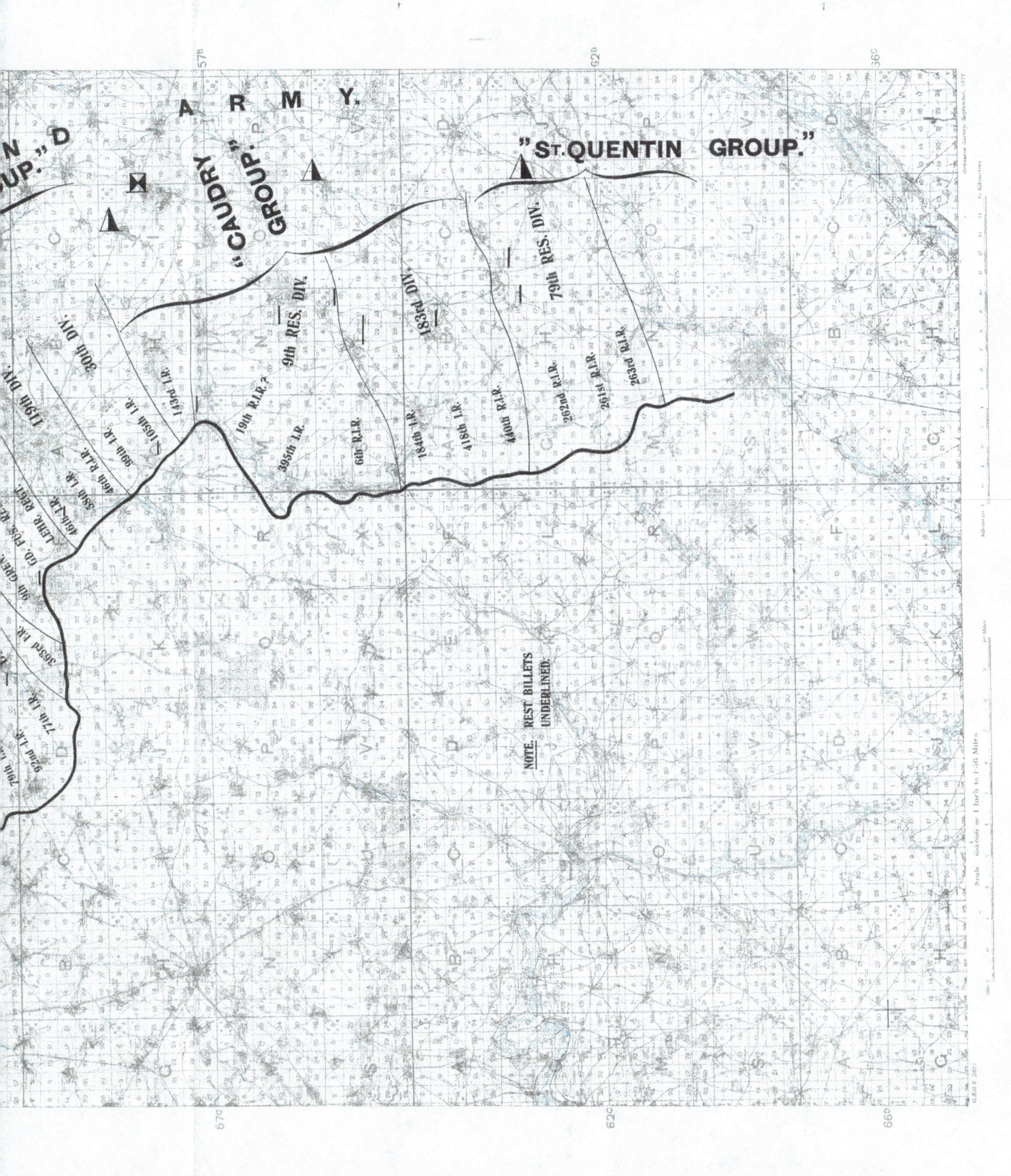

APPENDIX F.

BASED ON THE
WAR DIARY

WAR DIARY

9th Bn. No.H. Fus.

APPENDIX. F.

CAPTURED
BEIT HITTEL

WAR DIARY
9th Bn North'd Fus.

9 NF Vol 28

9TH BN NORTHD FUSILIERS.

WAR DIARY

VOLUME XXIV

DECEMBER.

1917.

Army Form C. 2118.

WAR DIARY
or
INTELLIGENCE SUMMARY.
(Erase heading not required.) 9th North'n Murray 12 Northumberland

Place	Date	Hour	Summary of Events and Information	Remarks and references to Appendices
TRENCHES	Dec 1917	2nd	The Battalion was still in Brigade Support. A Coy in ROOKERY, B Coy in CONCRETE TR, C Coy in EGRET TR, D Coy EGRET LOOP, H. Bn HQ at THE NEST. Two working parties were found by day & night for work under the R.E's. Working parties were found by day & night for work under the R.E's.	MWA
TRENCHES		3rd	The Batt relieved the 2/5th North'ns in the front line & the LEFT SUBSECTOR. The Adjutant in Coy was in H.Q. A Coy with B Coy in the left, & D Coy in Reserve. MALLARD TRENCH. A quiet relief, we were not shelled. Relief complete by 9 am. Our Trench Mortars carried out shoots on enemy trenches & trench board area between 1.30 & 3 pm. The enemy retaliated but we counted no casualties. Patrols were sent out by grand little Co during the night & we put up wire in front. An enemy Machine Gun which was firing on wiring parties in front, we put on doing some fixed lines by a patrol which we sent out. Shelled which retaliation was heard. The enemy seemed to have spent his Machine Gun ammunition firing from NO MAN'S LAND. It is hoped that some of the enemy were hit.	MWA
TRENCHES		4th	A very quiet day. We arrived in the trenches. Patrols were sent out during the night. Wiring carried on as usual.	MWA
TRENCHES		5th	Another quiet day. Wire & front. Patrols were sent out at night to ascertain if the enemy was holding his front line. Voices were heard & the enemy seemed to be in vicinity. At 9.45 pm the 10 Northd Fus relieved us & by 2.15/15 the Battn was in BRIGADE RESERVE in front line.	MWA
TRENCHES		6th	This was also a quiet day. Some shelling by Machine gun artillery, but no casualties were sustained by us. Patrols were sent out as usual during the night. No enemy was encountered in NO MAN'S LAND	MWA

Army Form C. 2118.

WAR DIARY
or
INTELLIGENCE SUMMARY
(Erase heading not required.)

Of ___ M.G. Bn ___ Major N.M.? ___

Instructions regarding War Diaries and Intelligence Summaries are contained in F.S. Regs., Part II. and the Staff Manual respectively. Title pages will be prepared in manuscript.

Place	Date	Hour	Summary of Events and Information	Remarks and references to Appendices
TRENCHES	Dec 7th		The ____ was relieved by the 10th N.F. [Northumberland Fusiliers] Regt. 10th Bgde. A number of our men could not reach our reliefs in the open till 12.30 pm. The ____ marched heavily and then in to camp at NORTHUMBERLAND LINES, where it arrived about 4 pm.	M.S.A.
CAMP	8th		NORTHUMBERLAND LINES. The day was devoted to cleaning up & ____ rearming. Some of the men were bathed & ____ men were inspected by their Coy Commanders. Capt. J.M. ____ assumed the duties of acting adjutant as 2 Lt. H.W. Brighouse had proceeded on any later for ____ ____.	M.S.A.
CAMP	9th		NORTHUMBERLAND LINES. During the morning Physical training was carried out. The Coy went to the baths during the morning. The afternoon was spent in fatigues & light Coy training. This was the ____ ____ ____ here.	M.S.A.
CAMP	10th		NORTHUMBERLAND LINES. Parades & training were carried out during the day.	M.S.A.
CAMP	11th		NORTHUMBERLAND LINES. Grenade training was carried out during the day & a musketry exam & ____ ____ ____ for the gun units.	M.S.A.
CAMP	12th		NORTHUMBERLAND LINES. The day was devoted to cleaning up of kit. The afternoon the battn was in field during the day by the Runner 15th N.F. The ____ ____ ____ to ____ with 15th N.F. which is ____ ____ an attack on the Div. round ____ ____ ____ should, it was thought, that the enemy were observed to retake his old HINDENBURG LINE. Accordingly, the battn left ____ ____ at 6 am and reached	M.S.A.

Army Form C. 2118.

WAR DIARY
or
INTELLIGENCE SUMMARY.
(Erase heading not required.)

Place	Date	Hour	Summary of Events and Information	Remarks and references to Appendices
CAMP.	13th		NORTHUMBERLAND LINES. Parades & training during the morning. The Commanding Officer inspected the horse lines &c. In the evening numerous working parties as for last week were found by the Battn.	
CAMP.	14th		NORTHUMBERLAND LINES. The 103rd Brigade having relieved the 102nd Brigade in the trench sector, the Bn is under orders to hold itself in readiness to move at 10 A.M. to Camp YORKLINES where A.Q.G. Corps & Brigade HQ were allotted. C.O. & Coy went forward to reconnoitre & make arrangements at the above mentioned, and proceeded there later at the hour of the Battn in the line in the left adjacent area by train in case [illegible]	
CAMP.	15th		YORKLINES. Parades & training were carried out during the day by the Companies in Camp. Working parties were found by the Battn for various [illegible] Companies.	
CAMP.	16th		YORKLINES. Bomb, Lewis Gun, Gas & Company training at 10.30 A.M. for remainder of the day. An inter-Coy platoon Lewis is carried on all week.	
CAMP.	17th		YORKLINES. Owing to the inclement weather and where & at it was impossible to carry out training during this day. The talk was spent in cleaning up & preparing for Bn sports the mid the following day.	

Army Form C. 2118

WAR DIARY or INTELLIGENCE SUMMARY

(Erase heading not required.) 9th (Nthn'brian) Bn Northumberland Fusiliers

Place	Date	Hour	Summary of Events and Information	Remarks and references to Appendices
CAMP & TRENCHES	Dec 18th		YORK LINES. A & B Coys & Batn: Headquarters paraded at 8 AM & marched by platoons to the OLD GUN BOOT STORE in N22 b 39 where they met C.D Coys who had marched there from trenches in N16c. Here guides met the later & conducted it to Coys respective places in the front line trenches where the latter relieved the 25th/Bn Nthrbrd Fusiliers. Against which we carried out relief was completed by 12.30pm. The disposition in the Battn area were as follows - A Coy Right Front Coy, B Coy Left Front Coy, D Coy Support Coy in reserve. Battn HQ was in SHOVEL TRENCH. The day has run quiet & except for slight shelling STONE TRENCH with 4.2's & lively machine gun fire. Each front line Coy sent out 2 patrols during the night. The Nth of these patrols was to deny NOMANS LAND to the enemy & also to find part of the enemy wire near N16 b 4 & map or if possible to note & ascertain A Coys patrol which went out before midnight under 2/Lt HILTON clashed with an enemy working party & they replied. The enemy ahead (train & then believed unfortunately Lt HILTON & 2 O.R.'s was wounded. Our patrol then returned to our lines when it was discovered that 2 men were missing. On reached home up later having been to a shell hole, but in the other was missing. On reached home up later having been fired on by the enemy lines by others who did not own the return of prisoners that he walked into Enemy lines by mistake. Was never seen in Coy's front when it was weak in sentries. The Nth T enemy put (24/27) November) shells over attempting to penetrate their lines between two fronts in an to attempt to capture or kill the officer during in no lands. These voluntaries information has reference to the enemy preparation for trench of reporter than a document which was found on a Bosch NCO of this patrol which shortly gave this information of the front.	MWB
TRENCHES	19th		A quiet day was spent in the lines. Work was carried on in trenches by Coy's even during the day. Wiring & ???? at night as in the 18th. The patrols discovered no traces of the enemy & the night was very quiet.	MWB
TRENCHES	20th		Morning during the day the enemy virulently shelled WANCOURT. About 3 minutes at about 3 minutes at about. We thought his heavy artillery was not up to nothing. During the afternoon the shelling ceased. At nothing this he kept quiet but the ??? of enemy's front line sticks. Patrols carried out a	MWB

Army Form C. 2118

WAR DIARY
or
INTELLIGENCE SUMMARY

(Erase heading not required.) 9th (North'd Fusiliers) Br. North'd Fusiliers

Instructions regarding War Diaries and Intelligence Summaries are contained in F. S. Regs., Part II. and the Staff Manual respectively. Title Pages will be prepared in manuscript.

Place	Date	Hour	Summary of Events and Information	Remarks and references to Appendices
TRENCHES	Dec 21st		The day input were taken. Quiet. Work proving. Defaults at night in no man's land & nothing of importance occurred.	M.A.
TRENCHES	22nd		The Battn. was relieved by the 25th N'mbld Fusiliers. A great interest was evinced in the relief which was completed by 12 noon. On which the Battn. moved back to HQ. The Right marched by the TILLOY-WANCOURT ROAD to NI6c. C Coy to (old) SHIKAR AVENUE O19c 27.75; D Coy MARLIERE CAVES. A & B Coys in field trenches muster'd (old) SHIKAR AVENUE in NI6c just North of SLOUGH STATION on the Light Railway. Battn HQ was in dugouts in NI6c. Work proving defaults were found by the trench garrisons in the intervening lines during the night.	M.A.
BILLETS	23rd 24th 25th		Army Quiet. Time was spent in cleaning up & defaults. The Bosch applied about 200 rounds of 5.9 shells ranging for wiring & work to the COTE 81 VALLEY.	M.A.
BILLETS & TRENCHES	26th		The Battn. relieved the 25th Batt. N'mbld Fusiliers in the Front & support sector. A quiet relief was carried out. Relief was complete by 10 A.M. The dispositions were as follows:- C Coy Right front. D Coy Left front. A Coy in support RAKE TRENCH, B Coy in reserve CHARLIERE CAVES. Battn HQ. was again in SHOVEL TRENCH. The remainder of the day & the night were very quiet. Working parties were at work at the wire. The enemy were inactive. Patrols of the third lines advanced to (?) within range of the Hun lines & whenever a working party was heard working. The patrols were able to disperse(?) them.	M.A.
TRENCHES	27th 28th 29th		Three very quiet days were spent in the line. The weather was extremely cold. Much was made of the improvements of defences. Work on wire could not be proceeded with owing to ground not breaking during the days. 25 to 30 shells per day were put into our positions & trenches. A working party at the evening wore of Enemy Artillery worked by moonlight at his front wire entanglements opposite the COTEUR RIVER in the afternoon of 27th Dec. & we came into action but nothing was achieved by the moonlight.	M.A.
TRENCHES	30th		The Battn. was relieved by the 25th N'mbld Fusrs. A normal relief was carried out and completed by 10.30 A.M. A. Minshaw C.D. Coys. Batt. HQ's proceeded to Camp at CARLISLE LINES WAILLY. A & B Coy marched to huts in N16c.	M.A.

1875 Wt. W593/826 1,000,000 4/15 J.B.C. & A. A.D.S.S./Forms/C. 2118.

WAR DIARY
or
INTELLIGENCE SUMMARY

(Erase heading not required.) 9th (NWF Arisa) Bn Northd Fusiliers

Army Form C. 2118

Place	Date	Hour	Summary of Events and Information	Remarks and references to Appendices
CAMP	Dec	31st	CARLISLE LINES. The day was spent in cleaning. Each Cy supplied a working party of 20 N.C.Os & men. Iv wire defensively commenced. Traveling to left flank section & coil of Barb. Wire had been ordered from Ordnance which by hal been unable to hand. In turn by the latter was then in support. Major J R Osborne returned to this Battn from the enemy African command at ALDERSHOT. The Customary New Years eve being observed had we enclosed of this Battn from to day date.	M.L.A.

J W Lafford
2.1.18

J R Osborne
Major
Commdg 9th (NWF Arisa) Bn
Northd Fusiliers

WAR DIARY or INTELLIGENCE SUMMARY

Army Form C. 2118

DECEMBER 1917.

(Erase heading not required.)

Instructions regarding War Diaries and Intelligence Summaries are contained in F.S. Regs., Part II. and the Staff Manual respectively. Title Pages will be prepared in manuscript.

Place	Date	Hour	Summary of Events and Information	Remarks and references to Appendices

Strength of Battalion at beginning of month — 38 Officers 741 ORs
" " " " end of month — 36 Officers 684 ORs

Casualties

	Killed	Wounded	Evacuations	Commissions	Transfers	Released to Mining
	1	8	50	18	2	3

Drafts:
Week ending 8th — 12
"   "   15th — 8
"   "   22nd — 2
"   "   29th — 2
Period ending 31st — 3
Total 82

Officers
Joined
Lieut. F.J. Smart #13
Major R.R. Osborne 30th

Wounded
Lieut. J.E. Melvin 19th
Lieut. H.P. Kettuck 22
Total 25

Posted to TMB
Lieut. H.P. Kettuck 22
Lieut. H.P. Keageer 27th

Struck off (Medical Board)
Lieut. Warm Lane 30th

Transfer to Tank Corps
Lieut. H.P. Keageer 27th

Decorations
57332 Pte. Oliver J. Mclean Medal

APPENDIX 'A'

LEWIS GUNS S.O.S. LINES
SUPPORT GUNS FOR A.A. +
POSTS THUS X
HORSE SHOE POST. DISUSED
sap filled in
LANE
LARK
SUPPORT
AVENUE
SWIFT
WREN ALLEY
MARTIN TR.
CURTAIN SUPPORT
Right Coy HQs
PIONEER
Centre Coy HQs
Bn. HQs.
LONE SAP
FOSTER AVENUE
Res Coy HQs
MALLARD RES.
Res Coy - (for Counter attack) 4 Guns
BULLFINCH SUPPORT
SHAWS AVENUE
NEW BYKER ALLEY
CUT
Left Coy HQs
Dead End
Lewis Gun Covering Valley.
12
14
15
16
17
18
19
20
21
22
S7
S8
S10
S11

[SECRET] **Operation Order No 3.** 2.12.17.

Ref. Map. 1/20,000. 51.B.S.W.
1/10,000 HENINEL Trench Map.

1. The 9th (Northd. Hussars) Bn. Northd. Fus. will relieve the 25th Bn. Northd. Fus. in the left Sub. sector, front line tomorrow Dec. 3rd.

2. Dispositions in the line will be as follows:—
   "A" Coy Centre will relieve "C" Coy of 25th Bn. Northd Fus.
   "B" " Right   "   " "A" " of 25th "   "   "
   "C" " Left   "   " "B" " of 25th "   "   "
   "D" " Reserve "   " "D" " of 25th "   "   "

3. Relief to be completed by 10.0. A.M. All movements will be by platoons at 200 yds interval.

4. Guides as follows will meet the outgoing unit:—
   Right Coy — Junction of PIONEER and CURTAIN 8.0 A.M.
   Centre "   —   "   "   "   "   "   8.20 A.M.
   Left   "   — Coy. H.Q. at 8.0 A.M.
   Reserve   — Junction of MALLARD & FOSTER AV. 8.15 A.M.

5. (a) An advanced party of 1 N.C.O. & 2 O.R. per Coy & R.S.M. from Bn. H.Q. will proceed to take over stores etc at 7.30 A.M.
   (b) One Officer per Coy to take over Coy H.Q. at 8.0 A.M.
   (c) An Officer from Bn. H.Q will take over at 8.30. A.M.

6. A full proportion of specialists will also be sent forward.
   Receipts of stores etc taken over will be forwarded to Orderly Room, also detailed Trench Strength & Disposition Return not later than 4.0 p.m.

7. The following will be handed over on relief:—
   (a) All trench maps, aeroplane photographs & defence schemes.
   (b) Statement of work in progress & proposed work.
   (c) All trench stores etc.

8. Camp kettles etc, the property of Bn. will not be handed over.

9. Coys will wire their arrival in the new areas by using the code-word "WINNIE".

[ACKNOWLEDGE]

W. Sutton Lt.
a/Adjt.

Lt. Col.
Comdg 9th (Northd Hussars) Bn. Northd Fusiliers.

Operation Orders 1   10/12/17.

The Battalion will stand to at 6.15 a.m. tomorrow in Battle Order. The men will remain in their huts.

Details with regard to preparations for any move will be as issued personally to Company Commanders.

      5. a.m. Reveillé
      5.30. a.m. Breakfast.
      6.15. a.m. Stand to.

Cooks will prepare an extra tea ration for all men.

If no movement takes place Orders will be given when to "Stand down"; on the receipt of this order the extra Tea-ration will be issued & the men turn in until time for Parade as stated in Battalion Orders of tonight.

In case of Battalion moving the Reg.t Band under C/pl. Holland will act as Camp Guard.

              Ambrose Craven
                    Capt &
                      Adjt.

War Diary

11.12.1917.

Operation Order No 2.

The Battalion will "Stand to" at 6.15 am tomorrow Battle Order.

Company Commanders and R.S.M. will Report to Orderly Room that Battalion is "Stood to" and ready to move. On receipt of this report the men will turn in and sleep with equipment to hand. One Sentry in each hut being posted to awaken the men in case of a sudden move.

The sounding of two G's will be the signal for the sentries in the huts to turn in also. This will signify "Stand Down"

Reveille will again be sounded at 11. am.
Tea will be provided at 11.30 am.

    5.0 am. Reveille
    6.15 am Stand To
    11.0 am 2nd Reveille
    11.30 am Tea.

Should the Battalion move the Regimental Band under Corporal Holland will act as Camp Guard.

J M Brose Craster

Capt & a/adjt
9th (Nrthd Hussars) Battn Nrthd Fusiliers

War Diary

SECRET Copy No. 1

9th (Northumberland Hussars) Battn. Northumberland Fusiliers
OPERATION ORDERS. No 6

RELIEF. The 103rd Infantry Brigade will relieve the 102nd Infantry Brigade in the left sector of the 34th Divisional Front tomorrow the 14th inst. The 9th (Northumberland Hussars) Battn. Northumberland Fusiliers will relieve the 22nd Battn. Northumberland Fusiliers in Brigade Reserve.

ORDER OF RELIEF. "A" and "B" Companies will move to YORK LINES.

"C" Coy. will be attached to 24/27th Battn. Northumberland Fusiliers in support in N.16.c. where it will relieve "A" Coy of the 22nd Battn. Northumberland Fusiliers.

"D" Coy will move to MARLIERE CAVES in N.23.B where it will relieve a detachment of the 22nd Battn. Northumberland Fusiliers.

GUIDES. Guides for "D" Coy, at the rate of 1 per platoon will be at the end of the duckboard track (N.21.A.70.90) at 9 am.
Guides for "C" Coy. at the rate of 1 per platoon will be at the end of the duckboard track (N.21.A.70.90) at 12 midday.
There will be no guides for "A" and "B" Companies.

ROUTES.
"C" and "D" Coys.   NORTHD LINES – MERCATEL CROSS ROADS. – NEUVILLE VITASSE – WANCOURT ROAD to DUCKBOARD TRACK (N.21.A.70.90)
"A" and "B" Coys.   SUNKEN ROAD WEST OF CAMP.

MEALS. Breakfast 5.45 am.
Dinners. ("C" and "D" Coys will carry unexpended portion of days ration and have dinner at destination of each Company respectively).
"A" and "B" Coys   12 midday.   at YORK LINES.

"D" Coy will move off at 7.15 am. }
"C" Coy will move off at 10.15 am. } Platoons will move at 200 yards
"A" and "B" Coys will move off at 10 am. } interval

OFFICERS CHARGERS. "D" Coy will be on SUNKEN ROAD by "D" Coy lines at 7.15 am.
"C" Coy will be on SUNKEN ROAD by "C" Coy lines at 10.15 am.

TRANSPORT. One limber will be on the SUNKEN ROAD by "D" Coy lines to convey Lewis Guns and Cooking utensils at 6.30 am.
One limber will be on the SUNKEN ROAD by "C" Coy lines to convey Lewis Guns and Cooking utensils at 9.30 am.
One limber will be on the SUNKEN ROAD by "A" Coy lines to convey "A" and "B" Coys Lewis Guns and stores to YORK LINES at 9.30 am.
Two limbers will be on the SUNKEN ROAD by the Orderly Room at 9 am to convey (a) Officers Mess Kit (b) Orderly Room and Signal Stores. (c) return for Officers Valises.

ADVANCE PARTIES. "A" and "B" Coys and Battn. Headquarters will each send 1 N.C.O. and 1 man to take over YORK CAMP at 8 am. They will sign and retain copies) of all receipts for stores and ammunition etc.
All Company Commanders will ascertain the numbers of preserved rations and amount of ammunition to be taken over and notify Battn. Headquarters of immediate requirements by wire.

STORES. Companies will hand over ammunition and preserved rations at present in Coy. reserve, receipts will be obtained in duplicate.
Receipts will also be obtained shewing that the huts, latrines and sanitary arrangements were clean on handing over to incoming unit.

COMPLETION OF RELIEF. will be wired to Battn. Headquarters using code word "HUSSAR" followed by name of Company Commander.

1. WAR DIARY
2. 2nd in Command.
3. "A" Coy.
4. "B" Coy.
5. "C" Coy.
6. "D" Coy.
7. T.O. an. Q.M.
8. I.O.
9. 22nd Bn. NORTHd FUS.
10. R.S.M.

Ambrose Craven
Captain and Adjt.
9th (Northd Hussars) Battn. Northumberland Fus.

13.12.17.

17/12/17

SECRET.   OPERATION ORDERS. No. 7.   Copy No.
9th. (Northumberland Hussars) Battn. Northumberland Fusiliers.

RELIEF. The 9th (Northumberland Hussars) Battn. Northumberland Fus. will relieve the 25th Battn. Northumberland Fus. in the LEFT SUB SECTOR tomorrow the 18th inst.

ORDER OF RELIEF
A. Coy. will relieve RIGHT FRONT Coy. 25th Bn.Northd.Fus.
B. Coy.   "   "   LEFT FRONT Coy. "   "   "   "
C. Coy.   "   "   SUPPORT   Coy   "   "   "   "
D. Coy.   "   "   RESERVE   Coy   "   "   "   "

GUIDES. One guide per Post will meet Front Line and Support Companies and one guide per platoon for Reserve Company at GUM BOOT STORE in N 22 b 3.9 at 10-0 a.m.

ROUTES. A. and B. Coys. and Headquarters, YORK LINES - MERCATEL - NEUVILLE VITASSE - Duckboard track in N 21 a 7.9 then along duckboard track via valley in N16 c to GUM BOOT STORE in N 22 b 3.9
C. and D. Coys.   Direct from N 16 c to GUM BOOT STORE.

MEALS. A. and B. Coys. and Headquarters.
5-30 a.m. Breakfast.
6-0 a.m.   Stand To
7-15 a.m. Tea provided
O.C. C.& D Coys. will make their own arrangements.
Unexpended portion of the days rations will be carried.

TIMES OF DEPARTURE. First platoon of A. Coy. will move off at 8-0 a.m. remainder at 200 yards interval between platoons.

OFFICERS CHARGERS
A. and B. Coys.   8-0 a.m. at YORK LINES.
Headquarters   8-30 a.m. at YORK LINES.

TRANSPORT. One limber per Coy. to be at YORK LINES at 7-30 a.m. to convey Lewis Guns, Rations, and Cooking utensils and Officers Mess kit.
One limber for Headquarters to be at YORK LINES at 8-0 a.m. to convey Headquarters Officers Mess kit and Signal stores.

OFFICERS VALISES PACKS ETC. Officers valises, mens packs and spare kit will be dumped at YORK LINES under charge of Company Quarter Master Sergeants.

STORES. All defence and pursuit schemes, aeroplane photographs, working party details and detail of work in hand and contemplated will be taken over on relief.
Receipts for Trench Stores and certificates of cleanliness of billets will be rendered in duplicate to Battalion Headquarters by 9-0 p.m. tomorrow. Trench Strength and Disposition Returns will be rendered at the same time.

17.12.17

COMPLETION OF RELIEF Will be wired to Battalion Headquarters using code word "TYNE DOCK" followed by name of Company Commander.

OPERATION ORDERS No. 7. (contd.)

[signature]

Captain and A/Adjutant.

9th.(Northd.Hussars) Bn.Northd. Fus.

Copy No. 1. War Diary.
2. Retained.
3. 2nd. in Command.
4. A. Coy.
5. B. Coy.
6. C. Coy.
7. D. Coy.
8. O.C. 25th Bn. Northumberland Fusiliers.
9. T. O. and Q.M.
10. R.S.M.
11. Master Cook.

SECRET   Copy No. 1

OPERATION ORDERS. NO. 8

9th (N.Md. Rangers) Bn. Northumberland Fusiliers.

1. RELIEF
The 25th Bn. Northumberland Fusiliers will relieve the 9th (N.Md. Rangers) Bn. N. Fd. Fusiliers in the LEFT (COTEUL) SUB SECTOR commencing 20th inst. On relief 9th (N.Md. Rangers) Bn. N. Md. Fusiliers will occupy Support trenches vacated by 25th Bn. N. Fd. Fusiliers.

2. ORDER OF RELIEF
A Coy. 9 N.Md. Rangers/N.Md. Bn: relieved by Coy 25th ..
B   "   do   do   do   do   do   do
D   "   do   do   do   do   do   do
C   "   do   do   do   do   do   do

The relieved Coys will move as under:—
A & B Coys and Bn. H.Qrs. to billets in N.16.c.
D Coy to MARLIERE CAVES.
C Coy to ERNET TRENCH at junction with SMIKAR AVENUE. N.17.c. & 77.78.

3. GUIDES
Guides at the pit of ? for Coys and ? Coys and 1 for Platoon ? Support Coy, ? ? ? ? at junction of SHOVEL TRENCH with SOUTHERN AVENUE at 10.30 A.M. Guides Support to the ? COTEUL RIVER & old Gun. ? at ? in N.22.B.5.7. at 9.30 A.M. There will be no guides for rear Coy or Bn.H.Q.

4. COOKERS
A Coy. Cookers will be at N.16.c at 11.0 A.M. and will cook for A & B Coys. Rations for A & B Coys for tomorrow will be prepared on this Cooker.

5. BLANKETS
Blankets for A & B Coys and Bn. H.Q. will be brought to N.16.c with rations of 22nd inst.
Blankets for D Coy will be brought to MARLIERE CAVES with rations for 22nd inst.

6. MEALS
Breakfasts STAND DOWN
Dinners   ? ? ? ? N.16.c.
              C & D Coys ? ? ? ? ?

7. TRANSPORT
Rations & Tea/rations to ? ? for A & B Coys and Bn. H.Q. will be brought to N.16.c at 4.0 A.M. The ? ? rations for other Coys will be brought up tonight.

8. STORES
All defence equipment ? ammunition, aeroplane flares/trench ? party details, details of ? ? ? ? ? taken over ? ? ? ? for ? stores handed over & taken over & ? ? ? ? the cleanliness of trenches will be rendered in duplicate

OPERATION ORDERS (CONTD).

8. STORES   [illegible text about Brigade supply, men & Platoon]
             N.B. [illegible] to be included in Trench
             Stores, and [illegible] found in [illegible] Coy. are
             to be [illegible] for lists.

9. ADVANCED 1 N.C.O. per Coy. will report at their respective
   PARTIES   destinations at 6.30. A.M. to take over Trench Stores,
             billets etc.

10. WARNING Company Commanders are reminded that
             any deficiency or over establishment of S.A.A.
             must be made up before going into trenches.

11. RELIEF   [illegible] 9th Battn. [illegible] will be at the
    COMPLETE [illegible] the [illegible] following by name of Company Commander.
             Company Commanders will notify N.C.O.
             [illegible] when their Companies have taken up their
             new positions.

             21.17.17.

                              Capt & Adjt.
                          9th (Northd. Fus.) Battn.
                              [illegible]

Copies To.
 1. [illegible]
 2. [illegible]
 3. OC. A Coy.
 4. " B "
 5. " C "
 6. " D "
 7. OC. 9th Bn. Northd.Fus.
 8. " "   "
 9. T.O. & Quartermaster
10. R.S.M.
11. [illegible]

SECRET

OPERATION ORDERS No. 9.   Copy No.

9th (Northd Hussars) Battn. Northumberland Fusiliers

1. RELIEF
The 9th (Northd Hussars) Battn Northd Fusiliers will relieve 25th Battn Northd Fusiliers on the LEFT (COJEUL) SUB SECTOR tomorrow 26th inst. Relief to be completed by 10 am.

2. ORDER OF RELIEF
- "C" Coy 9th (N.H.) Bn. Northd Fus. will relieve RIGHT FRONT Coy 25th Bn Northd Fus.
- "D" . . . . LEFT FRONT Coy do
- "A" . . . . SUPPORT Coy do
- "B" . . . . RESERVE Coy do

3. GUIDES
Guides at the rate of 1 per post for Front Line Coys and 1 per Platoon for Support Coy will be at junction of SHOVEL TRENCH with SOUTHERN AVENUE at 8 am.

Guides at the rate of 1 per post for posts South of the COJEUL will be at the junction of EGRET TRENCH with SHIKAR AVENUE at 8 am.

There will be no guides for RESERVE Coy or BATTN. HQRS.

4. OFFICERS' VALISES AND BLANKETS
For "A" and "B" Coys and Battn. HQrs. will be dumped outside Coy. and Battn HQrs and left in charge of 2 men per Coy and 2 men for Battn. HQr. who will rejoin the Battn when same are collected by Transport.

"D" Coy will dump Officers' Valises and Blankets at Reserve Coy. quarters in MARLIERE CAVES under charge of 1 man. This man will be relieved by a guard from "B" Coy as soon as B Coy arrives and will then rejoin his Company.

5. TRANSPORT
The Transport Officer will see that necessary transport for "A" and "B" Coys and Battn. HQrs. is at Battn Hd. Qrs by 8 am. for valises & blankets.

Transport for "D" Coy valises and blankets will be at MARLIERE CAVES at 5.30 p.m. tomorrow night the 26th inst where same will be taken over from "B" Coy.

Transport for the Canteen will be at Battn Hd. Qrs at 8 am and "A" Coy cooker will move back to Transport Lines at this time.

6. STORES
All defence and pursuit schemes, aeroplane photographs, working party details, and details of work in hand and contemplated will be taken over and handed over on relief. Receipts for trench stores taken over and handed over and certificates of cleanliness of trenches and billets will be rendered to Orderly Room by 9 pm. tomorrow 26th inst. in duplicate.

N.B. Gas Blankets are to be included in Trench Stores

7. RELIEF COMPLETE
Will be wired to Battn H Qrs using code word "WORKHOUSE" followed by name of Company Commander.

ACKNOWLEDGE.

Copies To:-
No 1. Retained
2. War Diary
3. 'A' Coy
4. 'B' Coy
5. 'C' Coy
6. 'D' Coy
7. O.C. 25th Battn Northd Fus.
8. T.O. and Qr. M.
9. R.S.M.

J. M. Rose Craven.
Captain and A/Adjutant
9th (Northumberland Hussars) Battn Northd Fusiliers

Dated. 25th December 1917.

Secret   COPY No. 1

OPERATION ORDERS No. 10
9th (Northd. Hussars) Battn Northumberland Fus.

1. RELIEF
The 25th Bn. Northd. Fusiliers will relieve the 9th (Northd. Hussars) Bn Northd Fusiliers in the LEFT (COJEUL) SUB SECTOR tomorrow the 30th inst. Relief to be complete by 10 a.m.

2. ORDER OF RELIEF
"C" Coy 9th (N.H.) Bn Northd. Fus. will be relieved by — Coy 25th Bn Northd Fus
"D"   "   "   "   "   "   "   "   "   "   "   "   "   "   "   "
"A"   "   "   "   "   "   "   "   "   "   "   "   "   "   "   "
"B"   "   "   "   "   "   "   "   "   "   "   "   "   "   "   "

After relief "C" and "D" Coys and Battn Hd.Qrs. will proceed to CARLISLE LINES. "A" and "B" Coys will proceed to old trenches in N.16.c. (central) when they will take over billets vacated by two Coys of 26th Bn Northd Fus.

3. GUIDES
Guides at the rate of 1 per post for front line Coys, one per platoon for Support Coy and 1 per platoon for the two platoons of Reserve Coy in RAKE TRENCH, will be at the junction of SHOVEL TRENCH with SOUTHERN AVENUE at 7.30 a.m.

Guides at the rate of one per post for Posts South of the COJEUL will be at the junction of EGRET TRENCH with SHIKAR AVENUE at 7.30 a.m.

There will be no guides for Battn Hd.Qrs. or the remainder of the Reserve Coy.

4. ROUTES
For "C" and "D" Coys and Battn Hd.Qrs.
SOUTHERN AV — OLD GUM BOOT STORE (N.22 B.3.9.) — DUCKBOARD TRACK to WANCOURT — NEUVILLE VITASSE ROAD — NEUVILLE VITASSE — MERCATEL — SUNKEN ROAD (M.22.B.) — CARLISLE LINES.

For "A" and "B" Coys.
SOUTHERN AV — OLD GUM BOOT STORE (N.22 B.3.9) — N.16.c. (central)

5. TRANSPORT
Officers' Chargers and limbers as under will be on the road near the old GUM BOOT STORE (N.22 B.3.9.) at 10.30 a.m.
1 Limber for Signals and Orderly Room Stores.
1 Limber for "C" and "D" Coys and Bn Hd.Qrs. Officers Mess Kit (at 9. a.m).
1 Limber for "C" and "D" Coys Lewis Guns.
1 Limber for "C" and "D" Coys and Bn. Hd.Qrs. Cooking utensils etc.

6. COOKERS
1 Cooker will be 50 yards along North Road of Cross Roads N.20.B. at 11.30 a.m. and will provide soup for "C" and "D" Coys and Battn Hd.Qrs.
1 Cooker will be at trenches in N.16.c. (central) at 10.30 a.m. when it will prepare dinners for "A" and "B" Coys. This cooker will remain with these Coys whilst the Battn is in reserve.

7. STORES
All defence and pursuit schemes, aeroplane photographs, working party details and details of work in hand and contemplated will be handed over on relief. Receipts for Trench Stores handed over and certificates for cleanliness of trenches will be rendered to Orderly Room by 9 p.m. tomorrow the 30th inst.

Coys will hand over details of work still to be done to complete requisite shelters for S.A.A. and Bombs in accordance with tables supplied. Coy Commanders and R.S.M. will ensure that all their men leave the trenches with their full complement of S.A.A.

8. ADVANCE PARTIES
"C" and "D" Coys and Bn Hd.Qrs. will each send a Senior N.C.O. to take over their respective quarters in CARLISLE LINES, all stores will be signed for and copies of same rendered to Orderly Room with Trench Store lists. Certificates of cleanliness will be given.

These N.C.O's will proceed to Battn Details tonight and report to 2nd Lieut Drysdale at CARLISLE LINES at 7. a.m. tomorrow 30th inst.
"A" and "B" Coys will each send a Senior N.C.O. to (N.16.c (central) to take over as above. The N.C.O's will be at N.16.c (central) by 8 a.m.

OPERATION ORDERS No 10 (CONTD)

GUARD O.C. "B" will detail a guard of 1 N.C.O. and 4 men to report at Divisional Bomb Store (NEUVILLE VITASSE) at 10 a.m. tomorrow 30th inst. when they will relieve a similar guard of the 26th Battn Nrthd Fusiliers. Rations will be delivered to them.

10 RELIEF COMPLETE. Will be wired to Battn H. Qrs. using code word "GOANNA" followed by Company Commanders name. Companies will also inform Orderly Room when their Companies are in billets.

ACKNOWLEDGE.

[signature]
Captain and Adjutant
9th (Nrthd Hussars) Bn Nrthd Fus.

Datd 29th December 1917

Copies to:-
No 1 – Retained
- 2 – War Diary
- 3-6 – OC Coys.
- 7 – T.O. & Q.M.
- 8 – OC 25th Bn Nrthd Fus.
- 9 – OC 26th Bn Nrthd Fus.
- 10 – R.S.M.
- 11 – Master Cook.

SECRET 9"(N-M)Bn North" Fusiliers Copy N° 2

Operation Order. N° 4.

1/ On the evening of the 5th inst the right Battalion boundary will be altered and will be PIONEER ALLEY inclusive to 9th Bn.

2/ Post N° 9, 9A will be relieved by the 24/27 Bn North Fus.

3/ The following alterations in dispositions will be made:—
Right Coy. will hold 10-12-14 Posts and a post at junction of SWIFT SUPPORT and PIONEER.— Counter attack plats in Swift and Curtain — support platoon will patrol MARTIN at intervals during the night

Centre Company will hold 15-16 17-18A posts with standing patrol by night between 15-16 posts groups from supporting plat should cover Dead Beech alley & Foster Avenue.

Left Company Dispositions remain unaltered.

4/ Time Right Coy will probably be relieved in Posts 9 and 9A about 2-30 p.m. Alterations given in para 3 will be carried out as quickly as possible.

Companies will wire as follows.
Right Coy when 24/27 Bn.} Code word
has taken over posts 91-99} FIFTH.

Right & Centre Coy when dispositions} FUSILIERS.*
given in para 3 are completed

* followed by name of Coy Comdr

5/ Coys concerned will reconnoitre
new positions at once; (section Comdrs
& men if possible) should go over the
ground by daylight

6/ ACKNOWLEDGE.

6/12/17   J Ambrose Craven
                        Capt & Adjt
                        9/(N) Bn North'd Fusiliers

Copies 1/ Retained
       2/ War Diary
       3/ O.C. A Coy
       4/ OC B "
       5/ OC C "
       6/ OC D "
       7/ OC 24/27 North'd Fus.

SECRET   OPERATION ORDER No 5.   COPY No.

RELIEF: The 101st Infy. Bde. will relieve the 103nd Infy. Bde. in the RIGHT Sector tomorrow the 7th inst.
The 10th LINCOLNS (101st Bde) will relieve the 9th (N.H) North'd.Fus. in the LEFT Subsector.

ORDER of RELIEF. Coys Sect.	10th LINCOLNS		9th North'd Fus.
RIGHT	B	will relieve	B.
CENTRE.	A	"	A.
LEFT	D	"	C.
SUPPORT	C	"	D.
Bn. H.Qrs	—		—

GUIDES. One per Platoon. + one for BN QRS. Guides for RIGHT Coy. will be at the junction of CUCKOO & PIONEER at 11 a.m., other guides will be at Bn. H.Qrs. at 11 a.m..

ROUTE OUT. Via HINDENBURG LINE – CRUCIFIX (N 33 D.30.95) – N.26 central – NEUVILLE VITASSE – MERCATEL – NORTHUMBERLAND LINES.

MEALS. Breakfast — in trenches.
DINNERS — Two cookers will meet Coys. at the Cross Rd. at N.32.b.7.8. at 1-30 pm.. Cookers will be

MEALS. CONTD. allotted as follows :— one for B&D Coys and one for A&C Coys. "B&D" Coy cooker must proceed beyond the crest of the hill towards NEUVILLE-VITASSE before the men have their meal, the cooker for A&C Coys. will remain south of the crest.

Care will be taken that no men remain standing on the crest.

TRANSPORT. One limber will be at the CRUCIFIX at 11am. for carrying H.Qr & Coy. mess kit — Batmen going out with this kit will proceed VIA FOSTER AV. Three limbers will be at the CRUCIFIX at 1 pm. to carry Lewis Guns & magazines, Signalling, orderly Room & other stores.

Officers changes will be at the CRUCIFIX at 1-30 pm.

ADVANCE PARTY. One N.C.O. per Coy. will proceed to NORTHUMBERLAND LINES tomorrow where they will report to 2nd Lt. Drysdale at 7-30 am. These men will leave tonight.

STORES. All trench stores, aeroplane photos, maps, defence schemes and programmes of work and proposed will be handed over and receipts obtained. A receipt will also be obtained to the effect that all dugouts, trenches, latrines &c., were handed over in a clean and sanitary condition. All receipts to be rendered to Btn. O.R. by 9 a.m. the 8th. inst.

COMPLETION OF RELIEF. Will be wired to Bn. Hd. Qrs. using code word "TYNE" and Coy Commanders name.

6.12.17.

COPIES Nº 1. Retained
2. WAR DIARY.
3. O.C. A. Coy.
4. O.C. B. Coy.
5. O.C. C. Coy.
6. O.C. D. Coy.
7. Trans. Offr.

SECRET.   COPY No......
Ref. Maps QUEANT
and HERMIES.   36th.(S)Bn.NORTHUMBERLAND FUSILIERS.
Sq.1: 1/10,000   OPERATION ORDER No.115.
                                                          2nd December.1917.

1. A raid, with the object of killing and capturing enemy and destroying
   dug-outs, will be carried out against the enemy trenches N.W. of
   FONTAINE LES CROISILLES on the night of the 5/6th.December 1917.

2. A party from D and A Coy under 2/LIEUT.W.W.MILN has been selected
   for this operation.

3. The locality to be raided is bounded as follows:-
        U.1.b.73.70.
        U.1.b.85.92.
        U.1.b.99.82.
        U.2.a.01.68.
        U.1.b.90.64.

4. In conjunction with the raid there will be an Artillery, Trench and
   Stokes Mortar and Machine Gun barrage, and a Chinese attack will
   take place on the enemy trenches in 0.32.a. and 0.26.a.

5. Detail of organization and action of parties has been communicated
   separately to those it concerns.

6. A party of 4 O.Rs from 257th. Field Coy.R.E. will accompany the
   second wave for the purpose of destroying enemy concrete shelters or
   other enemy material or emplacements that may be found.

7. The Time Table will be as follows:-
   (a) Zero minus 1¼ hours, parties to be assembled in SWIFT SUPPORT
       where hot soup will be served.
   (b) Zero minus 1 hour, parties leave SWIFT SUPPORT.
   (c) Zero minus 10 minutes, parties to be formed up 20 yds. in
       front of our wire in front of the top of FIRST AVENUE.
   (d) Zero hour, barrage commences.
   (e) Zero plus 3 minutes, barrage lifts to support line and
       parties enter enemy front line.
   (f) Zero plus 6 minutes, barrage lifts off support line and
       forms box barrage. Second wave advances on support line.
   (g) Zero plus 36 minutes, parties commence to retire.

8. Battalion Headquarters will open at Adv.Bn.Hdqrs. in dug-out at
   0.31.c.75.64. at Zero minus 3 hours.
                              the parties
9. While crossing NO MANS LAND will keep well closed up in their
   respective waves. If discovered crossing the wire the raiding troops
   will throw bombs and rush into the trench.

10. Prisoners will be passed back to O.C. Raid and will be immediately
    sent on direct to Advanced Battalion Headquarters.
    2/LIEUT.D.E.LAW and a party of 10 O.R. of B.Coy will be at Adv.Bn.
    Hdqrs.,will collect prisoners there and on receipt of orders will
    take them on to Brigade Headquarters.
    Strict precautions will be taken to prevent any intercourse between
    prisoners and destruction of documents by them.

11. Any anti-gas Apparatus, shoulder badges or other kit useful for
    identification purposes will be brought back.

12. During the retirement the Officer or N.C.Os in charge of parties
    will report "All Clear" to O.C. Raid as they pass.

                                                        (continued)

Operation Order No. 115. (continued)

13. MAJOR H.H.NEEVES. D.S.O., M.C. with 2 Runners and 2 Signallers will take up a position in our front line with an Artillery Liaison Officer. He will be responsible for sending back all information to Adv.Bn.Hdqrs. by wire or runner.
At Zero plus 24 he will send up a Golden Rain Rocket as a signal to the raiding troops to retire. From Zero plus 24 onwards pairs of Green Very Lights will be sent up to act as a guide for the return of the raiding troops. On their return a Blue Star Rocket will be sent up as a signal to the Artillery to cease fire. This will also be reported to Battalion Headquarters by wire.

14. LIEUT. F.A.GAMBLE with 3 N.C.Os and 9 men will assist MAJOR H.H.NEEVES. D.S.O., M.C. in the front line by checking the number of the party as they return. He will also establish Sentry Posts at selected spots to guide the party down FIRST AVENUE.

15. In addition to the above signals the O.C. Raid will order the retirement by French Horn or by runner using code word.
If the O.C. Raid considers the situation demands it, he will order the retirement earlier than laid down.
If MAJOR H.H.NEEVES. D.S.O., M.C. hears the French Horn sound before Zero plus 24 minutes he will immediately send up the Golden Rain Rocket and commence sending up Green Very Lights.

16. An Officers Patrol under 2/LIEUT. G.H.HALL will leave our front line at a time to be notified later at the top of FIRST AVENUE and lay tapes towards the gaps in the enemy's wire at U.1.b.8.9. and U.1.b.7.8.
This Patrol will also reconnoitre the gaps in enemy wire and will report completion of the work to O.C. Raid at LEFT SUPPORT.
2/LIEUT. G.H.HALL will then act as a guide to the party to the tapes.

17. The Lewis Gun Officer will arrange with O.C. Co/27th.NORTH'D FUSRS. for protection of the flanks of the raid with Lewis Guns.

18. 2 Signallers with the raiding troops will deal out a wire to connect O.C.Raid with MAJOR H.H.NEEVES.D.S.O.,M.C. Sergt.Gilmore will arrange communication between MAJOR H.H.NEEVES.D.S.O.,M.C. and Adv.Bn.Hdqrs.by D III and Lamp. The Brigade Signalling Officer is arranging communication between Adv.Bn.Hdqrs. and Brigade Hdqrs.

19. The following code will be used between O.C.Raid and Major H.H.NEEVES. D.S.O.,M.C.and thence to Adv.Bn.Hdqrs.
   I I I............Raid party has got in.
   C C C............Raid party cannot get in.
   H H H............Raid apparently proceeding satisfactorily
   O O O............Raid party are all out.

20. The Medical Officer will be at the Aid Post in Dug-out A 44 (N.36.d.9.6.). Four Stretcher Bearers from each of A and D Coys will be in the front line just to the left of FIRST AVENUE and 4 from each of B and C Coys will form a relay post at Adv.Bn.Hdqrs.

21. 2/LIEUT.T.J.WALLEN and 2 N.C.Os A.Coy will be at the junction of CONCRETE RESERVE and FIRST AVENUE at Zero plus 15 minutes. He will collect the party there after the raid and take them back to the HINDENBURG SUPPORT.

22. Details regarding Dress, Equipment, Synchronisation of watches and Zero Hour will be notified later.

23. ACKNOWLEDGE.

(signature)
CAPT. A/ADJT.
 9TH. (S) Bn. NORTHUMBERLAND FUSILIERS.

COPY No 1 - A.Coy
" No 2 - B.
" No 3 - C.
" No 4 - D.
" No 5 - RETAINED
" No 6 -
" No 7 - MAJ. H.H.NEEVES. D.S.O. M.C.
" No 8 - 103RD BRIGADE
" No 9 - RIGHT GROUP R.A
" No 10 - 24/24TH BN N.F.
" No 11 - 9TH BN N.F.
" No 12 - 20TH MIDDLESEX REGT.

SECRET.   COPY NO......3.

103RD INFANTRY BRIGADE.

OPERATION ORDER NO. 159.

Ref. Map 1/10,000 U.T.S. Sheet 272 Edition 10.

1. A Raid will be carried out by the 26th Bn. Northd. Fusiliers on the 5th December.

2. Object:- to kill or capture enemy and destroy dugouts.

3. Locality to be raided:-
   Enemy Front Line between
   U.1.b.75.75. to U.1.b.85.95.   *amended 3.12.'17.*
   and dugouts between
   U.1.b.97.80. and U.2.a.0.7.

4. Strength of Raiding Party-
   (a) Infantry Party- 3 Officers 60 O.R.
   (b) R.E. Party   - 4 O.R.

5. There will be an Artillery, Heavy, Medium and Light Trench Mortar, and Machine Gun Barrage from Zero hour till the Raiding party has withdrawn.

6. The Signal for all clear and cease fire will be sent from a Battalion Forward Command Post in our Front Line at 0.31.d.65.20. by wire and one Blue Star Rocket.

7. The detailed action of-
   (a) Infantry and R.E.
   (b) Artillery and Mortars.
   (c) Light Trench Mortars.
   (d) Machine Guns
       is forwarded herewith to Units concerned.

8. Battalions will arrange for the Trenches to be cleared with the exception of necessary Lewis Guns and Sentries from Zero hour until any hostile retaliation has died down.

9. Watches will be synchronised at Right Battalion Headquarters N.36.b.3.1. for all Units concerned at 10.a.m. and 5.p.m. on the 5th inst.,

10. ZERO hour will be notified later.

11. ACKNOWLEDGE.

A.F.G. Perkins
CAPTAIN.
BRIGADE MAJOR.
103RD INFANTRY BRIGADE.

3.12.17.

Issued through Signals at 9.a.m.

DISTRIBUTION.

Copies Nos. 1 & 2 retained.	Copy No. 11.	207th Fd. Coy R.E.
Copy No. 3.	9th Northd. Fus.	" " 12	101 Infy Bde.
" " 4.	24/27th Bn. Nor. Fus.	" " 13	102 " "
" " 5.	25th " " "	" " 14	Right Infy. Bde.
" " 6.	26th " " "	" " 15	174th Tun. Coy.
" " 7.	103rd M.G.Coy.	" " 16	102nd F.A.
" " 8.	103rd L.T.M.B.	" " 17	Staff Capt.
" " 9.	Right Group R.A.	" " 18	Bde. Sigs.
" " 10.	34th Div. "G"		

10/3⁴ 96/29

War Diary

9th (North Russian) Battalion North'd Fusiliers.

(January 1918.)

WAR DIARY or INTELLIGENCE SUMMARY

Army Form

(Erase heading not required.) 9th (North American) Regt North Fusiliers

Place	Date	Hour	Summary of Events and Information	Remarks and references to Appendices
CAMP	January 1918 1st		CARLISLE LINES. Ref. M16a.8.9 (51bSW.) At this time the Battn was in Brigade Support with disposition as follows. A & B Coys in old trenches in N16c. C & D Coys in Battn HQ in camp at CARLISLE LINES. Owing to the fact that the Intradrm was so difficult of access having regard to the winter, fatigues required turn inside to carry on work in camp. Each Coy found 20 Officers & 50 men for work every day improving & deepening reserve & communication trenches in Centre Sector of the Brigade Front & also wiring infront of Support trenches in this sector.	MSA
CAMP & TRENCHES	3rd		CARLISLE LINES. C & D Coys & Battn HQs paraded at 8am & marched by platoons via MERCATEL - NEUVILLE VITASSE - TILLOY WANCOURT ROAD to the LEFT (COTFOD) subsector. A & B Coys marched direct from the old trenches in N16c. The Battn relieved the 25th Battn NORTH FUSILIERS. A normal relief was carried out, relief having completed at 12 noon. The enemy shelled SOUTHERN AVENUE whilst the Battn was moving up, & relieving two men of C Coy wounded. The rest of the day was quiet in the line. Working parties were employed by the RE's at night wiring & also we carried out patrols were sent out by front line Companies; the enemy was not met & no patrols could be seen in NO MAN'S LAND. The disposition of Coys were as follows A Coy - RIGHT FRONT COY. - B Coy LEFT FRONT COY. - C Coy in RESERVE in RAKE TRENCH & D Coy in SUPPORT in HOE SUPPORT & LOCK TRENCH - D Coy in RESERVE in RAKE TRENCH Bn HQ Hqrs quarters in SHOVEL TRENCH.	MSA
TRENCHES	4th		A fairly quiet day was spent in the trenches. At 4.15pm the enemy put an occasional shell over N15 a's and TANK DUMP, apparently trying to knock at the huts of MERCATEL. SOUTHERN AVENUE was shown in a few places in front of this. At 10.15pm the enemy put a barrage down on our ELF sector about Nr. N16 c5 by PONCHY. The SOS was put up & our artillery immediately replied. The enemy was about 15 mins & every thing was quiet again. No raid mine canisters or whizz-bangs sent out but no real ...	MSA

1875. Wt. W593/326 1,000,000 4/15 J.B.C. & A. A.D.S.S./Forms/C.2118.

WAR DIARY or INTELLIGENCE SUMMARY

Army Form C. 2118

(Erase heading not required.) 9th Bn (North Ansac) Br North Trailers

Place	Date	Hour	Summary of Events and Information	Remarks and references to Appendices
TRENCHES	Jan'y 4th (cont)		Patrols. The night was very quiet & the enemy was not met in NO MAN'S LAND.	Illid.
"	5th & 6th		Two very quiet days were spent in the line. Snow shelving during the day. Many men were confined to caves. Patrols were sent out each night in C.L. but the enemy was not met. Working parties returned to work during snow shower.	Illid.
"	7th		The Battalion was relieved by the 25th Bn North Australian. A mountain relief was carried out & relief was complete at 2.30. Moving the Bath march into Brigade Support & company distributed as follows. A Coy in GRIEVE. B Co in WANCOURT-TILLOY Road (NIGD). B & C Coy in HARLIERE CAVES. D Co in EGRET TRENCH. Bath HQ at WANCOURT-TILLOY Road (NW). The Battn supplied working parties at night, mainly in front of NEW GANNET TRENCH	Illid.
BILLETS	8th, 9th 10th		Three very quiet days spent in support. The weather all through at NEUVILLE VITASSE and work during coding by working parties. Who supplied ration.	Illid.
TRENCHES	11th		The Battn relieved the 25th Battn North Aust'n in the LEFT (COJEUL) Sub sector. Approach march was carried out which was complete by 11.30 AM. The line was taken over with these Coys in the front line each with a platoon in support. One Coy in reserve. The disposition of Coys was as follows. Right Coy (SOUTH COJEUL) D Coy. Centre Coy C Coy. Left Coy B Coy. HQ Coy held 1 platoon in dug out in HIDE SUPPORT. A Coy was in reserve in BAKE TRENCH. Battn HQ at SHOVEL TRENCH. And two sections of Vickers guns were spent in the line. Working parties were carried out by Coys & end front line Coys and mid and Vickers parael. The enemy was not encountered on our patrols but on LANYARD TRENCH & front of his wire enemy left. The Battn was moved to the front on the night of 24/27 to Battn but were captured 3 men from enemy picket in NO MAN'S LAND who are valuable information that the enemy in the neighbourhood opposite us were relieved & night to attack by us throughout this period of tour.	Illid.

WAR DIARY
or
INTELLIGENCE SUMMARY

(Erase heading not required.) Of [N.W.] Hussars/br N.W. Hundred and Twelve

Army Form C. 2118

Place	Date	Hour	Summary of Events and Information	Remarks and references to Appendices
TRENCHES.	Jan 12th		A quiet day was spent in the line. Work was carried on improving the trenches. Wiring was done at night by Trenching Coy & each Coy sent out officer's patrols. The whole of NO MANS LAND was thoroughly patrolled, but active enemy patrols were found in front of the enemy trenches, no Germans were met in NO MAN'S LAND. At 5 PM the enemy put a heavy barrage on the front line & support trenches from 7 mm Lechn. Afterwards was No. NCH.Y. There was no evidence till further of hostile & two golden lights and S.O.S. were up & our guns commenced rapid fire. All was again quiet at 5.30 PM	MWR
"	13th		A very quiet day was spent in the line. Nothing unusual occurred. Work was carried on as usual & the wire protective was perfected. The enemy was very quiet the night passed without incident.	MWR
"	14th		At about 1.5 pm the enemy trench mortars opened on our front line with M.T.M.s. In all about 30 rounds were fired, including 1 dud. Shelling ceased at 1.55 pm. At 4 pm new 3 direct hits on the trench which we knew, & under 30 yards at spot, 014.a.75.25. He also cut a gap about 20 to 30 wide in our wire in front of this place. The enemy twice attempted to break in our wiring party, who went out to repair it & repair this gap. Actions of our wiring party to never went out & the enemy Coy Sergt. in that place got up [illegible] of the Gap during the relief & was shot. Also in front of NO MAN'S LAND was cleared of the enemy.	MWR
"	15th		The Battn was relieved by the 25th Battn NMWU 2nd. A quiet relief was carried out, relief was complete at 4h 30 am. The Battn moved into Brigade Reserve with 2 Coys & Battn HQs at CARLISLE LINES. Working parties of relief [illegible] & 2 Coys at Battle HQs at CARLISLE LINES. Working parties of [illegible] commanded by [illegible] were found by the Battn during the afternoon [illegible]	MWR

Army Form C. 2118

WAR DIARY
or
INTELLIGENCE SUMMARY

(Erase heading not required.) 9th (North Antrim) Bn. N.N.I.H. Fusiliers

Place	Date	Hour	Summary of Events and Information	Remarks and references to Appendices
CAMP.	Jan 16, 17, 18th		CARLISLE LINES. Working parties were supplied daily clearing main Communication Trenches. The two forward Companies returned to CARLISLE LINES on the 18th. On the 19th inst. this Battn. relieved the 21st Batt. N.N.I.F. in the LEFT (COTEUX) Subsector. The relief was commenced & was complete by 8pm. The night was quiet. Parties were sent out by each of the forward Coys to reinforce the enemy's wire in NO MAN'S LAND. The disposing of the Battn. after relief were as follows. D Coy on the right (SOUTH COTEUX) - C Coy on Centre - A Coy on Left. B Coy was in Support in RAKE TRENCH, Battn. HQrs in SHOVEL TRENCH.	M.W.X.
TRENCHES	20th		A very quiet day was spent in the line. Work clearing & revetting trenches was carried on by all Companies. Patrols sent out by front line Coys report all quiet.	M.W.A.
"	21st		Another quiet day was spent in the line. Nothing unusual occurred. The night was quiet & patrols sent out by front Coys reported no signs of the enemy whilst in NO MAN'S LAND.	M.W.A.
"	22nd		Nothing of importance happened during the day. Patrols discovered no enemy working parties in NO MAN'S LAND. The artillery on both sides enjoyed same. No patrols could otherwise -	M.W.A.
"	23rd		The Batt. was relieved by the 21st Bn. N.N.I.H. Fus. The relief was a moved one & was complete by 8pm. After relief the Batt. moved to Bois-pre Subsector with dispositions as follows. A & C Coys in MARLIERE CAVES. D Coy EGRETT TR. D Coy Battn HQrs. N16.C.	M.W.S.
Billets	24th		A very quiet day was spent. Working parties clearing C.T.s were furnished at night by the Battn.	M.W.S.

1875 Wt. W.593/326 1,000,000 4/15 J.B.C. & A. A.D.S.S./Forms/C. 2118.

WAR DIARY
or
INTELLIGENCE SUMMARY

Army Form C. 2118

(Erase heading not required.) 9th (Northd Hussars) Bn North Fusiliers

Place	Date	Hour	Summary of Events and Information	Remarks and references to Appendices
Billets	25th		A very quiet day was spent in the occupied area. The Batt. was relieved by the 2nd Batt. The Suffolk Regt. The relief was without incident and was complete by 8pm. M.M. the Batt. marched toward Company to MERCATEL via NEUVILLE VITASSE, ATHEMERLETEIL the Batt. entrained & proceeded to No 2 CAMP BLAIREVILLE arriving there about 10pm.	M.W.S.
Camp	26th, 27th, 28th 29th, 30th, 31st		Cleaning up, training etc were carried out according to programme.	M.W.S.

B.A.Wignall Lt Col.
commanding 9th (Northumberland Hussars) Battn.
Northumberland Fusiliers.

Army Form C. 2118

WAR DIARY
or
INTELLIGENCE SUMMARY
(Erase heading not required.)

JANUARY 1918.

Instructions regarding War Diaries and Intelligence Summaries are contained in F.S. Regs., Part II. and the Staff Manual respectively. Title Pages will be prepared in manuscript.

Place	Date	Hour	Summary of Events and Information	Remarks and references to Appendices

			Strength of Battalion at beginning of month — 36 Officers 684 O.Rs.
			 " " " end of month — 43 " 741 "
			
			 Casualties:
			 Killed Wounded Evacuations Commissions Transfers
			 1 10 51 1 5 = total 68
			
			 Drafts:
			 Period ending 5th Jany 1918 — 3
			 " " 12" " — 52
			 " " 19" " — 2
			 " " 26" " — 9
			 " " 31" " — 59
			 Total 125
			
			 Officers:
			 Joined Transfers to Eng.
			 Capt R.W.L. Dallas 9/18 2/Lt G. Young Lieut E. Guy 31/12/17
			 2/Lt Barker 9/18 " W. Catherlone 9/18 To senior Officers' Course
			 " " Brown 9/18 " R.H. Craig 12/18 Major J.S. Allen M.C. 1/18
			 " " Dawson " W. Broughton 13/18
			                          " A.D. McEwen 13/18
			
			 Decorations
			 Mentioned in Despatches Croix de Guerre
			 Lieut Col. T.A. Vignoles D.S.O. Lieut D.P. Kilpatrick 14787 Sgt. Stafford J.
			 Captain J.P. Brady
			 2/Lieut J.L. Milton, 10285 Col Marsh J. Distinguished Conduct Medal
			                                         12250 C.Sm Browett G.	

1875 Wt. W593/826 1,000,000 4/15 J.B.C. & A. A.D.S.S./Forms/C. 2118.

APPENDICES
to
WAR DIARY FOR JANUARY 1918

"A".   MAP SHEWING POSTS ON LEFT COJEUL SUB-SECTOR

"B".   OPERATION ORDERS Nos 11 TO 17

"C".   2 SPECIAL ORDERS OF THE DAY BY F.M. SIR DOUGLAS HAIG, COMMANDER IN CHIEF.

"D".   SPECIAL ORDER OF THE DAY BY MAJOR GENERAL C.L. NICHOLSON COMMANDING 34th DIVISION

"E".   CONGRATULATORY LETTER FROM THE INHABITANTS OF ASHINGTON.

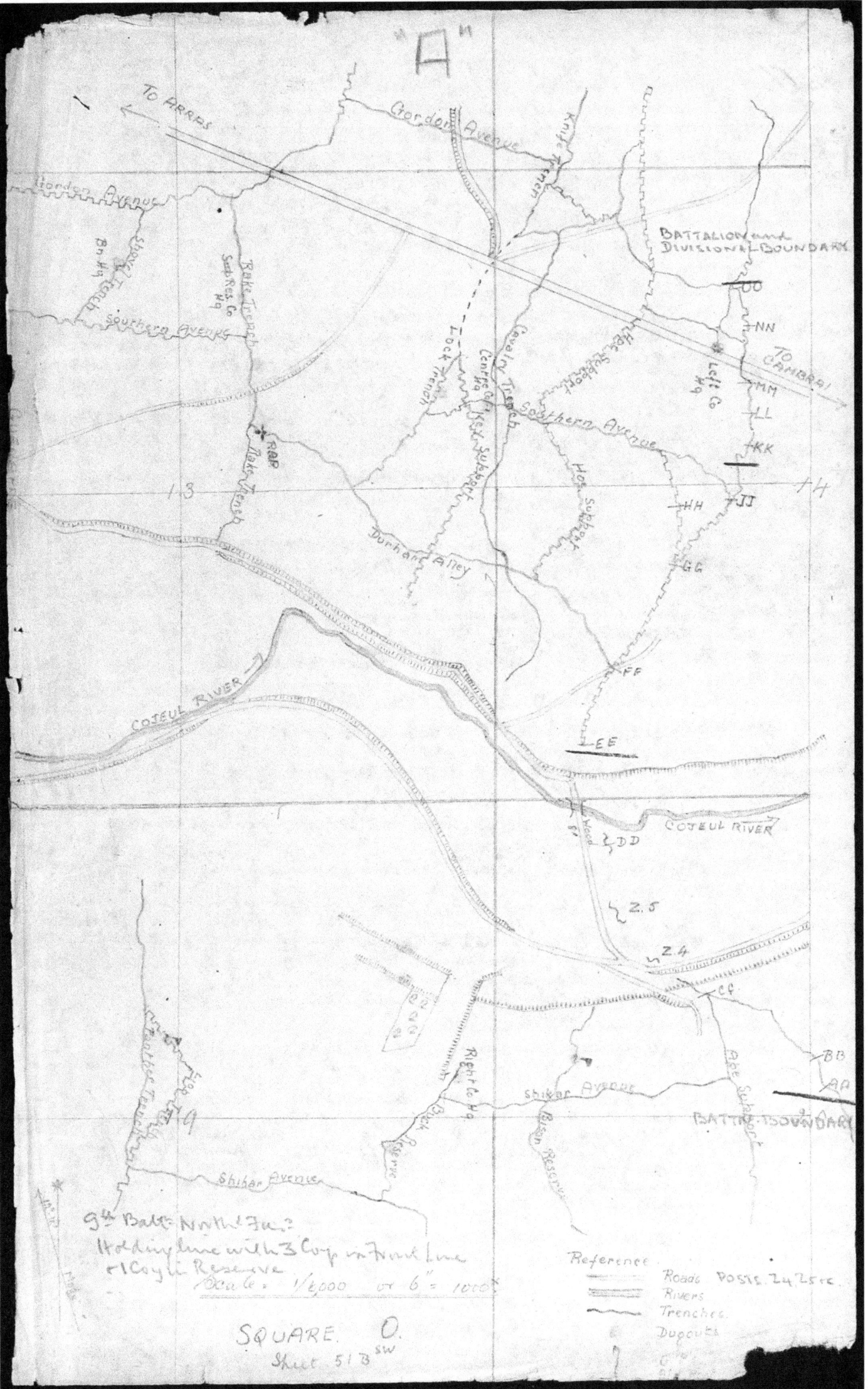

SECRET "B" **OPERATION ORDERS No 11** Copy No 1
                                            2nd Jany 18.
9t (Northld Hussars) Battn Northumberland Fusiliers

RELIEF
The 9th (Northd Hussars) Battn North Fusiliers will relieve the 25th Battn Northumberland Fusiliers in the LEFT (COJEUL) SUB SECTOR tomorrow 3rd inst.

ORDER OF RELIEF
"A" Coy will relieve RIGHT FRONT Coy 25th Bn Nthld Fus
"B" " " " LEFT FRONT Coy " " " "
"C" " " " SUPPORT Coy " " " "
"D" " " " RESERVE Coy " " " "

Guides
At the rate of 1 per post for front line boys and 1 per platoon for Support and Reserve boys will be at the junction of SHOVEL TRENCH with SOUTHERN AVENUE at 10.30 am. Guides at the rate of 1 per post for posts South of Cojeul will be at the OLD GUM BOOT STORE N22 B3.9 at 9.30 am.

Routes
"C" and "D" Coys and Headquarters. CARLISLE LINES - MERCATEL - NEUVILLE VITASSE - Duckboard track in N21a thence along WANCOURT - TILLOY Road.
"A" and "B" Coys direct from N16 C to Guides' rendezvous.

Meals
"C" and "D" Coys and Headquarters
6.30 am. Breakfast
"A" and "B" Coys will make their own arrangements. Unexpended portion of days rations to be carried.

Times of Departure
First platoon of "A" Coy at 9 am, others at 200 yards interval followed by "B" Coy at similar intervals.
First platoon of "C" Coy at 8 am, others at 200 yards interval followed by "D" Coy at similar intervals.
Headquarters - 9 am under Signal Officer.

Officers Chargers
"C" and "D" Coys - 8 am CARLISLE LINES
M. O. - 9 am do do
Headquarters - 9.30 am do do

Transport
1 limber per Coy for "C" and "D" Coys to be at CARLISLE LINES at 7.30 am to convey Lewis Gun, Rations, Cooking Utensils, Officers Mess Kit to OLD GUM BOOT STORE N22 B3.9.
1 limber for Orderly Room and Signal Stores and H. Qrs. II cooking utensils and
1 limber for Headquarters Officers' Mess Kit and Rations to be at CARLISLE LINES at 9 am to convey same to OLD GUM BOOT STORE N22 B.3.9.
A sufficient number of these limbers will be detailed to collect "A" and "B" Coys Officers messes and mess blankets in N16 C on their return journey and will bring them to CARLISLE LINES.

Officers Valises Packs etc.
Officers' valises, mens packs and blankets and spare kit will be dumped at CARLISLE LINES under charge of Coy. Q. M. Sergts.

Stores
All defence and pursuit schemes, aeroplane photographs, working party details, and details of work in hand and contemplated will be taken over and handed over on relief.
Receipts for trench stores taken over and certificates for cleanliness of billets will be rendered in duplicate to Battn Headquarters by 4 pm tomorrow 3rd inst. Trench Strength and Disposition Returns in accordance with proforma to be rendered at same time.
Marching out states will be rendered to Orderly Room before leaving CARLISLE LINES by "C" and "D" Coys and Headquarters. "A" and "B" Coys will send their marching out states to Battn Headquarters in SHOVEL TRENCH on their way to Front Line.

Operation Orders No 11 (Continued)   2.1.1918

1. Advance Parties

A proportion of all specialists will be sent up from Coys. and Battn Headquarters tonight where they will remain overnight.

1 Senior N.C.O per Coy, and the Battn Lewis Gun Sergt will be sent up tonight. They will check and take over all stores.

O.C. "D" Coy will detail an officer to proceed first thing tomorrow morning to supervise the taking over of trench stores by these N.C.O's.

2. Band

The Band will be attached to "D" Coy and will march out of camp with "D" Coy. They will be available for working parties.

3. Completion of Relief

will be wired to Battn Headquarters using code word "HINNY" followed by name of Company Commander.

ACKNOWLEDGE.

J.W. MacLiarn.
Captain and Adjutant
9th (Northd Hussars) Bn Northd Fus.

COPIES TO:-
No 1. War Diary
- 2 Retained
- 3-6 O.C. Coys.
- 7 O.C. 25th Bn Northd Fusiliers.
- 8 T.O. & Q.Mr.
- 9 Signal Officer
- 10 R.S.M.
- 11 Master Cook

SPECIAL ORDER OF THE DAY
By FIELD-MARSHAL SIR DOUGLAS HAIG
K.T., G.C.B., G.C.V.O., K.C.I.E
Commander-in-Chief, British Armies in France.

The following telegrams are published for the information of all ranks:—

To FIELD-MARSHAL SIR DOUGLAS HAIG FROM GOVERNOR-GENERAL, AUSTRALIA.
26-12-17.

On behalf of Government and people of Australia, I thank you for your good wishes and assure you of their continued confidence in you and the gallant troops you command. Heartfelt wishes for success and victory in 1918.

To FIELD-MARSHAL SIR DOUGLAS HAIG FROM GOVERNOR, NEWFOUNDLAND.
26-12-17.

Your telegram of 23rd instant has been received by Colony of Newfoundland with highest gratification. The Colony wishes you and your gallant Armies that complete success which is essential to the well-being of the civilized world.

To FIELD-MARSHAL SIR DOUGLAS HAIG FROM THE LORD PROVOST OF GLASGOW.
28-12-17.

On behalf of the Corporation and citizens of Glasgow, I desire to convey to you and the gallant men under your command cordial good wishes for the New Year, accompanied by an expression of our profound gratitude and admiration for the heroic and indomitable manner in which you and they are sustaining the glorious traditions of the British Army, and the earnest hope that during the year that is opening the war will be brought to a victorious termination.

FROM FIELD-MARSHAL SIR DOUGLAS HAIG TO THE LORD PROVOST OF GLASGOW.
28-12-17.

Please convey to the Corporation and citizens of Glasgow, on behalf of all ranks of the British Armies in France, our hearty thanks for your inspiring message, and assure them that every effort will be made to reach a successful conclusion in the coming year.

To FIELD-MARSHAL SIR DOUGLAS HAIG FROM THE WAR OFFICE, LONDON.
28-12-17.

High Commissioner for South Africa communicates following message from Botha, desiring to associate himself with its terms:—

"Sir Douglas Haig, his Officers and Men.—My greetings and best wishes that your heroic efforts may be crowned with the victory they deserve."

FROM FIELD-MARSHAL SIR DOUGLAS HAIG TO THE WAR OFFICE.
30-12-17.

Request that you will convey to the High Commissioner for South Africa and to General Botha my best thanks for their encouraging message, which will be communicated to the troops in France.

General Headquarters,
1st January, 1918.

D. Haig, F.M.
Commander-in-Chief,
British Armies in France.

"D"

SPECIAL ORDER OF THE DAY
by
Major General C. L. NICHOLSON, C. M. G.,
Commanding, 34th Division.

1st January 1918.

I desire to express to all Officers, N.C.Os., and Men of the Division which I have the honour to command, my great appreciation of the splendid service which they have rendered during the past year, and to congratulate you all on your brilliant achievements.

The Division has taken part in offensive operations five times during the year, viz: on the 9th and 28th April, 4th June, 26th August, and 22nd October.

On three occasions, you have met with the greatest success: on the other two occasions, though the actual results may not have been so great, the bravery, skill and endurance displayed were even more marked.

In recognition of these services, the number of decorations gained is as follows:-

	Immediate Reward.	Honours Gazette.
Victoria Cross,	3	-
C. B.,	-	1
C. M. G.,	-	3
Brevet Colonel,	-	1
Brevet Lieut. Colonel,	-	3
Brevet Major,	-	2
D. S. O.,	5	17
Bar to D. S. O.,	1	-
Military Cross,	78	36
Bar to Military Cross,	5	-
D. C. M.,	32	8
Bar to D. C. M.,	3	-
Military Medal,	423	-
Bar to Military Medal,	25	-
Meritorious Service Medal,	-	3
Croix de Guerre,	7	-
Medaille Militaire,	4	-
Italian Silver Medal,	1	-
Italian Bronze Medal,	5	-
Croix de Chevalier (French Legion of Honour)	1	-
Decoration Militaire (Belgian),	1	-
Mentions in Dispatches,	-	267
	599	341
Cards of Honour,	181	-

This is a record of which we may well be proud, and I feel sure that everyone will do his utmost to keep up the good name of the Division, and of the distinguished Regiments and Corps which are represented in it.

I feel confident that in the new year, every officer and man will continue to carry on with the same gallantry and devotion to duty as hitherto, until the final victory in the great cause for which we are fighting has been won, and I wish all ranks the best of luck for 1918.

Nicholson.

Major General,
Commanding, 34th Division.

War diary

We, the inhabitants of Ashington here assembled send our cordial greetings to the Northumberland Fusiliers: we express our sympathy with their hardships, our admiration for their achievements, and we pledge ourselves to support by every means in our power His Majesty's Forces who are fighting on land, on the sea, and in the air, until they shall have secured the conditions of a just and lasting peace.

COPY. "E" 103B/3/228.G.

Dr. Sir W.H.Hadow,
Armstrong College,
Newcastle-on-Tyne.

      The resolution adopted by the inhabitants of Ashington has been forwarded to this Brigade.

      The Officers and men of the 9th (Northd. Hussars), 24/27th, 25th and 26th Battns. Northumberland Fusiliers serving with this Brigade thank the inhabitants of ASHINGTON for their message of sympathy and pledge of support which strengthens their determination to secure a victorious peace.

(Sd) J.CHAPLIN,
Brigadier General,
17.1.18.   Commanding 103rd Infantry Brigade.

---- 2 ----   103B/3/229.G.

Officer Commanding,
9th (NF) Bn. Northd. Fusiliers.

      Herewith copy of resolution of Citizens of ASHINGTON, together with copy of the Brigade Commander's reply.

C.Hawes
CAPTAIN.
A/BRIGADE MAJOR.
103rd INFANTRY BRIGADE.

17.1.18.

SPECIAL ORDER OF THE DAY
By FIELD-MARSHAL SIR DOUGLAS HAIG
K.T., G.C.B., G.C.V.O., K.C.I.E
Commander-in-Chief, British Armies in France.

The following telegrams are published for the information of all ranks:—

To FIELD-MARSHAL SIR DOUGLAS HAIG FROM HIS ROYAL HIGHNESS, THE DUKE OF CONNAUGHT.
31-12-17.
Cordial greetings to yourself and all serving under you. May 1918 bring with it victory and an honourable peace.

FROM FIELD-MARSHAL SIR DOUGLAS HAIG TO HIS ROYAL HIGHNESS, THE DUKE OF CONNAUGHT.
1-1-18.
On behalf of all ranks, as well as for myself, I ask Your Royal Highness to accept our best thanks for your message and our best wishes for the New Year.

To FIELD-MARSHAL SIR DOUGLAS HAIG FROM GENERAL SIR H. PLUMER ITALY.
31-12-17.
We hope our big brothers in France will remember the youngest member of the family and accept from Italy heartiest greetings and good wishes for the New Year.

FROM FIELD-MARSHAL SIR DOUGLAS HAIG TO GENERAL SIR H. PLUMER.
2-1-18.
Your good wishes are heartily reciprocated by all ranks of the British Armies in France. We wish you all success and the best of good luck.

To FIELD-MARSHAL SIR DOUGLAS HAIG FROM THE LORD MAYOR, LONDON.
1-1-18.
On New Year's day the grateful thoughts of the Empire are centred in their soldiers and sailors, and the citizens of London beg you to accept personally and convey to your gallant forces their profound appreciation of all their services and sacrifices in the past and their best wishes and prayers that during the year the righteous aims of Great Britain and her Allies may be triumphantly realised and a lasting peace secured for the future happiness and prosperity of the World.

FROM FIELD-MARSHAL SIR DOUGLAS HAIG TO THE LORD MAYOR, LONDON.
2-1-18.
On behalf of all ranks serving in France I thank you personally and the citizens of London for your inspiring message. We fully appreciate what London is doing to help the Allied Forces in the field to bring about a lasting peace. We wish you all success and good fortune in 1918.

To FIELD-MARSHAL SIR DOUGLAS HAIG FROM HIS EXCELLENCY, THE PRESIDENT OF THE PORTUGUESE REPUBLIC.
2-1-18.   *(Translation.)*
On the occasion of the New Year I desire to send to the glorious Allied Army, on behalf of the Portuguese Nation, the most enthusiastic salutations, together with ardent wishes for your triumphs in the cause of liberty and justice for which we will fight until final victory. At the same time I desire to express to you the admiration of the Portuguese Army for the glorious feats of your brave troops and for the fine leadership of their Commander-in-Chief.
SIDONIO PAIS.

FROM FIELD-MARSHAL SIR DOUGLAS HAIG TO HIS EXCELLENCY, THE PRESIDENT OF THE PORTUGUESE REPUBLIC.
3-1-18.
On behalf of all ranks of the British Armies in France I thank Your Excellency and the Portuguese Nation for your inspiring message. We cordially reciprocate your good wishes.

General Headquarters,
5th January, 1918.

Commander-in-Chief,
British Armies in France.

SECRET Copy No. 2

OPERATION ORDERS No. 12
9th (Northumberland Hussars) Battn. Northumberland Fus.

1. RELIEF

The 25th Battn. Northumberland Fusiliers will relieve the 9th (Nthld. Hussars) Battn. Northumberland Fusiliers in the LEFT (COJEUL) SUB SECTOR tomorrow 7th inst.

On relief the 9th (Nthld. Hussars) Battn. Nthld. Fus. will move into Brigade Support and will take over billets evacuated by the 26th Battn. Nthld. Fusiliers. Relief to be complete by 3 pm.

2. ORDER OF RELIEF

"A" Coy. 9th Battn. will be relieved by RIGHT FRONT Coy of 25th Bn. Nthld. Fus.
"B" " " " " " " " LEFT FRONT Coy of " " " "
"C" " " " " " " " SUPPORT Coy of " " " "
"D" " " " " " " " RESERVE Coy of " " " "

After relief Companies will proceed as under:—
"A" Coy. to billets on WANCOURT-TILLOY ROAD near Battn. H.Q.
"B" and "C" Coys. to MARLIERE CAVES
"D" Coy. to EGRET TRENCH.

3. GUIDES

Guides at the rate of 1 per post for front line Coys and 1 per platoon for Support and Reserve Coys will be at junction of SHOVEL TRENCH with SOUTHERN AVENUE at 12.30 pm.

Guides at the rate 1 per post for posts SOUTH of the COJEUL will be at the OLD GUM BOOT STORE N.22.B.3.9. at 11.30 am.

There will be no guides for Battn. Hd Qrs.

4. ADVANCE PARTIES

1 N.C.O. per Coy will proceed to their various destinations tomorrow morning to arrive there by 8 am. These N.C.O.s will take over all stores etc.

1 Officer of "D" Coy will reconnoitre the route to EGRET TRENCH this afternoon.

2/Lieut Corner and the Battn. Lewis Gun Sergt will proceed to SUPPORT Battn. Hd Qrs by 9 am. tomorrow to take over.

5. TRANSPORT

No transport will be required but T.O. will ascertain necessary details for water supply from T.O. 26th Battn. Nthld. Fusiliers.

6. OFFICERS VALISES AND BLANKETS

For A. B. & C. Coys and Battn. Hd Qrs will be delivered as follows:—
"A" Company   4 pm.
"B" & "C" Coys   with rations
Battn. Hd Qrs.   2.30 pm.

7. RATIONS

All rations for day of relief will be brought up tonight.

Rations whilst Battalion is in SUPPORT will be delivered as under:—
"A" Coy and Battn. HQrs & Pushing Party (Consisting of 4 men per Coy and 1 NCO each from "A" and "B" Coys) at Battn. Hdtrs, or if by railway at SLOUGH Station

"B" and "C" Coys — MARLIERE CAVES, or if by railway LONDON DUMP.
"D" Coy — LONDON DUMP.
Cookers will not be required.

8. STORES

All defence and pursuit schemes, aeroplane photographs, working party details and details of work in hand and contemplated will be handed over and taken over on relief. Receipts for trench stores handed over and taken over and certificates for cleanliness of trenches and billets and parade states and disposition returns will be rendered to Orderly Room by 9 pm tomorrow 7th inst.

9. RELIEF COMPLETE

Will be wired to Battn. Hd Qrs. using code word "PIPSQUEAK" followed by name of Company Commander. Companies will also inform Orderly Room when their Companies are in billets.

ACKNOWLEDGE

DATED 6-1-1918

Copies to:
No 1. RETAINED   No 8. T.O. & Q.M.
  2. WAR DIARY   9. O.C. 25th Bn. Nthld. Fus
3-6. O.C. Coy's   10. " 26th " " "
  7. SIGNALLING OFFICER   11. R.S.M.
                          12. Master Cook.

J. M. Ross-Learn.
Capt. and Adjt.
9th (Nthld. Hussars) Battn. Nthld. Fus.

SECRET.   Copy No. 1.

OPERATION ORDERS No 13.
9th (Northumberland Hussars) Bn. Northumberland Fusiliers.

1. RELIEF.	The 9th (North'd Huss) Bn Northumberland Fusiliers will relieve the 25th Battn Northumberland Fusiliers in the LEFT (COJEUL) SUB SECTOR tomorrow 11th inst. The relief will take place on a 3 Company front, and will be completed by 12 noon.
2. ORDER OF RELIEF	D Coy 9th Battn will relieve Coy 25th Battn SOUTH OF COJEUL. C " " " " " CENTRE COY 25th Battn. B " " " " " LEFT COY " " A " " " " " COY 25th Battn in RAKE TRENCH.
3. GUIDES.	Guides at the rate of 1 per post for Coy SOUTH OF COJEUL will be at the junction of EGRET TRENCH with SNIKAR AVENUE at 9.30am. Guides at the rate of 1 per post for front Coys and 1 per platoon for reserve Coy will be at the junction of SHOVEL TRENCH with SOUTHERN AVENUE at 9.30 am. There will be no guides for Battn H.Qrs.
4. ADVANCE PARTIES.	1 N.C.O. per Coy and the Provost Serjt will be at their respective destinations at 8 a.m. to take over stores, particulars of work etc. 1 Officer from A Coy will supervise the taking over of these stores.
5. TRANSPORT.	The Transport Officer will arrange to have the necessary limbers to take back Officers Valises and Mens Blankets at the under-mentioned times A Coy and Battn H.Qrs. (H.H.C.) 10.30 am. B & C Coys (LONDON DUMP) 9 am. Companies will leave guards on the above, until collected by the Transport, when men will rejoin their respective Coys.
6. STORES.	All Defence & Survey schemes, aeroplane photographs, working party details and details of work in hand & contemplated will be taken over and handed over, certificates of cleanliness of billets and trenches and Disposition returns will be rendered to Orderly Room by 9 pm tomorrow night.
7. MARCHING OUT STATES.	Will be rendered to Orderly Room by 1 pm.
8. RELIEF COMPLETE.	Will be wired to Battn H.Qrs. using surname of Coy Commander.

ACKNOWLEDGE.

COPY Nº
1. War Diary.
2. Retained.
3. O.C. A Coy.
4. O C B "
5. OC C "
6. OC D "
7. T.O. & QM.
8. Signal Officer.
9. O C 25th Battn North'n Fus.
10. R.S.M.

J.M. Broun Cairn
Capt & a/Adjt.
9th (North'd Huss) Bn. North'n Fusiliers

DATED. 10/1/18.

SECRET   **COPY No. 1**

OPERATION ORDERS No. 14
9th (Northumberland Hussars) Battn Northumberland Fusiliers.

1. RELIEF.
The 25th Battn Northumberland Fusiliers will relieve the 9th (North'd Hussars) Battn Northumberland Fusiliers in the LEFT (COTEUL) SUBSECTOR tomorrow 15th inst. Relief to be complete by 12 noon.

2. ORDER OF RELIEF
"C" Coy 9th Battn will be relieved by CENTRE Coy 25th Battn.
"B"   "   "   "   "   "   "   LEFT Coy   "   "
"A"   "   "   "   "   "   "   RESERVE Coy   "   "
"D"   "   "   "   "   "   "   RIGHT Coy   "   "

3. GUIDES.
Guides at the rate of 1 per post for Coy South of COTEUL will be at junction of EGRET TRENCH with SHIKAR AVENUE at 9.30 a.m.

Guides at the rate of 1 per post for front Coys and 1 per platoon for Reserve Coy will be at junction of SHOVEL TRENCH with SOUTHERN AVENUE at 9.30 a.m. There will be no guides for Battn Hd Qrs.

4. TRANSPORT.
Officers Chargers for "A" and "B" Coys and Battn Hd Qrs. and limbers as under will be on the road near OLD GERMAN BOOT STORE N22 c.3.9. at 12 noon.
1 Limber for Signal and Orderly Room Stores
1   "   "   "A" and "B" Coys and Battn Hd Qrs Officers Mess Kit (at 10 a.m)
1   "   "   "A" and "B" Coys Lewis Guns.
1   "   "   "A" and "B" Coys and Battn Hd Qrs Cooking utensils etc.

5. COOKERS.
1 Cooker will be 50 yards along North road of Cross Roads N20 B. at 1 p.m. and will provide Soup for "A" Coy (less 50 o.r.) "B" Coy and Battn Hd Qrs.

Cookers will be at trenches N15 Central at 1 p.m. when they will provide dinners for "C" and "D" Coys and 50 o.r. of "A" Coy. The Cookers will return to Transport Lines after their meat has been served. "C" and "D" will do all further cooking in camp kettles. Haversack rations will also be brought up for the 50 o.r. of "A" Coy and tea rations for "C" and "D" Coys.

6. OFFICERS' VALISES AND BLANKETS
For "C" and "D" Coys will be delivered at N15 Central at 1 p.m.

7. STORES.
All defence and pursuit schemes, aeroplane photographs, working party details and details of work in hand and contemplated will be handed over on relief. Receipts for trench stores handed over and certificates for cleanliness of trenches will be rendered to Orderly Room by 9 p.m. tomorrow 15th inst.

8. ADVANCE PARTIES
"A" and "B" Coys and Battn Hd Qrs. will each send a senior N.C.O. to take over their respective quarters in CARLISLE LINES. All stores will be signed for and copy of same rendered to Orderly Room with trench stores lists at 9 p.m. tomorrow. These N.C.O's will proceed to Battn Details tonight and will report to 2/Lieut. W.H. Cerner at CARLISLE LINES at 8 a.m. tomorrow 15th inst.

"C" and "D" Coys will each send a senior N.C.O. to N15 Central to take over as above. These N.C.O's will be at their respective destinations by 8 a.m. tomorrow 15th inst.

O.C. "C" Coy will send an Officer to be at N15 Central at 3 p.m. today. He will personally take over full details of working parties for both "C" and "D" Coys.

9. GUARDS
O.C. "D" Coy will detail a guard of 1 N.C.O. and 4 men to report at Divisional Bomb Store (NEUVILLE VITASSE) at 10 a.m. tomorrow 15th inst. when they will relieve a similar guard of the 26th Battn Northumberland Fusiliers. Rations and Blankets will be delivered to them.

O.C. "B" Coy will detail a guard of 1 N.C.O. and 3 men to report at Coal Dump STONE SIDING at 10 a.m. tomorrow 15th inst. when they will relieve a similar guard of the 26th Battn. Northumberland Fusiliers. These men will report to the Quartermaster tonight.

OPERATION ORDERS No. 14. (CONTD)

10. WORKING PARTY

"A" Coy will supply a working party of 2 Officers and 50 O.Rs. This party will report to a representative of 2/Lieut Heslop. R.E. at the entrance to SHIKAR AVENUE (N24c 50.95) at 4 p.m. tomorrow 15th inst. 40 shovels and 20 picks will be drawn from DENTS DUMP and returned on completion of task. 5 hours work will be done.

Two lorries will be at WANCOURT (N23A) at 9 p.m. to convey party to CARLISLE LINES.

"C" Coy's Spoil and Timber party from 12 noon to 6 p.m. will not be required. "B" Coy will find party as usual.

11. GUM BOOTS:

All gum boots will be carried out and returned to store from which they were drawn. Receipts will be obtained for these.

12. RELIEF COMPLETE.

Will be wired to Battn Hd Qrs using surname of Company Commander. Companies will also inform Orderly Room when their Companies are in billets.

ACKNOWLEDGE.

COPIES TO.
- No. 1 Retained
- 2 War Diary
- 3 2nd in Command
- 4,5,6,7 O.C. Coys.
- 8 Signal Officer
- 9 T.O. & 2. M.
- 10 OC 25th Bn Northd. Fusiliers
- 11 OC 26th Bn   do
- 12 R.S.M
- 13 Master Cook.

[signature]
Captain and Adjutant
9th (Northd Hussars) Bn. Northd Fus

DATED. 14th January 1918.

[SECRET] [COPY No.]

OPERATION ORDERS No 15.
9th (Northumberland Hussars) Bn. Northumberland Fusiliers.

1. RELIEF
The 9th (N.H.) Bn North'd Fusiliers will relieve the 25th Battn North'd Fusiliers in the LEFT (COSEEL) SUB SECTOR tomorrow the 19th inst. No troops to pass the Control Post at N·21·c·8·9 before 5 p.m. All movement will be by platoons at 100 yards interval.

2. ORDER OF RELIEF
D Coy 9th Battn will relieve RIGHT Front Coy 25th Battn.
A "   "   "   "   "   LEFT   "   "   "   "
C "   "   "   "   "   CENTRE "   "   "   "
B "   "   "   "   "   RESERVE Coy "   "

3. GUIDES
Guides at the rate of 1 per post for Front Line Coys, 1 per platoon for Support Coy, and 1 for Battn Hd Qrs will be at the following places at times stated.
Left Coy, Centre Coy, Support Coy, & Battn Hdqrs at TRAM DUMP. N·13·c·26 at 6 p.m.
Right Coy Railway Track Junction (O·13·5·60·25) at 6 p.m.

4. RATIONS.
Rations for all Coys and Battn Hqrts will be delivered at PIONEER DUMP at 6 p.m.
1 Senior N.C.O. from each Coy and the Pioneer Sergt will be at the Dump by this time to take over their rations from C.Q.M.Ss.; and Coys with exception of D Coy will pick them up as they pass by.
O.C. B Coy will arrange to deliver rations to D Coy after relief is complete.

5. TRANSPORT.
Officers Chargers for Battn Hqrs will be at CARLISLE LINES at 4 p.m. and O.C. A & B Coys at 3-30 p.m. and OC C & D Coys at 4-15 a.m.
1 Limber for A & B Coys, and 1 limber for C & D Coys Lewis Guns will be at CARLISLE LINES at 3-30 p.m. and will proceed direct to PIONEER DUMP.
D Coys Guns will be offloaded at OLD GUMBOOT STORES (N·21·6·3·4) where they will be collected by D Coy Lewis Gunners.
1 Limber for Adjt Officers Mess Kit, Signal & Orderly Room stores will be at CARLISLE LINES by 3-30 p.m.
1 Limber for A & B Coys, & 1 Limber for C & D Coys Officers Mess Kit and cooking utensils will be at CARLISLE LINES at 3·30 p.m.

6. COOKERS.
1 Cooker for C & D Coys will be at N.Y. Central where it will have dinners prepared for these Coys at 12·30 p.m. This cooker will also prepare tea at 4 p.m.
1 Cooker for B Coy will be at N·Y·Y· Central at 3 p.m. where it will provide dinner for 50 O.Rs of B Coy.
These Cookers will return after meals are served.

7. ADVANCE PARTIES.
1 Officer, and 1 N.C.O. per Coy, and the Pioneer Sergt will proceed to their respective destinations by noon tomorrow to take over all stores. These stores will be carefully checked. 2 Signallers will also proceed to Bn Hqrs.

8. STORES.
All defence and pioneer schemes, aeroplane photographs, working party details, details of work in hand and contemplated will be taken over on relief. Relief for Trench stores takes over and certificate for cleanliness of trenches will be rendered to OC tomorrow 19th inst. by 10 p.m.
The "strength out" state, to be rendered to OR before leaving.

9. OFFICERS VALISES AND MENS BLANKETS
Will be collected and stored under arrangements by C.Q.M.Ss.

10. GUM BOOTS
Can be drawn at the rate of 23 pairs per Coy, and 8 pairs for Battn Hqrs from Gum Boot Store at MARLIERE CAVES.

OPERATION ORDERS No 15. CONTD.

11. WORKING PARTIES.
"A" party will be supplied by "B" Coy for work tomorrow morning as usual. No transport is available.
C & D Coys will be at their respective rendezvous from 9am to 12 noon. Transport to convey these men will be at embussing point at 7.30 am as usual. Meals for these parties are arranged for under para 6 of these orders.

12. RELIEF COMPLETE.
Will be wired to Battn Hdqrs using the code word "NIX" followed by surname of Coy Commander.

ACKNOWLEDGE

COPIES TO
1. Retained.
2. War Diary.
3/6. Coy Commanders.
7. Signal Officer.
8. T.O. & Q.M.
9. O.C. 25th Battn.
10. R.S.M.
11. Master Cook.

J. M. Ivor Craven
Capt & Adjt
9th (North'n Hussars) Bn North'n Division

DATED 18/1/18.

| SECRET. | OPERATION ORDERS No 16. | COPY No 2 |

9th (Northumberland Hussars) Bn. Northumberland Fusiliers.

1. RELIEF. The 25th Bn North'd Fus. will relieve the 9th (N.H.) Bn. North'd Fus. in the LEFT (COUEUL) sub-sector tomorrow the 23rd inst. No troops to pass the control post at N.21.a.8.9 before 5 pm.

2. ORDER OF RELIEF.
LEFT Coy 9th Batt'n will be relieved by Coy 25th Batt'n.
CENTRE " " " " " " " " " "
RIGHT " " " " " " " " " "
RESERVE " " " " " " " " " "

After relief D Coy & Batt'n H.Qrs will move to billets in N.16.C central.
A & C Coys will move to MARLIERE CAVES.
B Coy will move to EGRET TRENCH.

3. GUIDES. At the rate of 1 per post for LEFT & CENTRE Coys, 1 per platoon for reserve Coy, & 1 guide for Batt'n HQrs will be at TANK DUMP N.18.C.2.6 at 6 pm. Guides at the rate of 1 per post for RIGHT Coy will be at Railway Track Junction O.13.d.66.25 at 6 pm. OC B Coy will detail an officer to be at TANK DUMP at 5.45 pm to supervise the guides.

4. ADVANCE PARTIES. A Senior N.C.O. per Coy & the Batt'n L.G. Sergt will report at their respective destinations by 2.30 pm to take over billets & stores. These stores must be carefully checked.
2nd Lt. W.H. Corner will report at 3 pm to take over working party particulars.

5. TRANSPORT. 1 Limber for Orderly Room Stores will be at new ration dump at 6 pm. No other transport will be required but the Transport Officer will ascertain necessary details for water supply from Transport Officer 26th Bn North'd Fus.

6. OFFICERS VALISES AND BLANKETS. Officers Valises and men's blankets for D Coy & Batt'n HQrs will be delivered with rations.
Men's blankets for A. & C. Coy. will also be delivered with rations. Parties will be detailed to meet these.

7. RATIONS. Rations whilst Batt'n is in support will be delivered by Light Railway as under:-
A.B.& C. Coys at LONDON DUMP. 5 pm.
D Coy at SLOUGH STATION. 4.30 pm.
Batt'n HQrs & Pushing Party at BATT'N HQRS. 4.30 pm.
Ration parties will be sent by Coys to meet these.

8. PUSHING PARTY. Coys will each detail 7 men & B & D Coy. 1 N.C.O. each, to report to Sergt Little in Sunken Road N.22.a.4.3 before 12 noon on the 24th inst. unexpended portion of days rations to be carried. This parties will fetch their own rations nightly from Batt'n HQrs.

9. STORES. All defence & pursuit schemes, Aeroplane photographs, working party details & details of work in hand & contemplated will be handed over & taken over on relief. Receipts for Trench Stores handed over & taken over & certificates for cleanliness of Trenches & billets will be rendered to orderly room by 10 am 24th inst.

10. GUM BOOTS. All gum boots will be returned to GUM BOOT STORES on night of relief and receipts will be obtained for same.

11. AMMUNITION. IMPORTANT. All ammunition carried by men must be made up to Establishment before the men leave the Trenches.

12. RELIEF COMPLETE ACKNOWLEDGE. Will be wired to Batt'n HQrs using surname of Coy Commander, and Coys will report they are in billets.

COPIES TO. 1. Retained
2. War Diary.
3. 2nd in Command
4/7. O.C. Companies
8. Signal Officer
9. T.O. & Q.M.
10. OC 25th Bn North'd Fus
11. OC 26th Bn North'd Fus.
12. R.S.M.

DATED. 22/1/18.

J.W. Brosnan
Capt & /Adjt
9th (North'd Huss) Bn North'd Fusiliers

War Diary

[SECRET.]   **OPERATION ORDERS No. 17.**   [COPY No. 2.]

9th (Northumberland Hussars) Bn Northumberland Fusiliers

1. RELIEF.	The 2nd Battn Suffolk Regt. will relieve the 9th (N.H.) Bn North. Fus. in the support area tomorrow the 25th inst.
	On completion of relief the 9th N.H. Bn. North. Fus. will move to B.3. CAMP BLAIRVILLE – RENDECOURT area, embussing at MERCATEL.
	Transport will move independently as per orders received from Brigade.
2. ROUTE.	Direct to MERCATEL via WANCOURT – NEUVILLE VITASSE ROAD. All movement East of NEUVILLE VITASSE will be by platoons at 200 yds distance. West of that place by companies at 200 yds distance.
3. ORDER OF RELIEF.	B Coy 9th (N.H.) Bn North. Fus. will be relieved by Y Coy 2nd Suffolk Regiment
	A " " " " " " " W " " " "
	C " " " " " " " X " " " "
	D " " " " " " " Z " " " "
4. GUIDES.	Guides at the rate of 1 per platoon + 1 for Battn Hqrs will be at control post N.21.a.8.7 at 5 pm. O.C. D Coy will detail an officer to supervise the guides, he will report to Orderly room at noon tomorrow 25th inst for instructions.
5. TRANSPORT.	The Lewis Gun Limber of each Coy will be provided as under. Iboit limbers will also be used for Camp Kettles + Officers Mess Kits.
	A Coy – 5.30 pm MARLIERE CAVES
	C " – 5.30 pm do
	B " – 6.30 pm LONDON DUMP
	D " – 5 pm N.15.c.
	1 Limber for officers valises of Battn Hqrs will be at Battn Hqrs at 12 noon and the same limber will collect D Coys officers valises on its return at 6 pm. Mess Cart for Battn Hqrs Officers Mess Kit, Hqrs Cooking utensils, Signal + Orderly Room stores, + the Maltese Cart will be at Battn Hqrs at 5 pm.
6. ADVANCE PARTIES.	4th D.H. Corpls + 1 Senior N.C.O. per Coy will be at BLAIRVILLE by 2 pm tomorrow 25th inst to take over billets.
	The above NCOs fully equipped + with unexpended portion of the days rations will report to orderly room at 10 am tomorrow 25th inst.
7. PUSHING PARTY.	The PUSHING PARTY will be relieved by 12 noon 26th inst, + on relief will proceed to join the Battn. Rations for them for 26th inst will be delivered to Battn Hqrs at 12 noon tomorrow 25th inst by the limber for officers valises.
8. SOCKS.	All socks in excess of 2 pairs per man will be returned to R.Q.M.S. by 12 noon 25th inst.
9. STORES.	All defence + pursuit schemes, Aeroplane photographs, Trench + other maps, details of work in hand + contemplated, will be handed over on relief. Receipts for Trench Stores + Area stores (including store at Transport lines + Q.M. stores) handed over, + certificates for cleanliness of billets will be rendered to Orderly Room by 10 am on the 26 inst.
10. RELIEF COMPLETE	Will be wired to Battn Hqrs using surname of Coy Commander. O.C. Coys will also inform Orderly Room when their Coys are in billets.

ACKNOWLEDGE.

Copies to
1. Retained.
2. War Diary.
3. 2nd in Command.
4/7. O.C. Coys.
8. T.O. + Q.M.
9. Signal Officer.
10. R.S.M.
11. N.C.O. i/c Pushing Party.

[signature]

Capt + Adjt
9th (North. Hussars) Bn North. Fus.

DATED. 24/1/18.

SPECIAL ORDER OF THE DAY
By FIELD-MARSHAL SIR DOUGLAS HAIG
K.T., G.C.B., G.C.V.O., K.C.I.E
Commander-in-Chief, British Armies in France.

The following messages are published for the information of all ranks:—

FROM FIELD-MARSHAL SIR DOUGLAS HAIG TO FIELD-MARSHAL HIS IMPERIAL MAJESTY THE EMPEROR OF JAPAN, K.G.

23/1/18.

May I be permitted, in the name of the British Armies in France, most respectfully to offer to your Imperial Majesty our warmest congratulations on Your Majesty's appointment as Field-Marshal in the British Army. We rejoice to think that the Alliance which has existed between Japan and Great Britain for so long should be thus still further strengthened; and it is a source of deep satisfaction to the troops under my command and to me personally, to feel that the Ruler of our far Eastern Allies should hold the highest rank in our Army.

TO FIELD-MARSHAL SIR DOUGLAS HAIG FROM FIELD-MARSHAL HIS IMPERIAL MAJESTY THE EMPEROR OF JAPAN, K.G.

25/1/18.

I have received with sincere thanks and pleasure your telegram conveying to me the sentiments of yourself and the gallant troops under your command on the occasion of the conferment upon me of the rank of a British Field-Marshal. His Majesty the King, my constant Ally, has conferred on me an honour which I most deeply appreciate and which only one thing could enhance, namely this assurance that his gracious act is welcome to his magnificent Armies whose spirit and achievements in the field are beyond all praise. I am proud to be associated with their great work and I beg you to thank all ranks in my name for their congratulations.

D. Haig, F.M.

General Headquarters,
30th January, 1918.

Commander-in-Chief,
British Armies in France.

| SECRET | OPERATION ORDERS N° 18. | COPY N° |

9th (Northumberland Hussars) Batt. Northumberland Fusiliers

1. Destination — The Battalion will move to No 2 Camp BLAIRVILLE by Route march tomorrow the 28th inst. distance approximately 11 miles.

2. Route — GOUY-EN-ARTOIS — BEAUMETZ — RIVIERE — BLAIRVILLE
Starting Point cross roads Q.19.a.8.7.

3. Routine —
Reveille 5.30 am
Breakfast 6.30 am
Kit Parade 5.0 pm to night
Dinners at destination on arrival.

4. Parade — 7.35 am. Battalion will be ready to move off at this time.

5. Order of March — Batt. H/qrs, "D" Coy, Band, "C" Coy, B Coy, and A Coy, and Transport. Head of column to be at cross roads P.15.a.6.3. (where Band played March past on arrival of Battalion) facing FOSSEUX.

6. Dress — As for today viz. Battle Order with mess tin slung under haversack on Packing straps.

7. Marching out States — Will be rendered to Orderly Room by 8.0 pm tonight.
2 Lieut C. Wilkinson will be at starting point by 8.15 am tomorrow. He will synchronise his watch and also take the parade state.

8. Officers Mess Kit and Valises — Will be packed ready for the Lorries and Mess Cart by 7.0 am when they will be collected from the various messes.

9. Mens Blankets — Will be rolled in bundles & labelled ready for the Lorries which will collect them at 7.0 am from Coy. Stores.

10. Rear Parties — Each Coy will detail a party of 1 N.C.O. and 4 men to remain behind and finally clean all billets. Lt. A. Derwent will remain with these parties who will meet him at 9.40 am at the cross roads from which the Battalion moves off.
He will report at the starting point Q.19.a.8.7. at 11.0 am.

11. Guards —
1 man per Coy will travel on the Blanket Lorries.
1 man from A Coy will travel on the Officers Valise Lorry.

12. March Discipline — The Battalion will march to the right of the road, the inner file to be changed at each halt.
The Platoon Officer will march on the left at the head of platoon. The Platoon Sergt will march on the right at the rear of platoon.

ACKNOWLEDGE.

COPIES TO
1. War Diary
2. Commanding Officer
3. 2nd in Command
4. Adjutant
5-12 Companies
13. Medical Officer
14. R.S.M.
15. Master Cook
16. Quartermaster
17. Transport Officer

Ambrose Craven
Capt & a/Adjutant
9th (North. Hussars) Bn. North. Fusiliers

27.2.18

War Diary

OPERATION ORDERS N° IV. (Contd).

10. March Discipline

Strict March Discipline will be maintained - at halts, each Coy Comm' will give the order to halt; men will halt at once and <u>not close up</u>. Coy Comm'ˢ will then give "Right Turn fall out on the right." Men will march straight off the road and at once take off their equipment. On falling in men will <u>not close up.</u> Water bottles will not be used without an order, or the permission of an officer.

11. Move Complete.

Companies will report when in billets.

12. Cross Country Team.

The Cross Country race will take place tomorrow the 27ᵗʰ inst.

A Lorry will report at BUNEVILLE at 10am to pick up members of the Batt'ⁿ Team in this village, it will then pick up the remainder of the Team at MONTS EN TERNOIS.

Lieut. E. R Hooper will accompany the team. After the race the party will be taken to BARLY where they will rejoin the Battalion.

<u>Equipment</u> as in above orders will be taken by the team on the lorries, and the <u>unexpended</u> portion of the days rations will also be carried.

<u>Team.</u> The members of the team should draw running shorts to night. They will run in service boots.

<u>Time.</u> Competition commences at 4.0pm.

<u>ACKNOWLEDGE.</u>

COPIES TO:-
1. War Diary
2. Commanding Officer.
3. 2ⁿᵈ in Command
4. Adjutant.
5-12 Companies
13 Medical Officer
14 R.S.M
15 Master Cook
16 Quartermaster
17 Transport Officer

DATE. 26-2-18.

J. Ambrose Dawe
Capt & ?/Adjutant.
9 (York's Hussars) Bn North'ᵈ Fusiliers

Lieut Col W.S. Synnot DSO
War Diary

War Diary

February 1918.

9th (T.A.) Bn. Northumberland Fusiliers

Vol 30
9 NF

WAR DIARY
or
INTELLIGENCE SUMMARY

(Erase heading not required.) 92 (N.4) Bde North'n Div'n

Army Form C. 2118

Instructions regarding War Diaries and Intelligence Summaries are contained in F.S. Regs., Part II. and the Staff Manual respectively. Title Pages will be prepared in manuscript.

Place	Date	Hour	Summary of Events and Information	Remarks and references to Appendices
CAMP.	FEBRUARY 1st to 7th inclusive		BLAIREVILLE No. 2 CAMP. The Batt'n carried out training & parades according to programme. Nothing of unusual interest occurred during these few days.	M.A.
	8th		The Batt'n paraded at 7:30 a.m. & marched to the Corn Roads in BLAIREVILLE where it took its position in the Brigade which was moving to the concentration which had taken place in the Div'n who were comprised as follows:— 92 (N.4) De North'n 1st Bde East Lancs 10th Bde Lancs.	M.A.
	9th		The Brigade marched V' at 8am for LE CAUROY and & proceeded via BRETTENCOURT, BEAUMETZ, SIMENCOURT, WANQUETIN, HAUTEVILLE to AVESNES LE COMTE. Here a halt was made & dinners were served. Afterwards the batt'n proceeded via BEAUFORT to LIENCOURT where H.Q. & A. "D" Coy billeted for the night. B. "C" Coys went on to DENIER & billeted there. The Batt'n paraded at 12.45 p.m. & proceeded by route march via DENIER, & MAGNICOURT to MONTS EN TERNOIS where A. "B. Coy. & H.Q. billeted. D. Coy. went on to BUNEVILLE & billeted there. From there the final destination of the Division who was now in G.H.Q. Reserve	M.A.

WAR DIARY
or
INTELLIGENCE SUMMARY

(Erase heading not required.)

Army Form C. 2118

Instructions regarding War Diaries and Intelligence Summaries are contained in F.S. Regs., Part II. and the Staff Manual respectively. Title Pages will be prepared in manuscript.

Place	Date	Hour	Summary of Events and Information	Remarks and references to Appendices
Bn Hd Qrs A B C togr at BUNEVILLE. A & B Coys TRANSLY MONTS-EN-TERNOIS	10th		The Battn. having arrived at its final destination, the day was devoted to general cleaning up and interior economy. Billets were good, the Battn. occupied two villages, making it necessary to supply Coy Guards for A & B Coys and a Quarter Guard for BUNEVILLE. The Colonels of both villages were obtained for Relaxation Rooms which proved to be of much benefit to the men	[initials]
do	11th		Training commenced, the hours being 9am – 1pm which the afternoon was given up to Recreation. Two football fields Engineered. Training consisted mainly of P.T & BF and Guards & Sentries which latter was both interesting to the men and helped greatly towards smartening the men after their long spell in the trenches. The Running Team commenced to train in travel for the Corps Race.	[initials]
do	12th		General Training as for 11th inst with steady hard Training of specialists commenced, also special classes for Rifle Grenadiers. Three classes were formed with a view of a rapid production of wire trained men and Instructors for their work in the villages. A letter was received from the Divnl. General expressing his satisfaction of the smart turn out in the trenches was published in the orders. General Training retarded owing.	[initials]
do	13th		as for 12th inst.	
do	14th		It was decided to have a Battn. Hd Qrs. Call followed viz Regimental Call followed by 2 G.S.	
do	15th		General as per programme. "W" Coy men were busted E.S.M. amongst who has of R.S.M. for nearly 2 yrs with the Battn. receiving confirmation in his rank of R.S.M. Platoon football competition commenced	

Army Form C. 2118

WAR DIARY
or
INTELLIGENCE SUMMARY
(Erase heading not required.)

Instructions regarding War Diaries and Intelligence Summaries are contained in F. S. Regs., Part II. and the Staff Manual respectively. Title Pages will be prepared in manuscript.

Place	Date	Hour	Summary of Events and Information	Remarks and references to Appendices
do.	16th		Training as per programme. Billeting continues.	
do	17th		Church parade. Work was commenced on a Zero range which was required for the A.R.A. Platoon competition.	
do.	18th		Training as per programme. A tactical scheme was held during the afternoon for all officers. Platoon Sergeants working on range continued.	
do	19th		Brigade Route March. Route: BUNEVILLE – TERNAS – GOUY-en-TERNOIS – MAGNICOURT – HOUDIN – MONCHEAUX, BUNEVILLE.	
do	20th		Training as per programme. The Equipment of the Bttn. being inspected it was decided that Battn. equipment should be under rifle, necessary exchanges were made: 9th (N.H.) Bn. Northumberland Fusiliers Scatter 10th Bn. Lincolnshire Regiment do 1st Bn. East Lancs. do. Warning was received that the Battn. would be inspected by the Divisional Commander on the 21st inst.	
do	21st		Parade Morning – Cleaning of billets &c. Whole Battn. paraded with transport 2 P.M. G.O.C.'s Inspection. The General expressed himself as pleased with the general turnout movement of the Battn. Coys. lagoons had to man their Coys. and the form "D Coy" movement of the Battn. which found by a march passed "D" Coy. drills. The General then inspected	

WAR DIARY or INTELLIGENCE SUMMARY

Army Form C. 2118

(Erase heading not required.)

Instructions regarding War Diaries and Intelligence Summaries are contained in F. S. Regs., Part II. and the Staff Manual respectively. Title Pages will be prepared in manuscript.

Place	Date	Hour	Summary of Events and Information	Remarks and references to Appendices
do	22nd		Training as per programme. The 300x Range being completed it was allotted to "A" & "C" Coys. for the day. In view of the coming B.T.A competition time was devoted during the afternoon to rapid loading & disappearing.	
do	23rd		Practice for competition. The platoon football final took place. 12 plat. of "B" Coy v. 15 plat. of "D" Coy. "D" Coy. winning by 1–0.	
do	24th		Church parade. During the afternoon the best plat. in each coy. competed to represent the Batt. in the B.T.A Competition. No 7 platoon of "B" Coy. under 2nd Lt. W. Broughton won this.	
do	25th		W.T.I. no training. The Brigade was inspected by the Corps Commander at Gouy in Artois prior to moving to the forward area.	
do	26th			
do to BARLY	27th		The Batt. moved to BARLY (GOUY in ARTOIS) by route march a distance of 13 miles. The Batt. moved off at 9.15am. and reached its destination without casualties. ROUTE. BUNEVILLE- MONTS in TERNOIS – MAGNICOURT – AMBRINES – GIVENCHY le NOBLE – AUBIGNY la COMPTE – BARLY. Billets were good & the Batts. reoccupied her own night.	
BARLY to No2 CAMP BLAIRVILLE	28th		The Batt. moved off at 7-30am. by route march to BLAIRVILLE. (dist 11 miles.) ROUTE. PICHEUX – GOUY in ARTOIS – BEAUMETZ – RIVIERE – BRETENCOURT- BLAIRVILLE. On leaving BEAUMETZ the Batt. marched passed the Divisional General on arriving in Camp hhueries was served & the Bn. settled down for two or three days.	

1875 W. W.593/826 1,000,000 4/15 J.B.C. & A. A.D.S.S./Forms/C. 2118. -

WAR DIARY
or
INTELLIGENCE SUMMARY.   FEBRUARY 1918.

Army Form C. 2118.

Place	Date	Hour	Summary of Events and Information	Remarks and references to Appendices
			Strength of Battalion at beginning of month — 43 Officers 741 O.R.	
			" " " end " " — 50 Officers 978 O.R.	
			Casualties	
			Wounded Evacuations	
			1 48 31 Total 80	
			Drafts: strength incoming 9th = 293	
			" 16th = 13	
			" 23rd = 6	
			" 28th = 5	
			Total 317	
			Officers: Joined	Transfers
			Lieut. H.S. Fitzgerald 17/2/18	2 Lieut Yarkley 14/2/18 ? to RFC
			" D.S. Prover 25/2/18	" E.P. Orow 23/2/18
			" —— Evacuated	Lieut A.P. Hutchinson 15/2 - to Sick Guards
			Lieut O. Bellaby 19/2/18	Lieut D. Auton 21/2 - to Home Establt.
			" " "	2 Lieut H.C. Freeman 1/2 - " " "
			Officers: Joined	
			Lieut R. Bilany ⎫	
			" —— Dunean ⎪	
			" C.F. Walker ⎬ 3/2/18	
			" H.C. Jamieson ⎪	
			" L.P. Brocklehurst ⎭	
			" J.H. Heaton	
			" G.W. Borland ⎫	
			" J.A. Loughlin ⎪	
			" J. Fitzgerald ⎬ 6/2/18	
			" F. McDonnell ⎪	
			" Capt. Wm. Goodall ⎭	
			2 Lieut. N.J. Whaley	

WAR DIARY
or
INTELLIGENCE SUMMARY
(Erase heading not required.)

Army Form C. 2118

Place	Date	Hour	Summary of Events and Information	Remarks and references to Appendices
			During the month the composition of the Brigade was altered owing to the reduction in the number of Battns in the Brigades throughout the Armies from 4 to 3. The 25th Can. from Northumberland was transferred to the 102nd Brigade, another 24th & 21st and 26th Battns were disbanded, a number of men being drafted from these Battns to the 9th Battn. The 10th Lincolns were transferred from the 101st to the 103rd Brigade and the 1st North East Lancashire Regt joined from another Division. It was expected that the Division would remain in rest until about March 14th but the Corps Commander, Lt Gen Haldane in a speech to the Brigade on the 26th said that Genl. Von Mackensen was reported to be on the 3rd Army front and a big German attack was expected. The Division was therefore being moved back into the line under orders from G.H.Q.	

W. Wyndes Lt Col

| SECRET | | MOVEMENT ORDER No. 1 | COPY No 1 |

9th (Northd Hussars) Battn. Northumberland Fusiliers

MOVE
The 9th (Northd Hussars) Battn Northd Fusiliers will proceed to LE CAUROY AREA, by route march on the 8th and 9th inst.

DESTINATION FIRST DAY
Headquarters, "A" and "D" Coys NEUVOCOURT. "B" and "C" Coys DENIER

ROUTINE
Reveille 5.0 a.m
Breakfast 5.45 a.m
Sick Parade 6.15 a.m.

PARADE
Parade on roads in column of route at 7.30 a.m in following Order: "D" Coy, "C" Coy, Band, "B" Coy, "A" Coy, and Headquarters. Transport with lump ?? in rear of the Battalion. Head of column to be opposite the Guard Room facing BLAIREVILLE.
Drill Battle Order.

SYNCHRONISING OF WATCHES
2/Lieut Amell will report at 7.45 a.m to Brigade Major at Cross Road, BLAIREVILLE to synchronise watches

BLANKETS
Blankets will be tightly rolled in bundles of two, tied and labelled with letter of Coy, Headquarters, Band, Signallers etc as the case may be.
Blankets of Headquarters, Signallers, Band etc will be dumped on R.Q.M. Sheds and those of Companies in hut nearest road in Company lines by 6.30 a.m.
1 Blanket per man to be ... also as above to be piled in above huts ... use on night of 8th inst and to be kept separate from remainder which will be despatched to final destination

PACKS
Mens packs will be dumped in same huts as blankets by 6.30. Each pack to be clearly marked with man's name, number and letter of Company. Leather jerkins and P.H. Helmets to be packed in the packs.

OFFICERS' VALISES
Officers valises will be taken to R.Q.M Stores by 6.30 a.m and will be conveyed to final destination

OFFICERS' KITS AND MESS KIT FOR THE JOURNEY
One limber for "A" and "D" Coys and limbers for "B" and "C" Coys and the Mess Cart for Headquarters Officers will be outside Officers huts to convey such Officers Kits and Mess Kit as may be required on the journey. Limbers to be loaded by 7.0 a.m

MESS BASKETS
Mess Baskets with the remainder of kit will be stacked with Company Blankets at 6.30 a.m. to be despatched to final destination

CANTEEN, ORDERLY ROOM ?? and CAMP KETTLES
These will be handed in to R.Q.M. Stores by 7.0 a.m.

COOKERS
Dinners will be prepared en route ready to be served at 11.30 a.m during mid-day halt. ?? for teatime also should be ready in Cookers in order to ?? ?? at arrival at destination

WATER CARTS WATER BOTTLES
will be filled before starting

BAGGAGE GUARDS
Each Company will detail 6 men who are unfit to march to report to Lieut. W. Hutton at 6.15 a.m. These men will act as Baggage Guards

STORES
All camp stoves, palliasses, tables and forms and other area stores will be taken to RECREATION HUT by 6.30 a.m

MOVEMENT ORDER No 1. (CONTINUED)

REAR PARTY — 2/Lieut W. Hutton, the Sanitary Corporal and 2 men will be left behind to hand over to Area Officer. 2/Lieut W. Hutton will be in possession of a list of stores in duplicate, one will be handed to Area Officer and the other kept. Certificate for cleanliness and sanitation of camp will be obtained from Officer taking over. The party of 2 will follow on with the last lorry.

CLEANING CAMP — O.C. Companies will be held responsible that tents, lines, Cook houses and ground in the vicinity are left in a clean and sanitary condition. The Medical Officer will inspect the camp at 7.0 a.m.

MARCHING OUT STATES — will be rendered to Orderly Room by 7.0 a.m.

ARRIVAL — Companies will report when they are settled in billets and number of absentees.

ACKNOWLEDGE.

Dated 7th February 1916.

Copies to
No 1. Retained
2. War Diary
3. O.C. 'A' Coy
4. O.C. 'B' Coy
5. O.C. 'C' Coy
6. O.C. 'D' Coy
7. Medical Officer
8. Transport Officer
9. Quartermaster
10. R.S.M.
11. Master Cook

[signature]
2/Lieut & a/Adjutant
9th (North'n Hussars) Batn North'd Fus.

War Diary.

Copy No 2

MOVEMENT ORDER No 2.
9th (Northd Hussars) Batn Northumberland Fusiliers

1. MOVE — The Battalion will proceed by route march tomorrow 9th inst to MONTS EN TERNOIS.

2. ROUTINE —
Reveille 7.30 a.m.
Breakfasts 8.0 a.m.
Sick Parade 8.30 a.m. for "A" and "D" Coys & Battn H.Qrs.
   do   10.30 a.m. for "B" and "C" Coys (O.C. B Coy will select a suitable place).
Dinners 11.30 a.m.
Teas. On arrival.

3. PARADE — Parade in column of route as below:—
Band, "D" and "H" Coys and Battn H.Qrs on road outside Guard Room at 12.45 p.m. ready to march off at 1.0 p.m. Head of column to be opposite "D" Coy's H.Qrs facing NORTH WEST.
"B" and "C" Coys 1.0 p.m. on main road through RENIER ready to join column as it passes.

4. BLANKETS — Rolled, tied and labelled as for today to be dumped in suitable places selected by Company Commanders. Location of place chosen will be handed in to Orderly Room by 4 p.m. tonight.

5. OFFICERS KITS and MESS KIT — Transport Officer will detail half a limber per Company and the Mess Cart for Headquarters Officers to collect Officers Kits and Mess Kit from their respective Headquarters in time to move off with the column.

6. CLEANING BILLETS. — O.C. Companies will render to Orderly Room by 6.0 p.m. tomorrow a certificate stating that they have personally inspected the billets and that they were left in a clean and sanitary condition. If necessary Companies will leave behind a small party to clean up billets. Such parties to proceed to final destination independantly; each under a responsible N.C.O.

7. MARCHING IN STATE. — Will be rendered to Orderly Room by 6.0 p.m. tomorrow 9th inst.

8. ARRIVAL — Companies will report when they are settled in billets and number of absentees.

ACKNOWLEDGE
8.2.1918

Copies to
1. Retained
2. War Diary
3. 2nd in Command
4. O.C. A Coy
5. O.C. B Coy
6. O.C. C Coy
7. O.C. D Coy
8. Medical Officer
9. Transport Officer
10. Quartermaster
11. R.S.M
12. Master Cook

[signature]
2 Lieut and a/Adjutant
9th (Northd Hussars) Batn. Northd. Fus.

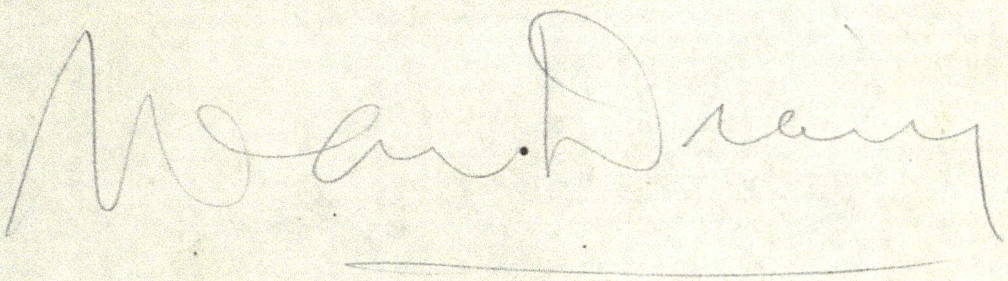

SECRET   OPERATION ORDERS. No. IV.   **COPY No 3**

6 (Northumberland Fusiliers) Battn, Northumberland Division.

1. Destination	The Battalion will move to BARLY by route march tomorrow the 27th inst. Approximate distance 13 miles.
2. Routine	Reveille 6·0 am. Breakfasts 7·0 am. Sick Parade 6·30 am. Dinners. On the march, or after arrival as arranged by Coys. Haversack rations may be carried if preferred. Tea. on arrival.
3. Parade.	Companies will be ready to move off as follows:-
8·45am	Band, Hd Qts & "D" Coys. BUNEVILLE. Head of Battn H.Qs. to be opposite H.Qs. mess as for to-days inspection.
9·5am	"A" & "B" Coys on road opposite "A" Coy mess. Head of "A" Coy at road junction opposite Q.M. Stores as for to-days inspection.
9·5am	Transport on the GOUY—MONTS-EN-TERNOIS Road. Head of column opposite Q.M. Stores.
4. Dress	Battle Order with Steel Helmets. Packs and Greatcoats will not be carried.
5. Blankets	Lorries will collect blankets as under:- 1 for A & B Coys and Transport. 1 for C & D Coys and Battn H.Qrs. All blankets should be stacked in Coy stores, in rolls of 10. (labelled) by 8·0 am. Should lorries be too late to be packed by Coys before they move, the rear party will load them.
6. Officers Mess Kit and Valises	Such Kit as is necessary for immediate use will be packed in bags and dumped outside the various messes at times shown. A & B Coys at 8·30 am. C & D Coys and Battn H.Qrs at 8·0 am. The above will be collected by the Mess Cart. All other kit will be packed in one mess basket and dumped at Coy and Battn H.Qrs with Officers Valises by 8·0 am. a lorry will pick these up.
7. Dumps.	For packs, surplus blankets, and any surplus kit will be as follows: A & B Coys, Transport & Q.M. Stores at Q.M. Stores. C & D Coys & Battn H.Qrs. at Regimental Aid Post.
8. Guards.	Lorries. 1 man per Coy will travel on the blanket lorries. 1 man from "A" Coy on the Officers Valise lorry. Dumps as above. O.C. "D" Coy will detail a guard of 3 men for the Regimental Aid Post under the pioneer Sergt. and O.C. "B" Coy a guard of 1 N.C.O. and three men for the Q.M. Stores. These parties will be provided with 3 days rations.
9. Rear Party.	Each Coy will detail a party of 1 N.C.O. and 4 men to remain behind and finally clean up all billets. R.S.M. Dorrant will remain with these men. They will report to him at the Q.M. Stores at 12·0 noon and proceed to FREVILLE COURT by 1·0 pm where Brigade party will be formed under Senior Officer present and marched to destination of the Battalion.

OPERATION ORDERS Nº 14. (Cont'd).

10. March Discipline	Strict March Discipline will be maintained at halts, each Coy Comm^r will give the order to Halt; men will halt at once and <u>not close up</u>. Coy Comm^r will then give "Right Turn fall out on the right." men will march straight off the road and at once take off their equipment. On falling in men will <u>not close up</u>. Water bottles will not be used without an order, or the permission of an Officer.
Move Complete.	Companies will report when in billets.
2. Cross Country Team	The Cross Country race will take place tomorrow the 24th inst. A Lorry will report at BUNEVILLE at 10.am to pick up members of the Battⁿ Team in this Village, it will then pick up the remainder of the Team at CROIX EN TERNOIS. Lieut. C. A. Hooper will accompany the team. After the race the party will be taken to BAILY where they will rejoin the Battalion. Equipment as in above orders will be taken by the team on the Lorries, and the <u>unexpended</u> portion of the days rations will also be carried. Team. The members of the team should draw running shorts to night. They will run in service boots. Time. Competition commences at 4.0pm.

ACKNOWLEDGE.

COPIES TO:-
1. War Diary.
2. Commanding Officer.
3. 2nd in Command
4. Adjutant.
5-12 Companies
13 Medical Officer
14 R.S.M
15 Master Cook
16 Quartermaster
17 Transport Officer

DATE. 26·2·18.

Capt & Adjutant
9th (York & Lancs) Bn. York & Lancs.

OPERATION ORDERS Nº 14. (Cont'd).

| SECRET | OPERATION ORDERS N°17. | COPY N° 1 |

9th (Northumberland Hussars) Battn. Northumberland Fusiliers.

1. Destination
The Battalion will move to BARLY by route march tomorrow the 24th inst. approximate distance 13 miles.

2. Routine
Reveillé 6·0 a.m.
Breakfasts 7·0 a.m.
Sick Parade 6·30 a.m.
Dinners. On the march, or after arrival as arranged by Coys. Haversack rations may be carried if preferred.
Teas. on arrival.

3. Parade.
Companies will be ready to move off as follows:-

8·45 am Band, Bn. H.Qs. C & D Coys. BONEVILLE. Head of Batt. H.Qs. to be opposite H.Qs. mess as for today's inspection.

9·5 am "A & B" Coys on road opposite "A" Coy mess. Head of "A" Coy at road junction opposite Q.M. stores as for today's inspection.

9·5 am Transport on the CODY - MONTS-EN TERNOIS Road, Head of column opposite Q.M. stores.

4. Dress
Battle Order with steel helmets.
Packs and Greatcoats will not be carried.

5. Blankets
Lorries will collect Blankets as under:-
1 for A & B Coys and Transport.
1 for C & D Coys and Batt. H.Qrs.
All blankets should be stacked in Coy stores, in rolls of 10. (labelled) by 8·0 am.
Should lorries be too late to be packed by Coys before they move, the rear party will load them.

6. Officers Mess Kit and Valises
Such kit as is necessary for immediate use will be packed in bags and dumped outside the various messes at times shown.
A & B Coys at 8·30 am.
C & D Coys and Batt. Hqrs at 8·0 am.
The above will be collected by the Mess Cart.
All other kit will be packed in one mess basket and dumped at Coy and Batt. Hqrs with Officers Valises by 8·0 am. A lorry will pick these up.

7. Dumps.
For packs, surplus blankets and any surplus kit will be as follows: A & B Coys, Transport & Q.M. stores at Q.M. stores C & D Coys & Batt. Hdqrs. at Regimental Aid Post.

8. Guards.
Lorries. 1 man per Coy will travel on the blanket lorries. 1 man from "A" Coy on the Officers Valise lorry.
Dumps as above. O.C. D Coy will detail a guard of 3 men for the Regimental Aid Post under the pioneer Sergt. and O.C. "B" Coy a guard of 1 NCO and three men for the Q.M. stores.
These parties will be provided with 3 days rations.

9. Rear Party
Each Coy will detail a party of 1 NCO and 4 men to remain behind and finally clear up all billets. Lt. C. Dumont will remain with these men. They will report to him at the QM stores at 12·0 noon and proceed to MAGNICOURT by 1·0 pm where Brigade party will be formed under Senior Officer present and marched to destination of the Battalion.

ROCLINCOURT

1:10,000

la Targette · Neuville-St-Vaast · les Tilleuls
aux Rietz
Maison Blanche
Ecurie
Madagascar
Roclincourt

G.S.G.S. 3062

REFERENCE.

Prominent Haystacks

Scale 1:10,000

TRENCH MAP.
ROCLINCOURT.
51ᴮ N.W. 1.
EDITION 8·A
Scale 1:10,000.

		Coke oven.		Nacelle	Ferry.		Remblai	Embankment.
		Glove Factory.		Orme	Elm.		Remise (des Machines)	Engine shed.
		Station.		Orphelinat	Orphanage.		Réservoir, Rést	Reservoir.
		Warren.		Ostensio	Oast-beds		Route cavalière	Bridle road.
		Garrison.		Ouvrage	Fort.		Rubanerie	Ribbon Factory.
		Gasometer		Ouvrages hydrauliques.	Water works.		Ruine	
		Mirror Factory.					Ruines	Ruin.
		Ice factory.		Papeterie	Paper-mill.		En ruine	
		Crane.		Parc	Park, yard.		Ruiné - e	
		Fuel.		,, aérostatique	Aviation ground			
		Sentry-box, Turret.		,, à charbon	Coal yard		Sablière	Sand-pit.
		Signal-box (Ry.)		,, à pétrole	Petrol store.		Sablonnière, Sablon	Pit tree.
				Passage à niveau P.N.	Level-crossing.		Sapin	Willow tree.
		Halt.		Passerelle, Pass**	Foot-bridge.		Saule	Salt-works.
		Shed, Hangar		Pépinière	Nursery-garden		Saunerie	Sos-mill.
		Hospital.		Peuplier	Poplar tree.		Scierie, Sᵉ**	Boring.
		Town hall.		Phare	Light-house.		Sondages	Spring.
		Colliery.		Piton, Pit	Pont.		Source	Sugar factory.
		Oil factory.		Plaine d'exercice	Drill ground.		Sucrerie, Sucʳᵉ	
Impʳⁱᵉ		Printing works.		Pompe	Pump.		Tannerie	Tannery.
				Poncees	Culvert.		Tir à la cible	Rifle range.
		Fire.		Pont	Bridge.		Tissage	Weaving mill.
		Rolling mills.		,, levis	Drawbridge.		Tôlerie	Rolling mill.
haute		High water mark.		Poste ,, de garde	Guard-guard		Tombeau	Tomb.
mo____				Station ,, ,, ,, ebts station.			Tour ,,	Tower.
se passe		Low ,,		Poterie Pⁱᵉ	Post.		Tourbière	Peat-bog, Peat-bed
ière				Pôtère	Pottery.		Tourelle	Small tower.
		Forester's house		Poudrière, Pondʳᵉ	Powder magazine.		Tuilerie	Tile works.
		Malt-house.		Magasin à poudre				
		Marble works.		Prise d'eau	Water supply.		Usine à gaz	Gas works.
		Marsh.		Puits	Pit-head, Shaft, Well.		,, électrique	Electricity works.
		Saltern.		,, Artésien	Artesian well.		,, d'électricité	
		,, Salt marsh.		,, d'orage			,, metallurgique	Metal works.
		Market.		,, ventilateur	Ventilating shaft.		,, à agglomérés	Briquette factory.
		Pool.		,, de sondage	Boring.			
		Rick.					Verrerie, Verrⁱᵉ	Glass works.
		Mine.		Quai	Quay, Platform.		Viaduc	Viaduct
		Monastery.		,, aux bestiaux	Cattle platform.		Vivier	Fish Pond
		Mill.		,, aux marchandises	Goods platform.		Voie de changement	
		Steam mill.					,, de déchargement	
		Wall.		Raccordement	Junction.		,, d'évitement	Siding.
		Loop-holed wall		Raffinerie	Refinery.		,, formation	
				,, de sucre	Sugar refinery.		,, manœuvre	
				Râperie	Beet-root factory.		Zingnerie	Zinc works.

GLOSSARY.

Abbaye, Abbᵉ	Abbey
Abreuvoir, Abᵛ	Watering place
Abri de douaniers	Customs-shelter
Aciérie	Steel works
Aiguilles	Points (Ry.)
Allée	Alley, Narrow road
Ancien, -ne, Anᶜⁿᵉ	Old
Aqueduc	Aqueduct
Arbre	Tree
éventail	fan-shaped
déchaussé	bare
fourchu	forked
isolé	isolated
penché	leaning
Arbrisseau	Small tree
Arc	Arch
Ardoisière, Ardʳᵉ	Slate quarry
Arrêt	Halt
Asile	Asylum
d'aliénés	Lunatic asylum
de charité des pauvres de refuge	Asylum
Auberge, Aubᵉ	Inn
Avec	Able-tree
Bac	Ferry
à traille	
Bains	Baths
aux bains	Bathing place
Balise	Beacon, Beacon
Banc de sable	Sand-bank
vase	Mud-bank
Barrage	Dam
Barrière	Gate, Bar
Bascule à flacons	Weigh-bridge
Bassin	Dock, Pond
d'échouage	Tidal dock

Bassin de radoub	Dry dock
Bateau phare	Light-ship
Blanchisserie	Laundry
B.K. (borne militaire)	Mile stone
Bⁿᵉ (borne kilométrique)	
Boulonnerie	
Fabᵗ de boulons	Bolt Factory
Bouée	Buoy
Brasserie, Brassᵉ	Brewery
Briqueterie, Briqᵗᵉ	Brickfield
Brise-lames	Breakwater
Bureau de poste	Post office
de douane	Custom house
Butte	Butt, Mound
Cabane	Hut
Cabaret, Cabᵗ	Inn
Câble sous-marin	Submarine cable
Calvaire, Calᵛ	Calvary
Canal de dessèchement	Drainage canal
Canal d'irrigation	Irrigation canal
Fabᵗ de caoutchouc	Rubber factory
Carrière, Carʳᵉ	Quarry
de gravier	Gravel-pit
Caserne	Barracks
Champ de courses	Race course
manœuvres	Drill-ground
tir	Rifle range
Chantier	Building yard
	Ship-yard
	Dock yard
Chantier de construction	Slip-way
Chapelle, Chᵖᵉ	Chapel
Charbonnage	Colliery
Château d'eau	Water tower
Chaussée	Causeway, Highway
Chemin de fer	Railway
Cheminée, Chⁿᵉᵉ	Chimney
Chêne	Oak tree
Cimetière, Cimᵗ	Cemetery
Clocher	Belfry
Clouterie	Nail factory
Colombier	Dove-cot

Corons	Workmen's dwellings
Cour des machines	Goods yard
Couvent	Convent
Croisier	Sling heap
Croix	Cross
Darse	Inner dock
Démoli -e, Démᵒˡⁱ	Destroyed
Détruit -e, Détᵗ	
Déversoir	Weir
Digue	Dyke, causeway
Distillerie, Distᵉ	Distillery
Douane	Customs-house
Bureau de douane	
Entrepôt de douane	Custom warehouse
Dynamitière, Dynᵐ	Dynamite magazine
Dynamiterie	Dynamite factory
Écluse	Sluice, Lock
Écluette, Ecˡᵗᵉ	Sluice
École	School
Écurie	Stable
Église	Church
Émaillerie	Enamel works
Embarcadère, Embʳᵉ	Landing-place
Estaminet, Estamᵗ	Inn
Étang	Pond
Fabrique, Fabᵗ	Factory
Fabᵗ de produits chimiques	Chemical works
Faïencerie	Pottery
Ferme, Fᵐᵉ	Farm
Filature, Filᵗ	Spinning mill
Fonderie, Fondᵉ	Foundry
Fontaine, Fontⁿᵉ	Spring, fountain
Forêt	Forest
Forme de radoub	Dry dock
Forge	Smithy
Fosse	Mine, Pit
Fossé	Mont, Ditch
Four	Kiln
à chaux	Lime-kiln

Four à coke	Coke oven
Ganterie	Glove Factory
Gare	Station
Garenne	Warren
Garnison	Garrison
Gazonnière	
Gazomètre	Gasometer
Glacière	
Fabᵗ de glaces	Mirror Factory
Glacière	Ice factory
Grue	Crane
Gué	Ford
Guérite	Sentry-box, Turret
à signaux	Signal-box (Ry.)
Halte	Halt
Hangar	Shed, Hangar
Hôpital	Hospital
Hôtel-de-Ville	Town hall
Houillère	Colliery
Huilerie	Oil factory
Imprimerie, Impᵉ	Printing works
Jetée	Pier
Laminerie	Rolling mills
Ligne de haute	High watermark
de basse marée	Low
Maison Forestière Mon forᵉ	Forester's house
Malterie	Malt-house
Marbrerie	Marble works
Marais	Marsh
Marais salant	Saltern, Salt marsh
Marché	Market
Mare	Pool
Meule	Rick
Minière	Mine
Monastère	Monastery
Moulin, Mⁿ	Mill
à vapeur	Steam mill
Mur	Wall
crénelé	Loop-holed wall

Nacelle	
Orme	
Orphelinat	
Usine	
Ouvrage	
hydrauliques	Waterworks
Papeterie	
Parc	
aéronautique	
à charbon	
à pétrole	
Passage à niveau P.N.	Level crossing
Passerelle, Pasˡᵉ	
Peuplier	Poplar
Phare	Lighthouse
Pilier, Pilʳ	Pillar
Plaine d'exercices	
Pompe	Pump
Poteau	Post
Post Indic. de guide	
Station côte	
Poteau Pᵘ	Post
Poterie	Pottery
Poudrière, Poudʳᵉ	
Magasin à poudre	
Prieuré	
Puits	Well
artésien	
d'aérage ventilation	
de sondage	
Quai	Quay
aux bestiaux	
aux marchandises	
Raccordement	
Raffinerie	
de sucre	
Râperie	

Army Form C. 2118

WAR DIARY
or
INTELLIGENCE SUMMARY
(Erase heading not required.)

9th [N.H.] Bn. NORTHUMBERLAND FUSILIERS.

WAR DIARY – MARCH 1918 –

APPENDICES ATTACHED –

O.O. Operation Orders Nos 19 to 27 –
A – Instructions for Reconnaissance Parties –
B – Map of sector held by 34th Div. March/18.
C1 Sketch Map – Attack on 9th Bn. North'd Fus.
  afternoon of 21-3-18 –
C2 do   do – Dispositions 8am. 22-3-18 –
C3. do   do – Final dispositions before withdrawal.
D – Report on operations at St. LEGER. March 21/22/1918.
E – Special order of the day by G.O.C. 34th □ in" – 29/3/18.
F   do   do   do   3/4/18.
G   do   do   by O.C. 9th Bn. North'd Fus –
H. do   do   do   by the C-in-C.

Army Form C.2118

WAR DIARY
or
INTELLIGENCE SUMMARY

(Erase heading not required.)

9th (N'ld & Hussar) Batt'n Northumberland Fusiliers

MARCH 1918

Instructions regarding War Diaries and Intelligence Summaries are contained in F.S. Regs., Part II. and the Staff Manual respectively. Title Pages will be prepared in manuscript.

Place	Date	Hour	Summary of Events and Information	Remarks and references to Appendices
	MARCH 1918			
BLAIRVILLE	1st 2nd		In R.2 Camp BLAIRVILLE. Parades and training carried out, including rapid fire wearing & box respirators; all men wore box respirators for an hour each day as it was anticipated that the enemy would use a large quantity of gas in the coming offensive.	
	3rd	2.am	The 34th division moved into the line in the centre sector of the VI. Corps front, taking over from the 178th Inf. Brig. of the 59th Div'n. and on the right and the 8th Brigade of the 3rd Div'n on the left. The 101st and 102nd Brigades took over the line, the 103rd Brigade being in Div'l Reserve. The Batt'n from BLAIRVILLE to ERVILLERS (ENISKILLING CAMP) via FICHEUX - BOISLEUX-AU-MONT - HAMELINCOURT -	Operation order no. 19.
	4th to 6th		Training was carried on, firing with gas box respirators on. Reconnaissance parties went forward to the Div'l area and the trenches in the left Batt'n area of the Right Brigade subsector. A general reconnaissance was carried out with a view to finding routes to forward area in case the Brigade in reserve was ordered forward in support of the forward Brigades. Gaps were cut in the wire in the rear area to allow for passage of troops in platoons in file.	Instructions appendix A.
	7th		The Batt'n relieved the 25th Can. Batt'n as left Batt'n of the right Brigade. Coys moved at 10 minute intervals commencing 6.30 p.m. via MORY - HOMME MORT - B'n HQs in BUNHILL ROW using PELICAN AVENUE. Relief complete 1.30 am.	O.O. 20.

WAR DIARY or INTELLIGENCE SUMMARY

Army Form C. 2118

9th Bn. Northumbd. Fus- Page 2.

MARCH 1918.

(Erase heading not required.)

Place	Date	Hour	Summary of Events and Information	Remarks and references to Appendices
IN THE LINE.	MARCH 7th to 12th		Dispositions. Left Batt: of Right Brigade. HQrs in BUNHILL Row in U.25.a, 6.5 – Three Cos holding front line each Co in depth holding pots in TUNNEL TRENCH with Supports in BUR & SUPPORT – order of Cos Right to Left A - B - C. Reserve Co in STRAY RESERVE.— This was modified later B Co being withdrawn to RESERVE in BUNHILL Row near Bn HQs, A+C each taking half the front previously held by B. Seeing the period enemy was very quiet though he could be seen working on his trenches by day, and although continually fired on by 18 pounders continued the work. Prisoners taken at various points on the British front, all told stories of Divisions being specially trained in rear for the coming offensive, and stated that they had been ordered to evacuate front-line posts on any sign of a raid to prevent identifications being obtained. Very few enemy patrols were met with, the enemy evidently was to lull us into a false security. The enemy overshot the mark, and his very quietness caused suspicions to be entertained that something abnormal was in preparation. On the 12th the warning was received that a prisoner had stated the attack was to commence on the early morning of the 13th. The prisoner, he was a deserter (a Lorrainer) gave a great deal of detail about the operation most of which in the event proved to be accurate.—	SEE MAP APPENDIX B.

WAR DIARY
or
INTELLIGENCE SUMMARY

7th a March 1918.

Army Form C. 2118

(Erase heading not required.)

Place	Date MARCH	Hour	Summary of Events and Information	Remarks and references to Appendices
TRENCHES	12th		During the night the Corps Artillery carried out a heavy bombardment of the enemy's trenches. "COUNTER PREPARATION", the enemy did not reply except with a few trench mortars.	
	13th		Before stand to, the Support Co moved in TIGER TR., a new trench with a good field of fire on which work had been pushed forward with all speed, and the Reserve Co to STRAY RES. On the evening of this day the Battn was relieved by the 10th Bn the Lincolnshire Regt and went into Brigade Res. Dispositions- Bn HQs. Rly Cutting U.25.8.9.1 C.Co. Road U.25.a.4.8 A Co. Rly embankment T.24.d.8.3 B+D Cop in the fork roads in T.23.d Co in shelters in case of threatened attack, Coys moved before STAND TO to Battle positions in BUNHILL Row from U.25.8.9.1 along trench in front of the FACTORY and CROSILLES to the road at T.18.c.5.4 order (Right to left) D - C - A - B.	O.O. 21. Map appendix B.
	14th to 19th		During these days the Battn was employed digging and improving TIGER trench; the Battn "stood to" each morning from 4am. to 7am. in battle positions. The enemy continued very quiet, and made very little reply to the "Counter Preparation" which was carried out at intervals each night. There were no definite signs on the Divisional front of an attack being in preparation, but the very fact that the enemy did not reply to our	

WAR DIARY or INTELLIGENCE SUMMARY

9th Bn. North'd Fus.
Army Form C. 2118
Page 4
MARCH 1918

Place	Date	Hour	Summary of Events and Information	Remarks and references to Appendices
Trenches.	MARCH 14th to 19th		Our bombardment was suspicious. Prisoners & deserters taken on various parts of the British front confirmed previous statements that a big offensive was in preparation, but stated it had been postponed for a few days. From these statements it appeared that the night of the attack would be either at BULLECOURT or on the SENSEE River. One prisoner stated that they were to attack BULLECOURT & passing through it were then to swing S/E the right. This is what the enemy actually did.	
	19th.		The Batn. was relieved at night by the 25th Bn. North'd Fus. 102nd Bde. & as part of the 103rd Brigade went into Divisional Reserve. Dispositions. Bn HQrs. - Reg. Cutting U.20.B.1.1. A. Co. in Reg. Cutting to S.E. of Bn. HQs. B & D. Cos in shelters in banks in U.20.d. C. Co. in shelters in banks near BANK COPSE U.21.c.	OO.22. See MAP APPENDIX B.
	20th.		Officers went forward & reconnoitre routes to and the ground in rear of first and second line systems.	
	21st	4am to 5am	Warning was received during the evening that a prisoner had stated that the offensive would commence on the morning of the 21st. Between 4am & 5am the enemy commenced a heavy bombardment of our front systems and batteries, & as being largely used. About noon, as far as is known, the Infantry attack commenced by ST. QUENTIN. It appears that the 34th Div. were not attacked frontally, but that the 59th were driven back, and the enemy coming through BULLECOURT swung to the right and captured or killed the personnel of the Battn. HQs. (Third Battle of the 102nd Brigade) in BUNHILL ROW	

Army Form C. 2118

WAR DIARY
or
INTELLIGENCE SUMMARY

9th Bn. Rattd. Fus

MARCH 1918.

Page 5.

(Erase heading not required.)

Place	Date MARCH	Hour	Summary of Events and Information	Remarks and references to Appendices
	21st		The enemy appear to have captured ECOUST at an early hour, and then proceeded due East towards ST. LEGER crossing the N.E. end of the ridge known as the HOGS BACK. This was the approximate situation when this Battn. began to take part in the fight.	
	21st	2.10pm	The Battn. moved under orders of the Brigade to the wood on the S. side of ST. LEGER, occupied the trenches in time to stop the enemy's advance. The enemy attacked until dark, under cover of m.g. fire from the HOGSBACK, and a barrage by Heavy Artillery. All attacks were beaten off; a battery of the 160 R.F.A. firing from a position on the right of the Battn. continually broke up the enemy formations as they came over the HOGSBACK. The night was fairly quiet; the guns of the battery were withdrawn, the Battn. was reorganized the position being held in depth.	SEE Sketch MAP. APPENDIX C.1 SK.map C.2.
	22nd	8am.	The enemy again attacked but was beaten off.	
		Noon 4pm	The enemy made a series of determined attacks under cover of an intense barrage of 5.9 & 2.10pm guns. All attacks were driven off until 4 p.m. when the frontline was lost owing to troops on the right giving way.	
		5.0pm	The enemy was driven out of the frontline he had taken by the Artillery. Severe casualties were inflicted on the enemy as he retired. There was then a lull.	
		Dusk.	At dusk the enemy made another attempt to take the position, but was again driven back, the support line holding firm.	

WAR DIARY or INTELLIGENCE SUMMARY

9th Bn. North'd Fus.
MARCH 1918
Page 6.

Army Form C. 2118

Place	Date	Hour	Summary of Events and Information	Remarks and references to Appendices
	MARCH 22nd		This attack drove our men back on the right (40th Division) and the enemy signals were seen being fired from the direction of B.1.b.6. while a machine gun was firing behind Bn. HQrs. (B.4.d.3.B) from a position B.1.a.d. Our troops on the N. side of the ST. LEGER CROISILLES valley had previously retired to the Railway in T.27.a. and 20.d.;	For details of fighting see report Appendix II SKMAP APPENDIX C 3.
		8-15.	Acting on instructions from the Brigade orders were issued to withdraw from the position. This was done without loss, and the Division being relieved the Battn. moved back to HAMELINCOURT. The men turning in to sleep (in huts) by 4 a.m.	
	23rd	10 a.m.	The officers who took part in the fighting were:—	

Headquarters
O.C.   Lt. Col. W.A. VIGNOLES. D.S.O.
R.M.C.   MAJOR. D.R. OSBORNE
Adjt.   2/Lt. M.W. DRYSDALE.
Sig.Off   2/Lt. W.H. CORNER.
I.toll.Off 2/Lt. L. FLETCHER
M.D.   CAPT. K.D.C. MACRAE. R.A.M.C.

A.Coy.
CAPT. R.V.L. DALLAS. M.C.
2/Lt. J.L. HOPKINS.
2/Lt. R.H. CRAIG
2/Lt. C.H. WALKER
2/Lt. H.B. JAMIESON

B.Coy.
CAPT. G. DAVIES
LT. H.S. ROWE
2/Lt. W. BROUGHTON
2/Lt. G.D. YOUNG.
2/Lt. V. MASON.

C.Coy.
CAPT. W.S. ALLAN. M.C.
2/Lt. J.A. GODFREY
2/Lt. W.L. BROWN.
2/Lt. F.L. BROCKLEHURST
LT. H.G. HADDOCK.
2/Lt. G.M. BORLAND.

D.Coy.
CAPT. I.G.C. BRADY
LT. E.B.L. PIGGOTT
2/Lt. H. ANSELL
2/Lt. F.L. FEATHERSTONE
2/Lt. A.G. OWEN.

Other officers of the Bn. were on leave or on courses —

| | | 10 a.m. | The Battn. moved out of HAMELINCOURT to the West of MOYENNEVILLE & rested in the open in Artillery formation awaiting orders. While moving through MOYENNEVILLE Co.Sgt. Major HENDERSON was killed and several men wounded by an enemy shell H.E. of heavy calibre. | |
| | | 2 p.m. | The Battn. moved and bivouaced as part of the 103rd Bde. on the west side of the AYETTE - BUCQUOY Road. | |

Army Form C. 2118

WAR DIARY
or
INTELLIGENCE SUMMARY
(Erase heading not required.)

9th Bn North'd Fus
Page 7
MARCH 1918.

Instructions regarding War Diaries and Intelligence Summaries are contained in F.S. Regs., Part II. and the Staff Manual respectively. Title Pages will be prepared in manuscript.

Place	Date MARCH	Hour	Summary of Events and Information	Remarks and references to Appendices
	24th	3.5 p.m.	Moved by route march to LABHERLIERE via BUCQUOY - HANNESCAMP - BIENVILLERS to billets.	O.O.23.
	25th	8.45 a.m.	Moved by route march to GRAND RULLECOURT. Route SAULTY- SOMBRIN near AUXI-LE-CHATEAU	
	26th	7.50 a.m.	Moved by route march to WAVANS. Route REBREUVIETTE - FREVENT - VACQUERIE - LE BOUCQ. It is understood that the move to this area was a precautionary measure. A certain number of civilians were moving W. on the road from DOULLENS, have fled from the zone behind the battle line E. of AMIENS	O.O.24.
	27th	11.45 p.m.	Moved to FREVENT to entrain - route VILLERS L'HOPITAL and BONNIERES. A portion of the transport proceeded with the Batn.	O.O.25.
	28th	10 am	remainder moved by Route March to ESTAIRES. First Army area - Batn. detrained at STEENBECQUE and marched to CAUDESCURE near VIEUX BERQUIN. In billets by 10 pm.	
	29th	1.15 p.m.	Moved to ESTAIRES by route march.	O.O.25A.
	30th	2.45 p.m.	Moved to forward area, huts & billets at LA ROLANDERIE FM. South of ERQUINGHEM-LYS. Map Ref H.11.c. Central. Sheet 36.	O.O.26.
	31st.		The Batn. relieved the 2/5 Bn K.O.R.L. Regt. as night sub-sector of the Divisional front. On holding from I.20.d.45.15 to I.21.a.85.70. Sheet 36.N.W.4. Scale 1/10,000. Relief complete 11 pm. Details of sector in next month's diary.	O.O.27.

WAR DIARY
or INTELLIGENCE SUMMARY.
(Erase heading not required.)

MARCH 1918. Page 5.

Army Form C. 2118.

Strength of Battalion at beginning of month — 50 Officers 978 O.R.
" " " end " — 43 Officers 887 O.R.

Casualties:

Killed	Wounded	Missing	Evacuations	Transfers	Conversions
29	81	10	44	40	3

Total 207

Details:

Week ending 9" = 48
" " 16" = 29
" " 23" = 13
" " 31" = 26

Total 116

Officers:

Killed:
2nd Lieut. H.G. Clay 1/3/18
" W.F. Walker } 27/3/18
" A.G. Owen }

Wounded:
2nd Lieut. R.H. Craig 31/3/18

Evacuations (sick)
2nd Lieut. F. Thompson 28/2/18
" H. Gatenby 22/3/18

Wounded:
2nd Lt. F.L. Brookhurst 23/3/18
" J.L. Hopkins 22/3/18
" J.R. Hooper 21/3/18
" H.G. Jamieson 21/3/18
" G.L. Brown 22/3/18 (remained at duty)

Transfers:
Captain Jas. Fred. Garvin to M.G.C. 25/3/12
Lieut. J.W. Livingston to R.A.F. Dymé 1/3/18
2nd Lt. J.A. Garrard to R.F.C. 6/3/18

H.B.Winger Lt. Col.

34th Division.
103rd Infantry Brigade.

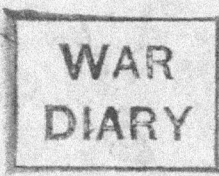

9th BATTALION

THE NORTHUMBERLAND FUSILIERS

MARCH. 1 9 1 8

Report on Operations 21st-22nd March 1918 attached

SECRET

WAR DIARY — March 1918. APPENDIX CO 14

OPERATION ORDERS. N°19.   COPY. N°2.

9th (Northumberland Hussars) Battn. Northumberland Fusiliers.

1. Relief	The 34th Division will relieve the 8th Infantry Brigade of the 3rd Division and the 148th Infantry Brigade of the 39th Division in the Centre Sector of the VI Corps Front. The 103rd Brigade will be in Divisional Reserve in the HAMELINCOURT–ERVILLERS area.
2. Move	The Battalion will move to INNISKILLING CAMP, ERVILLERS tomorrow the 3rd inst.
3. Route	BLAIRVILLE – FICHEUX – BOISLEUX-AU-MONT – HAMELINCOURT – ERVILLERS. Distance approximately 8 miles.
4. Starting Point	Cross roads B.2.d.4.8.
5. Routine	Reveillé 5.30 am. Breakfast 6.30 am. Kit Parade 7.0 am. Dinners on arrival.
6. Parade	8.0 am. On the road passing through the Camp. Head of the column at the Guard Room facing BLAIRVILLE.
7. Order of March	Battn Hd Qrs, "A" Coy, "B" Coy, Band, "C" Coy, "D" Coy and Transport. Coys will march at 100 yards interval. Transport to march 100 yards behind rear Coy.
8. Dress	BATTLE ORDER. Leather jerkins to be worn over jackets.
9. Officers Mess Kit & Valises	Necessary mess kit will be dumped by the road at end of the Officers Lines by 7.15 am. The mess Cart will collect this. Valises and surplus kit will be dumped as above by 7.15 am where they will be collected by a lorry.
10. Blankets	Will be rolled in bundles of 10 and labelled. They will be dumped at the end of Coy Lines by 7.0 am when a lorry will collect them.
11. Rear Party	Each Coy will detail 1 N.C.O. and 4 men to remain behind as a rear party, and finally clean the Camp. These parties will report to Lieut Godfrey at 11.0 am, who will march them to the cross roads at B.2.d.4.8 where Brigade party will proceed to destination under the senior Officer present.
12. Camp Furniture	All Camp furniture will be returned to the recreation hut by 7.30 am.
13. Marching out states	To be rendered to Orderly Room by 7.0 am.
14. Packs	Mens Packs will be dumped at Coy Stores before breakfast.

ACKNOWLEDGE.

Copies to:
1. War Diary
2. Retained
3. Commanding Officer
4. 2nd in Command
5–8. Companies
9. Quartermaster
10. Transport Officer
11. R.S.M.
12. Master Cook
13. Medical Officer

J. Groat Crawh
Capt & Adjutant.
9th (North'n Hussars) Bn. North'n Fusiliers

DATE. 2-3-18.

Retained

APPENDIX II

9th (NORTH⁴ HUSSARS) BATT⁴ (NORTH⁴ FUSILIERS)
REPORT ON OPERATIONS
ROUND ST. LEGER
MARCH 21ST AND 22ND 1918.
REF. MAPS. 1/20,000 SCALE SHEETS 51ᵇ S.W. and 57ᶜ N.W.

MARCH 21ˢᵗ

The Battalion as part of the 103rd. Brigade was in Divisional Reserve, and on the night of the 20th/21st was in shelters in banks and in the Railway Cutting in T.20.d, (Sheet 51ᵇ S.W.

2.0.p.m. Orders were received to move the Battn. forthwith to B.6. (Sheet 57ᶜ N.W.)

A Coy. moved within 5 minutes, other Coys. following, the Battn. proceeded across the SENSEE VALLEY through T.26. c and D avoiding ST. LEGER which was being heavily shelled. B.4.d. was reached without casualties.

2.50.p.m. An officer met the O.C. "B" Coy. with orders for the Battn. to press on with all haste, stating the enemy was in BUSHILL ROW, and instructions for the O.C. Battn. to report to G.O.C. 102nd Brigade.

On reaching B.4.d. the enemy could be seen coming over the HOGS BACK in waves; he was being engaged by a battery of the 160 Brigade R.F.A. at about B.4.d.9.4. firing with open sights. One or more Coys. of the 1st EAST LANCASHIRES were engaged with the enemy, holding the front line of the THIRD SYSTEM about B.5.a and c.

On reporting to the G.O.C. 102nd Bde. the 9th Battn. was ordered to hold the wood and high ground on the S. side of ST. LEGER

9th Batt. Fus. REPORT   Page 2.

MARCH 21st

at all costs.

The following positions were taken up as the various companies arrived.

Bn Hqs. B.4.d.3.8.

'A' Coy. T.29.c.7.1. to T.29.a.5.0. in the trench on the N.E. edge of ST. LEGER WOOD (Front line Third System).

'B' Coy. B.4.d.65.10. to B.5.a.05.10. (Support line Third System).

'C' Coy. In support line in ST. LEGER WOOD B.4.b.9.2. to about T.28.d.4.3.

'D' Coy. In reserve in sunk road B.4.b.4.6. to B.4.b.1.5. with a post at B.10.b.9.3 to command the valley.

A Coy. of R.E. reported and were ordered to hold the line between 'B' and 'C' Coys.

4.0. p.m. Orders had apparently been given to the 1st Battn. EAST LANCASHIRES to reorganize on the road in B.10.b. and B.11.c. to make a counter attack against ECOUST, and about 4.0 p.m. the Coys. in the front line of the Third System began withdrawing in accordance with these orders, with the exception of one Coy. which the O.C. 9th North'd Fusiliers ordered to stand fast. The result of this withdrawal was that the enemy entered the front line Third System in B.5.c. and was never entirely ejected.

The enemy in the meantime had been advancing over the HOGS BACK in a series of waves and though broken up by artillery fire, Machine Gun fire from 4 guns about B.4.d.5.4. and long range Lewis Guns and rifle fire a number of men had reached the dead ground in B.5. central.

Page 3.

MARCH 21st

large numbers must have been used as fresh waves continually replaced those that were broken up.

The enemy re-formed in the dead ground in B.5.b. and advanced to attack the S.E. Corner of the wood.

'A' Coy. had pushed posts in front of the trench and inflicted casualties on the advancing enemy. These posts were driven in by heavy M.G. fire from B.6. central.

The enemy was seen on the HOGS BACK doubling forward carrying M.Gs. like a stretcher.

Under cover of this fire the enemy reached our wire and opened fire on the trench but was driven back by rifle fire.

5.0 pm to 6.0 pm — One platoon of 'C' Coy. was ordered to hold the trench on the left of 'A' Coy. in T.29.a. to cover the left and prevent an advance up the CROISILLES VALLEY; one platoon of 'D' Coy. to prolong 'C' Coy's left in the support line and get in touch with the Battn. on the left in the bottom of the valley.

About this time it was discovered that details of the 25th Battn. North'd. Fus. were holding out in the north end of sunken road in T.29.b. or trenches near this.

5.15 pm — 2/Lt. H.G. JAMIESON advanced with No.3 Platoon and reinforced the details mentioned in previous paragraph.

5.30 pm — 2/Lt. C.H. WALKER advanced through the wire with No.1 Platoon at the S.E. Corner of the wood killing 20 of the enemy and capturing 2 M.Gs. He eventually occupied the road in T.29.d.

About this time a special R.E. Coy. about 50 rifles came up through the wood and reinforced 'A' Coy. in the trench in front of it.

Page. 4.

5.45.pm — Two platoons of the 102nd Bde. "PIONEER COY", 3 officers and 50 O.Rs. came along the trench in front of the wood from the North and joined up with 'A' Coy.

6.30.pm — The two platoons of 102nd Bde. Pioneer Coy. with No. 4 platoon 'A' Coy. were ordered to form up in front of the trench and to advance to sunken road in T.29.b. to close the gap between No. 1 platoon 'A' Coy. and the 25 Btn. further left. This was carried out.

7.30.pm — Units of the 40th Division came in on the right.

Dispositions were then, as far as can be ascertained:-

A forward line as follows

From T.29.c.75.35 to T.29.b.45.35. thence along sunk road to Cross Roads T.23.d.9.3. and trench from T.29.b.70.85 to T.23.d.3.2. held from right to left by 2 platoons of 'A' Coy. 9th Btn. Nthd. Fus. — 2 platoons 102nd Bde Pioneer Coy — Details of 25th Btn. Nthd. Fus.

Front Line

From B.5.a.8.7 (about) along N.E. edge of wood.
One Coy. of 13th YORKSHIRE REGT — One platoon of 'C' Coy. 9th Battn. 2 platoons of 'A' Coy. — 2 platoons 12 Yorkshires — J Coy. R.E. Left in touch with 10th LINK Right of B.5.8.7. the enemy were in the front line.

Support Line — Right to Left.

2 Platoons 12th Suffolks.
'D' Coy East Lancashires — 3 platoons B 9th Nthd. from B.4.d.65.10. to B.5.a.05.10. with a post in front of the battery at B.4.d.9.4. — one platoon special Coy. R.E. — one platoon East Lancashire one platoon 'B' Coy. 9th Nthd. Fus. — 3 platoons 'C' Coy. 9th Nthd. Fus to left of T.28.d.25.60.

Page 5.

The guns of the battery at B.4.d.9.4. were withdrawn after dark under cover of the post established by 'B' Coy. 9th North'd. Fus.

8.0 pm 'D' Coy. was ordered to take over the trench (Front Line) to the right of 'A' Coy, i.e. Trench running S. through B.5.a. It was not known at this time that the enemy were in it. 'A' Coy of the Yorkshire Regt. were found to be pushing down the trench to try and get in touch with the 12th Suffolks holding the front line on the HOGS BACK, and in front of BANKS WOOD. With the assistance of 'D' Coy. 250 yds of trench was gained but further progress could not be made as the enemy was in force in the trench.

9.0 pm Orders were received from Bde. to reorganize the Battn. and to take over the frontage T.29.c.7.0 to T.28.b.9.5. with 13th YORKSHIRES on the right and 10th LINCOLNS on the left, and to withdraw the troops in the forward position in T.29.b.and.d. This was done. The details of 102nd Bde. and the R.E. Coys. in the front and support lines withdrew to other areas.

11.30 pm A Coy. took over trench in front of the wood after withdrawing from forward position.

During the night the dispositions were altered:-
Right to left on the frontage allotted to the Battn. — 'A' Coy — 'C' Coy — 'D' Coy. each with 2 platoons in front line and 2 in support — a platoon of 13th YORKSHIRES appear to have remained on the left of 'C' Coy in the front line

It was not found possible to move 'B' Coy into the area allotted to Battn. as the 13th Yorkshires were too weak to hold their sector, 'B' Coy therefore remaining in the trench they had held during the day.

March 22nd.
3. Am to 5.30am

The alteration in dispositions was carried out without casualties; the night was fairly quiet completion of moves reported to Bde. at 6.20 am.

Lt. V. MASON and SGT. BENNET went out as a patrol from the support line. They proceded W. and S. of BANKS WOOD over the front line, which they found at this point to be held by us, and out along the HOGS BACK to 2nd System which was found to be held by the enemy. A prisoner of the 221st SAXON DIVISION was captured during the night. Prisoners captured earlier in the day belonged to a BAVARIAN DIVISION. During the night the 13th YORKSHIRES tried to drive the enemy out of the front line trench, but found he was firmly established between B5a.E.3 and BANKS WOOD.

8.0. am.

Between 7.0 am and 8.0 am observers on the left saw a number of cavalry come forward and dismount and advance towards ST. LEGER WOOD.

At 8.0.am. a large party of the enemy were seen from our trenches advancing to attack the S.E. corner of the wood. Lt. C.H. WALKER 'A' Coy. withheld the fire of the men until the enemy were up to the wire when fire was opened

Page 7.

causing the enemy many casualties and driving him back.

The enemy then began to dig at T.29.d.4.2.; owing to the configuration of the ground it was not possible to fire on the men working on it, but artillery was directed on them later in the day.

2/Lt. H. ANSELL and 2/Lt. W.L. BROWN took out daylight patrols beyond our wire and brought back valuable information.

The enemy made his attack at this time under cover of artillery fire of heavy calibre directed on the support line and the road near Battn. HQrs. which were at about B.4.d.3.8.

9.0 am to noon. The remainder of the morning was fairly quiet, artillery fire being intermittent, but observers on the left saw that the enemy were continually bringing up fresh troops which were massing out of sight from our trenches.

11.45 am. During the morning it was decided in consultation with OC. 13th Yorkshires to get the artillery on to the front line trench in B5.a. and c. held by the enemy; this was done and at 11.45 am. a Coy. of the Yorks. attacked and gained their objective with slight loss, driving the enemy into a large part of a trench previously held by them.

12 noon. A patrol of cavalry was seen on the hill about T.22.b.

12 noon to 4.0 pm. Between noon and 4 pm. the enemy made a series of determined attacks under cover of an intense barrage of shells of all calibre,

12.noon to 4.0.pm	but mostly 210 M/M. or 240 m/m directed on the Support line and on the road by Battn. HdQrs. Notwithstanding this barrage the Coy. and Battn. runners continued to carry messages between the Front Line and Battn. HdQrs. without delay.

A Major and Subaltern of artillery continued observing and were of the greatest assistance in obtaining Field Artillery Support when it was required. Support of the Heavy Batteries was obtained through the 103rd Inf. Bde.

Though the Bde. HdQrs. were at GOMIECOURT a line was maintained most of the day, the Brigade Signallers under Sgt. RISING. R.E. repairing the line as often as it was cut.

All attacks were beaten back, by rifle, L.G. and rifle grenades (the latter directed beyond the crest of the hill) until 4.0 p.m. when the Yorkshires on the right withdrew from the front line, causing the right of the 9th N'thd Fus. to withdraw also, and the left being induced to conform. The men were practically all rallied on the Support line. |
| 4.30pm | 2Lt. W. L. BROWN seeing the enemy had not entered the trench in force collected men of his platoon and with Sgt. CAMPBELL and assisted by Pte. O'NEIL made a counter-attack, re-entered the trench killing about 20 of the enemy. Finding that he was unsupported, he then withdrew. |

Page 9.

4.30 pm A post was established at T.28.b.6.3. to cover the left front. This post inflicted at least 20 casualties on the enemy.

The 9th North'd. Fus. were still in touch with the Lincolns on the left and the Coy. of EAST LANCS. were standing firm in the support line on the right. The 40th Division on the right though heavily attacked were holding out.

When the front line gave way, the enemy entered the trench on the S.E. of the wood and pushed up it to about B.5.a.4.5.

Lt. H.S. ROWE 9th North'd Fus. went forward and organised a party of the YORKS who were retiring down this trench and bombed the enemy back; he shot four of the enemy himself. At 5.0 pm. the enemy worked up the trench again and were driven back by Lt. H.S. ROWE, Cpl. WATSON, and the bombers of the left platoon of 'B' Coy 9th North'd. Fus.

The enemy retreated over the ridge suffering casualties as they retired and the YORKS re-occupied the trench.

A number of the enemy were killed in these two bombing fights.

B. 26 b 8.3 should presumably read T 26. b. 8. 3.

Page 10

March 22 On hearing that men were retiring on the left of the Battalion front, all available personnel of Battalion HQ's were organised and led forward through the wood by 2/Lieut: L. FLETCHER. (Intelligence Officer) and W.H. CORNER (Signalling Officer) and R.S.M. ARMITAGE. This party advancing rallied men who were retiring and reinforced the Support line. R.S.M. ARMITAGE and SGT. WILKINSON were wounded; the party moved up through the barrage in extended order.

5.0 pm About this time our artillery was directed (through the F.O.O.) to fire on the front line trench in front of the wood which the enemy had gained; the enemy was seen to leave this trench in large numbers our men firing and inflicting severe casualties on him.

It is thought that the trench could have been regained if a reserve had been available but every man was in action.

At 6 p.m. Enemy was seen concentrating M.G's at B.5.d.4.2 the Artillery were informed and dispersed them.

6.0 pm It seemed at this time as if the attack had been definitely beaten off, but at dusk large numbers of our troops were seen to be retiring from HILL SWITCH in T.22 back to the Railway in T.20d followed by the enemy who fired signals as he advanced, and quickly reached T.22.c.1.3. The enemy at the same time made another determined attack against ST LEGER WOOD.

The Lincolns on the left withdrew about this time. D Coy was then ordered to withdraw a platoon from the line and form a defensive flank to left along the railway on the N.W edge of the wood.

6-7 pm Between 6 and 7 pm the YORKS who had a Battalion HQ's in the road at about B.4.b.05.80 were asked to send a patrol down the road to watch the exit from village, but the message was not delivered as the HQ's had withdrawn.

March 22 7.0 pm	A message was sent to the O.C. 12th SUFFOLKS at the MORT HOMME when it was found that this Battalion was retiring to the Army line. As it got dark the attack on ST LEGER WOOD was finally beaten off but the enemy could be seen firing his signal lights from the MORT HOMME and a M.G. fired from some point on B.10.d through B.11 central. The signal lights were at 8.0 oclock being fired from the direction of B.16.b.
7.30 pm	The Coy of East Lancs. and a platoon of B Coy 9th North Fusiliers were ordered to form a flank facing S.E.
8.0 pm	After reporting situation to the G.O.C. 103rd Brigade the Battalion was ordered to withdraw.
8.15 pm	Orders were sent to Companies to withdraw in the order D, A, C, B. Coy of E. Lancs each covering its own withdrawal.
8.30 pm to 9.30 pm	The East Lancs covered the right during the withdrawal and a patrol from D Coy with Lewis Gun covered the left. The enemy appeared to be pushing slowly towards ST LEGER from the MORT HOMME. The withdrawal was conducted in an orderly manner, pouches were refilled before leaving, Lewis Guns that were undamaged and magazines and the wireless set and signal apparatus were brought out. Each Coy Commander reported to Battn Hd Qrs as his Coy got clear. Battn Hd Qrs withdrew after the Coys were clear covered by the last platoon of the East Lancs. The retirement was carried out through B.11 and B.3 central, thence N across the valley to the SENSÉE SWITCH which the Battalion had been ordered to hold. This trench was found to be full of troops, so the Battalion was concentrated at B.26 c & d.3.

March 22nd

Orders were eventually received to withdraw to HAMELINCOURT as the Division was being relieved.

The only casualties during the withdrawal, were from a chance shell fired at the SENSEE SWITCH.

Miscellaneous Notes

Enemy Aeroplanes

During the afternoon of the 22nd a squadron (4 or 5) enemy planes took part in the attack on the wood, flying low over the trenches, dropping lights as signals to the Artillery and firing into the trenches with MG's. B Coy in support fired on them each time they came over with rifles and L.G's and appeared to drive them away. Very few if any casualties were caused by the planes.

Rations

Rations, previously cooked, were brought up by 1st line Transport to Battalion HQ's on the night of the 21/22nd. Water was obtained from ST LEGER. No casualties occurred in delivering these.

Ammunition

The ammunition for the firing line third system had been dumped in shell holes behind the line. It would have been better to have had it in the trench as the dumps were difficult to find while under shell and M.G. fire. All the ammunition was used, and further supplies were carried on the evening of the 22nd from the dump at ST LEGER.

The M.G's also ran out of ammunition and a party was supplied from Battalion HQ's 9th Northd Fusiliers which carried 20 or 30 boxes to the guns.

Page 13

Weapons Used:
The principal weapons used were the Rifle, Lewis Guns, Machine Guns, and Artillery. Bombs and No 23 grenades were used to clear the trench of the enemy and the rifle grenades (No 24) were used against M.G's which withdrew behind the crest when fired on with rifles. They were very effective.

Communications:
Communication with Brigade H.Q. was by telephone; it worked well, and though the wires were cut several times the break was soon repaired. The fact that the line was buried was of the greatest advantage. It is certain that that communication would have been constantly broken more often had the wires been in the open as the barrage was deep.

Visual was never established. This was a great disadvantage as when the line was cut all communication was gone (as the wireless was out of order) with the exception of the pigeons.

Two pigeons were available, one was flown and it is understood the message reached the Corps Staff in 8 minutes.

Morale:
The morale of the men remained excellent throughout, though very exhausted by the continuous fighting.

Officers:
All the Officers did excellent work, and showed great initiative and a knowledge of the use of the weapons at their disposal. CAPT R.V.L. DALLAS M.C. Commanding "A" Coy especially showed a quick grasp of the situations that arose and a willingness to take responsibility that was of the greatest value.

Page 14

<u>Casualties</u>. Killed, wounded and missing about 120 including

<u>Officers</u>. Killed 2/Lieut. R.H. CRAIG.
Wounded. Lieut E.R. HOOPER
2/Lieut T.L. HOPKINS
2/Lieut H.G. JAMIESON
Lieut F.L. BROCKLEHURST
2/Lieut W.L. BROWN (at duty)

R.S.M. ARMITAGE wounded later died of wounds.

Dated 2nd April 1918

Comdg.
Lieut Colonel
9th (Northumberland Hussars) Battn.
Northumberland Fusiliers.

SECRET   APPENDIX A   COPY No.

Instructions for Reconnaissance Parties

Detail of Parties 4 Parties each consisting of 2 Officers and 2 Platoon Sergeants (1 Officer or 1 Sergeant from each Company) will carry out reconnaissance as under.

Party No. 1 Will proceed to Left Brigade Hd. Qrs. at T.21.c.5.9. (Sheet 51 B.S.W. on 1/20,000 Scale) (51.B.S.W on 1/10,000 scale), thence to the Left Battalion Hd. Qrs., thence to the Front Line.

They will take note of :—
(A) Route to ST LEGER and CROISILLES
(B) HENIN HILL in T 4, 5, 10 and 11.
(C) Third, Second and Front line systems as given on map circulated to Companies.

Party No. 2 As for Party No. 1 but will proceed from Left Brigade Hd. Qrs. to Right Battalion Hd. Qrs. thence to front line etc.

Party No. 3 Will proceed to Right Brigade Hd. Qrs. at B.19.a.8.7. (Sheet 57c N.W. 1/20,000 scale) thence to Left Battalion Hd. Qrs. of Right Bde., thence to front line.

They will take note of :—
(A) The approaches to CROISILLES and ST LEGER
(B) The HOGS BACK in B 6 and 11 (Sheet 51 S.W.) and U 25 c and d (Sheet 57c N.W.)
They should also locate each system of trenches as shown on map circulated to Companies.

Party No. 4 As for party No. 3 but will proceed from Right Brigade Hd. Qrs. to Right Battalion Hd. Qrs. thence to front line.
They will also note position of ECOUST and LONGATTE.

Guides The above parties should ask at the Brigade Hd. Qrs. for guides or directions as to finding the way.

Routes Parties 1 and 2 through ST LEGER
Parties 3 and 4 through MORY.

Dress Skeleton order and rifles - ground sheets rolled on belts

Time Parade at 8.30 a.m. at Orderly Room and proceed under Senior Officer of each party.

Rations A Haversack ration will be carried.

Intelligence Officer Will proceed with one of above parties.

Runners 1 Battn. Hd. Qrs. Runner will proceed with each party. Company runners will proceed with parties as under.

	A. Coy.	B. Coy.	C. Coy.	D. Coy.
No 1. Party	1	1		
No 2. "			1	1
No 3. "	1	1		
No 4. "			1	1

ACKNOWLEDGE.

DATED 3rd March 1918.

Copies to: No 1. Commanding Officer
            " 2. 2d in Command
            " 3-6. Company Commanders
            " 7. Intelligence Officer

Captain & Adjutant
7th (Works Sussex) Bn North'n Regt

9th Bn North'd Fus.

WAR DIARY

MARCH 1918

APPENDICES C₁
C₂
C₃

Sketch Maps

9th Bn North'd Fus-
WAR DIARY

MARCH 1918
_____

APPENDICES C₁
C₂
C₃

Sketch Maps
_____

WAR DIARY.

APPENDIX C2

SKETCH SHOWING APPROXIMATE DISPOSITIONS. 8 AM. 22nd 1918.
ST. LEGER WOOD. OF 9th Bn NORTD FUS.

TO BE SUPERIMPOSED ON MAP. APPENDIX B

21

T B

3

10th LINCOLNS

1 PN E. YORKS

ST. LEGER

D Co
C Co
A Co

1 Co 15th E. YORKS

BN HQS 9th N.F.

B Co

1 Co EAST LANCS

ENEMY SEEN THROUGHOUT THE DAY ADVANCING TO REINFORCE

ATTACK AT 8 A.M.

ENEMY

12th SUFFOLKS

13th E. YORKS

40th DIVn

13 E. YORKS must be an error for 13 YORKS. (121 Bde 40 Divn.)

WAR DIARY
APPENDIX C3
15

SKETCH SHOWING FINAL
POSITION AT ST LEGER
AND WITHDRAWAL.

TO BE SUPERIMPOSED ON
MAP. APPENDIX B.

——— BRITISH
——— ENEMY.

LINE HELD.

SIGNALS FIRED.

SENSEE SWITCH.

ENEMY ATTEMPTING TO BOMB US OUT

ST LEGER WOOD.

9th North Fus.

WITHDRAWAL.

ONE Co EAST LANCS

HALLY COPSE

M.G. SIGNALS FIRED.

APPENDIX "D"
precedes War Diary.

APPENDIX E/F/G

34th Div. No. A/222.

Order of the Day

1. The following letter has been received from the G.O.C., VIth Corps, dated 23rd March :-
   " The heavy loss the 34th Division has suffered and the trying
   " work that has fallen upon it during the last three days, makes
   " it unavoidable that it should leave the VIth Corps. Will you
   " please thank all ranks for their work during the opening stage
   " of the great battle now in progress. The task that they had
   " to carry out was not an easy one, and I fear that their losses
   " have been great. "

2. On my own behalf, I wish to record my high appreciation of the gallantry and the stubborn power of resistance shewn by all ranks and arms of the Division on the 21st and 22nd March.

3. When the full story of those days is known the gallant fight of the 102nd Brigade and part of the 101st Brigade on the 21st March when outflanked and almost surrounded, the stubborn and protracted resistance of the 11th Suffolks on the left of the Division on the 21st and 22nd March, and the steady disciplined gallantry of the 103rd Brigade on the 21st and 22nd March, will go down to history among the greatest achievements of the War.

4. A separate order has already been issued to the Artillery of the Division, and it is only necessary to say here that their conduct was worthy of the highest traditions of the Royal Regiment.

5. The 34th M.G. Battalion, recently organised as it is, laid, during the 21st and 22nd March, the foundation of a tradition of its own. No higher praise can be given to it than to say that the orders issued to the Battalion that each gun was to be fought to the last man and the last round of ammunition, were carried out in all cases, in the spirit of the order and in many cases, to the letter of the order.

6. As admirable as the gallantry displayed in action, has been the high standard of discipline, endurance and cheerfulness shewn by all during the days which have elapsed since the Division was withdrawn from the line.
   During these days also, the work of the A.S.C. carried out under great difficulties, has been beyond all praise.

   It is now necessary for the Division again to go into the line, but I feel more than ever confident that no call can be made upon the 34th Division which will not be instantly and cheerfully responded to.

J. Nicholson.

Major General,
Commanding, 34th Division.

26th March, 1918.

APPENDIX F

SPECIAL ORDER OF THE DAY
by
Major General C.L. NICHOLSON, C.B., C.M.G.,
Commanding, 34th Division:

3/4/18.

The Divisional Commander has received the following letter from the G.O.C., Third Army, and wishes it to be read at the head of each unit on parade, or otherwise communicated to all ranks of the Division.

Lieut.Colonel,
A.A.&.Q.M.G., 34th Division.

* * * * * *

Third Army,

2.IV.18.

" I cannot allow the 34th Division to leave the Third
" Army without expressing my appreciation of their splendid
" conduct during the first stages of the great battle now in
" progress.
" By their devotion and courage they have broken up
" overwhelming attacks and prevented the enemy gaining his
" object, namely, a decisive victory.
" I wish them every possible good luck.

J. BYNG,
General. "

APPENDIX G

Special order of the day
by Lt Col.

9th (NF) Battn. Northd Fusiliers.

The following is a copy of letter received by the Divisional Commander from the G.O.C. Third Army.

I cannot allow the 34th Division to leave the Third Army without expressing my appreciation of their splendid conduct during the first stages of the great battle now in progress.

By their devotion and courage they have broken up overwhelming attacks and prevented the enemy gaining his object, namely, a decisive victory.

I wish them every possible good luck.

(Signed) J. Byng, General

Special order of the day by Lt Col. W. A. VIGNOLES. D.S.O. commanding 9th Bn Northumberland Fusiliers.

To. The Officers. W.Os. N.C.Os and men of the 9th (NF) Battn. Northd Fusiliers

I had hoped to have been able to speak to you all before this, to tell you how proud I am to command a Battalion that fought as this one did on March 21st – 22nd. By its steadiness and discipline, under the most trying circumstances, it held up the enemy's attack over a front much larger than the one it actually occupied, and when the withdrawal was ordered it was able to get away in good order without a casualty.

While the present spirit animates the Battalion, it will, I am certain, give a good account of itself whenever and however it meets the enemy.

Again let me say I am proud to command such a Battalion.

W.A.Vignoles
Lt Col.

Dated 5th April 1918.

S E C R E T   Copy No........

103rd INFANTRY BRIGADE ORDER No.187.

Reference Map
FONTAINE & CROISILLES,
    U.T.S., 1;10,000.

                                                     10.3.18.

1. The 10th Lincolns will relieve the 9th (N.H.) Northd. Fusiliers in the LEFT Subsection of the Brigade Sector on the night 13th/14th March, 1918.
    On relief, the 9th (N.H.) Northd. Fus. will withdraw to the Reserve Battalion positions.
    Relief not to commence before 7.45 p.m.

2. All details of relief to be arranged between Commanding Officers concerned.

3. All Ammunition, Grenades, S.O.S. lights, reserve rations and water and other trench stores will be handed over, and consolidated lists forwarded to Brigade Headquarters 24 hours after completion of relief.
    Maps of the Sector, aeroplane photographs, Defence Schemes, details of work in hand or proposed, Intelligence, etc., will also be handed over.

4. The working parties being found by the two Battalions concerned, will be handed over on relief without any cessation of work taking place.

5. Completion of relief to be wired to this office using the code word "LOVE"

6.   A C K N O W L E D G E.

                                                   CAPTAIN.
                                            A/BRIGADE MAJOR.
                                         103rd INFANTRY BRIGADE.

DISTRIBUTION :

Copies Nos. 1 & 2 Retained.	Copy No. 10	101st Inf. Bde.
Copy No. 3 9th (N.H.) Bn. N.F.	" " 11	177th Inf. Bde.
" " 4 10th Lincolns.	" " 12	102nd Inf. Bde.
" " 5 1st East Lancs.	" " 13	34th Div. "G".
" " 6 103rd L.T.M.B.	" " 14	Right Group, R.A.
" " 7 208th Field Co. R.E.	" " 15	18th Bn. Northd. Fus.
" " 8 103rd Field Amb.	" " 16	34th Bn. M.G.C.
" " 9 No.4 Coy. Div. Train.	" " 17	Staff Captain.
	" " 18	B.S.O.
	" " 19	B.T.O.

Issued through Signals at 8 φ.m.

S E C R E T.   Copy No.......

103rd INFANTRY BRIGADE ORDER No. 188.

Ref. Maps,
CROISILLES &
FONTAINE Sheets.
    1:10,000.   And 51B S.W. 1:20,000.

1. The 103rd Infantry Brigade will be relieved in the line by 102nd Infantry Brigade on 19th March, 1918, in accordance with attached Table 'A'.

2. On relief, 103rd Infantry Brigade will move to positions at present occupied by 102nd Infantry Brigade in 3rd Battle System and will be in Divisional Reserve.

3. Guides from Units of 103rd Infantry Brigade, for Battalions taking over Front Line, at the rate of 1 per platoon and 1 per Coy. Headquarters will be provided by Units at their Headquarters.
    In the case of Reserve Battalions, 1 per Coy. and 1 per Battalion Headquarters will meet relieving Unit at T.29.a.55.80.

4. All moves will be by platoons at 200 yards interval. Transport will move after dark.

5. All Defence Schemes, aeroplane photographs, reserve S.A.A., Grenades, L.T.M. bombs, S.O.S. signals, and all other trench stores, also Counter Preparation targets, and line patrols can go to, will be handed over on relief. Receipted lists of stores handed over will be forwarded to Brigade Headquarters by 12 noon, March 20th.

6. All information about the enemy and details of work in hand and proposed, will be handed over on relief.

7. Units 103rd Infantry Brigade will each send advance parties not exceeding one Officer and 5 o.r's per Battalion to take over bivouacs and shelters in the Reserve Brigade Area at 3 p.m. 19th March. Taking over receipts to be forwarded to Brigade Headquarters by noon March 20th.

8. All other details of relief will be arranged direct between O's.C. concerned.

9. Completion of relief will be reported to Brigade Headquarters by telegraphing the code word "GILBEY".

10. Command of the Right Section will pass to G.O.C. 102nd Infantry Brigade on completion of the relief.

11. Brigade Headquarters will close at B.4.b.2.6 on completion of relief and re-open at T.2.b.8.2 at the same hour.

12. A C K N O W L E D G E.

                                        R. L. Romford.
                                        CAPTAIN.
                                        A/BRIGADE MAJOR.
18.3.18.   103rd INFANTRY BRIGADE.

            DISTRIBUTION :
Copies Nos. 1 & 2 Retained.   Copy No.10   102nd Inf. Bde.
Copy No.2   9th (N.H.) Bn. Northd.Fus.   "   " 11   101st Inf. Bde.
 "   " 3   10th Lincolns.   "   " 12   177th "   "
 "   " 4   1st East Lancs.   "   " 13   34th Div. "G".
 "   " 5   103rd L.T.M.B.   "   " 14   Rt. Group, R.F.A.
 "   " 6   208th Fld. Coy. R.E.   "   " 15   209th Fld. Co. R.E.
 "   " 7   "C" Coy. 34th Bn. M.G.C.   "   " 16   34th Bn. M.G.C.
 "   " 8   103rd Fld. Ambce.   "   " 17   Staff Captain.
 "   " 9   No.4 Coy. Div. Train.   "   " 18   B.S.O.
                                          "   " 19   B.T.O.
Issued through Signals at 2 pm.

ORDER.

103rd INFANTRY BRIGADE.

34th. Divn.
CROISILLES &
NORREUIL Sheet.
1/10,000. 2nd Cdn S.R. 1909.

1. The 103rd Infantry Brigade will be relieved in the Line by 102nd Infantry Brigade on 10th November 1917, in accordance with attached Table "A".

2. On relief, 103rd Infantry Brigade will take over positions at present occupied by 102nd Infantry Brigade on the ST. LEGER-CROISILLES and will be in Divisional Reserve.

3. Guides from Units of 103rd Infantry Brigade at present holding the line will be provided at the rate of 1 per platoon and 1 per Coy. Headquarters, at the point of relief. In the case of reserve Battalions 1 per Coy. and 1 per Battalion Headquarters will meet relieving Unit.

4. All moves will be by platoons at 200 yards interval. Transport will move after dark.

5. All Defence Schemes, accompanying diagrams, operation S.A.A., Trenches, L.T.M. Bombs, S.O.S. Signals, and all other stores etc. also Counter Preparation targets, and line patrols out by L.T.M.B. will be handed over on relief. Receipts, 4 lists of stores handed over will be forwarded to Brigade Headquarters by 12 noon, following relief.

6. All information about the front and dumps or snipers' nests now prepared, will be handed over carefully.

7. Units 102nd Infantry Brigade will, the day previous and having parties not exceeding one Officer and 2 N.C.O. per Battalion to take over bivouacs and shelters in the Reserve positions from the Units at present taking over receipts that are handed in to Brigade Headquarters by noon 10/11/17.

8. All other details of relief as per operation orders issued from C.R.E., 34th.

9. Completion of relief will be reported at Brigade Headquarters by telephone using the code word "DIXIE".

10. Command of the 34th. Div. Section will hand over to O.C. 103rd Infantry Brigade on completion of the relief.

11. Brigade Headquarters will be at B.C. Croisilles in conjunction with relief and re-open at T.2.b.0.5. at the same time.

12. ACK.W. PARKER.

TABLE 'A'.
To accompany 103rd Infantry Brigade Order No. 182.

Serial No.	UNIT.	Relieved by	TIME IN	ROUTE.	REMARKS
1.	103rd L.T.M.B.	102nd L.T.M.B.	Right Section.	CROISILLES - ST. LEGER. Takes over positions from guides.	Relief to be complete by dusk.
2.	10th Lincoln Regt.	23rd N.F.	5 p.m. at T.20 central. Left Subsection. Bn. H.Qrs. BOIRY BECQUERELLE.	do	Units to move via CROISILLES as long as it is light, after dark by most direct route.
3.	9th (N.F.) N.F.	25th N.F.	6 p.m. at T.29.a.55.30. Brigade Reserve. Bn. H.Qrs.	do	
4.	1st E.Lancs.Regt.	22nd N.F.	7 p.m. at T.20 central. Right Subsection. Bn. H.Qrs. ST. LEGER.	do	

MARCH TABLE to accompany O.O.190.

Serial No	Date	Unit	From	To	Route	Time of passing Starting point
1	24/3/18	Brigade HQrs Sig. Sectn. 2.T.M Battery	Camp in F.2.2	La Cauchie	Bucquoy — Hannescamp Bienvillers	3 p.m.
2	do.	9th Nothumbld	do	Lamerliere	do. —	3.57 p.m.
3	do.	10th Linchs	do	La Cauchie	do. —	3-15 p.m.
4	do.	1st Easthans	do	Bienvillers	do.	3.25.

To accompany 103rd Inf.t Brigade's
O. Order 191.

MARCH TABLE

Serial No	Date	Unit	From	To	Route	Will pass Starting Point, Four Roads at the "S" in Staltan Laherliere	Remarks
1	25th	Brigade Head Quarters Signals T.M. Battery	LaCauchie	Liencourt	Laherliere - Saulty - Sombrin	11 A.M	Following the halt at 11.50am there will be a 1 hour halt for mid-day meal. March to re-commence at 1 p.m
2	do.	10th Lincolns	do	Berlencourt	do.	11.5 A.M	
3	do.	9th Batt. N. Fus.rs	Laherliere	Grand Rullecourt	do.	11.15 A.M	
4	do.	1st East Lancs.	Bienvillers	do.	do.	11.25 AM	

MARCH TABLE

To accompany O.O.192

Serial No	Date	Unit	From	To	Will pass Starting Point/Crossroads immediately N of N in VACQUERIE	Route	Remarks
1	26/3/12	Brigade Headquarters Signals & Trench M. Battery	Liencourt (Spargo Pk)	Chateau de Beauvoir	8.30 A.M.	Rebreuviette – Frevent – Vacquerie – Le Boucq.	Halt will take place at 10 minutes before the clock hour, irrespective of the time of starting. Following the halt at 12.50 p.m. there will be no hour halt for dinner. March to recommence at 2 p.m.
2	Do	10th Lincolns	Berlencourt	Noeux	8.35 A.M.		
3	Do	1st East Lancs	Grand Rullecourt	Do.	8.45 A.M.		
4	Do	9th (N.H.) N.F.	Do.	Navars St Beauvar – Riviere.	9.10 A.M.		

SPECIAL ORDER OF THE DAY
By FIELD-MARSHAL SIR DOUGLAS HAIG
K.T., G.C.B., G.C.V.O., K.C.I.E
Commander-in-Chief, British Armies in France.

The following telegrams are published for the information of all ranks:—

FROM FIELD-MARSHAL SIR DOUGLAS HAIG TO ADMIRAL KEYES, DOVER.
22-3-18.
    Delighted to hear of your Naval success off Dunkirk last night. Heartiest congratulations to you and all who took part in it.

TO FIELD-MARSHAL SIR DOUGLAS HAIG FROM ADMIRAL KEYES.
22-3-18.
    Very many thanks for your congratulations, which are much appreciated by myself and officers and men concerned.

D. Haig, F.M.
Commander-in-Chief,
British Armies in France.

General Headquarters,
23rd March, 1918.

SPECIAL ORDER OF THE DAY
By FIELD-MARSHAL SIR DOUGLAS HAIG
K.T., G.C.B., G.C.V.O., K.C.I.E
Commander-in-Chief, British Armies in France.

To ALL RANKS OF THE BRITISH ARMY IN FRANCE AND FLANDERS.

We are again at a crisis in the War. The enemy has collected on this front every available Division, and is aiming at the destruction of the British Army. We have already inflicted on the enemy in the course of the last two days very heavy loss, and the French are sending troops as quickly as possible to our support. I feel that everyone in the Army, fully realising how much depends on the exertions and steadfastness of each one of us, will do his utmost to prevent the enemy from attaining his object.

D. Haig. F.M.
Commander-in-Chief,
British Armies in France.

General Headquarters,
23rd March, 1918.

PRINTED IN FRANCE BY ARMY PRINTING AND STATIONERY SERVICES.   PRESS A—3/18.

SPECIAL ORDER OF THE DAY
By FIELD-MARSHAL SIR DOUGLAS HAIG
K.T., G.C.B., G.C.V.O., K.C.I.E
Commander-in-Chief, British Armies in France.

The following telegrams are published for the information of all ranks:—

To FIELD-MARSHAL SIR DOUGLAS HAIG FROM LORD DERBY, WAR OFFICE.
23-3-18.

    We watch you and the Army in this great ordeal with the utmost admiration and gratitude. You are in all our thoughts. We are endeavouring to help you in every way, and you may be assured we shall spare no effort to second your undaunted efforts.

FROM FIELD-MARSHAL SIR DOUGLAS HAIG TO LORD DERBY.
23-3-18.

    I beg you to accept on my behalf and on that of all ranks under my command engaged in this great battle our most grateful thanks for your generous message of confidence and gratitude for what the Army is doing. It is specially encouraging at this moment to know of the great efforts now being made to provide the Army with all its needs.

To FIELD-MARSHAL SIR DOUGLAS HAIG FROM THE LORD MAYOR, LONDON.
23-3-18.

    The City of London, watching with profound emotion and grateful admiration the splendid resistance which the British and Overseas Forces under your command are heroically offering to the attacks of the enemy, renews the assurance of its full confidence in our gallant and devoted troops and their ultimate and complete victory. They will remain in our prayers and thoughts throughout these anxious days.

FROM FIELD-MARSHAL SIR DOUGLAS HAIG TO THE LORD MAYOR, LONDON.
23-3-18.

    Grateful thanks from all ranks of the British Armies in France for the inspiring message which you have been good enough to send us on behalf of the City of London. Your expression of the manly confidence of the citizens of our great capital is a special source of encouragement to us all at this critical time.

To FIELD-MARSHAL SIR DOUGLAS HAIG from THE COMRADES OF THE GREAT WAR, LONDON.

23-3-18.

The Comrades of the Great War salute their valiant comrades in the trenches, assure them of support, confident that heritage of unbroken front will be maintained until victory crowns our arms.

From FIELD-MARSHAL SIR DOUGLAS HAIG to THE COMRADES OF THE GREAT WAR (THROUGH WAR OFFICE, LONDON).

23-3-18.

All ranks join with me in sending grateful thanks to the Comrades of the Great War for their message of confidence and encouragement at this time of crisis.

D. Haig, F.M.
Commander-in-Chief,
British Armies in France.

General Headquarters,
24th March, 1918.

PRINTED IN FRANCE BY ARMY PRINTING AND STATIONERY SERVICES.

PRESS A—3/18.

SPECIAL ORDER OF THE DAY
By FIELD-MARSHAL SIR DOUGLAS HAIG
K.T., G.C.B., G.C.V.O., K.C.I.E
Commander-in-Chief, British Armies in France.

The following telegrams are published for the information of all ranks:—

To FIELD-MARSHAL SIR DOUGLAS HAIG FROM THE LORD MAYOR OF BRISTOL.

23.3.18.

A great meeting of Bristol citizens to-night listening to addresses of Ministers of the Crown, send greetings to you and all our fellow countrymen fighting to uphold the honour of the Empire. We remember you and all to-night in our thoughts and prayers in this your hour of trial. We are behind you and will do all in our power at home to help in winning the war.

FROM FIELD-MARSHAL SIR DOUGLAS HAIG TO THE LORD MAYOR OF BRISTOL.

23.3.18.

The message which you have sent me has been welcomed with gratitude by all ranks of the British Armies in France. On their behalf and on my own I beg you to be good enough to convey to the citizens of Bristol our deepest thanks. May I be allowed to congratulate you and them on their splendid spirit at this critical time.

D. Haig, F.M.

Commander-in-Chief,
British Armies in France.

General Headquarters,
25th March, 1918.

SPECIAL ORDER OF THE DAY
By FIELD-MARSHAL SIR DOUGLAS HAIG
K.T., G.C.B., G.C.V.O., K.C.I.E
Commander-in-Chief, British Armies in France.

The following telegrams are published for the information of all ranks:—

To FIELD-MARSHAL SIR DOUGLAS HAIG FROM THE LORD MAYOR OF BRISTOL.

23.3.18.

A great meeting of Bristol citizens to-night listening to addresses of Ministers of the Crown, send greetings to you and all our fellow countrymen fighting to uphold the honour of the Empire. We remember you and all to-night in our thoughts and prayers in this your hour of trial. We are behind you and will do all in our power at home to help in winning the war.

FROM FIELD-MARSHAL SIR DOUGLAS HAIG TO THE LORD MAYOR OF BRISTOL.

23.3.18.

The message which you have sent me has been welcomed with gratitude by all ranks of the British Armies in France. On their behalf and on my own I beg you to be good enough to convey to the citizens of Bristol our deepest thanks. May I be allowed to congratulate you and them on their splendid spirit at this critical time.

D. Haig, F.M.

Commander-in-Chief,
British Armies in France.

General Headquarters,
25th March, 1918.

PRINTED IN FRANCE BY ARMY PRINTING AND STATIONERY SERVICES.   PRESS A—3/18.

SPECIAL ORDER OF THE DAY
By FIELD-MARSHAL SIR DOUGLAS HAIG
K.T., G.C.B., G.C.V.O., K.C.I.E
Commander-in-Chief, British Armies in France.

The following telegrams are published for the information of all ranks:—

FROM HIS MAJESTY THE KING, BUCKINGHAM PALACE, TO FIELD-MARSHAL SIR DOUGLAS HAIG.

25.3.18.

I can assure you that the fortitude, courage and self-sacrifice with which the troops under your command are so heroically resisting greatly superior numbers is realised by me and my people. The Empire stands calm and confident in its Soldiers. May God bless and give them strength in their time of trial.

To HIS MAJESTY THE KING, BUCKINGHAM PALACE, FROM FIELD-MARSHAL SIR DOUGLAS HAIG.

25.3.18.

Your Majesty's gracious message has given universal encouragment to the whole of the Army in France.

I beg your Majesty to accept our respectful and grateful thanks, and the assurance that we will stedfastly continue to do our utmost to deserve the inspiring confidence your Majesty and the People throughout the Empire have placed in us in this hour of national stress.

D. Haig, F.M.

General Headquarters,
25th March, 1918.

Commander-in-Chief,
British Armies in France.

SPECIAL ORDER OF THE DAY
By FIELD-MARSHAL SIR DOUGLAS HAIG
K.T., G.C.B., G.C.V.O., K.C.I.E
Commander-in-Chief, British Armies in France.

The following telegrams are published for the information of all ranks:—

To FIELD-MARSHAL SIR DOUGLAS HAIG FROM THE PRIME MINISTER.
25-3-18.

The British Cabinet wishes to express to the Army the thanks of the Nation for its splendid defence. The whole Empire is filled with pride as it watches the heroic resistance offered by its brave troops to overwhelming odds. Knowing their steadfastness and courage whenever the honour of their country depends on their valour, the Empire awaits with confidence the result of this struggle to defeat the enemy's last desperate effort to trample down the free nations of the world. At home we are prepared to do all in our power to help in the true spirit of comradeship. The men necessary to replace all casualties and the guns and machine-guns required to make good those lost are either now in France or already on their way, and still further reinforcements of men and guns are ready to be thrown into the battle.

FROM FIELD-MARSHAL SIR DOUGLAS HAIG TO THE PRIME MINISTER.
26-3-18.

All ranks of the British Army in France have received with gratitude the message of confidence which you have sent me on behalf of the British Cabinet. The assurance that no effort will be spared at home to give us all assistance is of great encouragement to us. We will do all in our power to maintain the honour of the Empire in this hour of trial and to prove ourselves worthy of the trust that is reposed in us.

To FIELD-MARSHAL SIR DOUGLAS HAIG FROM THE DUKE OF DEVONSHIRE, CANADA,
26-3-18.

My advisers desire me to convey to you the profound admiration of the Canadian people for the magnificent valour and endurance of the Forces under your command in withstanding the enemy's desperate attacks. We have complete confidence that the German drive will be adequately met and that the final victory will crown the Allied arms.

FROM FIELD-MARSHAL SIR DOUGLAS HAIG TO THE DUKE OF DEVONSHIRE, CANADA.
26-3-18.

The inspiring message of comradeship and confidence which you have been good enough to send me on behalf of the Canadian people is encouraging to all ranks of the British Army in France. I beg you to convey to your advisers our grateful thanks for their message and the expression of our determination to do all that men can do to uphold the honour and safety of the Empire in the great battle which is now raging.

To FIELD-MARSHAL SIR DOUGLAS HAIG from THE MAYOR OF LEICESTER.
25-3-18.

    Accept Leicester's unbounded confidence in the hour of our country's destiny. Convey citizens' profound admiration and deepest gratitude to her brave sons for their heroic stand.

From FIELD-MARSHAL SIR DOUGLAS HAIG to THE MAYOR OF LEICESTER.
26-3-18.

    Please convey to the citizens of Leicester, on behalf of all ranks of the British Armies in France, our heartfelt thanks for your welcome message. It is a great encouragement at this critical time to the whole Army in France to feel merited Leicester's confidence.

To FIELD-MARSHAL SIR DOUGLAS HAIG from THE BLACKBURN DISCHARGED SAILORS' AND SOLDIERS' ASSOCIATION.
26-3-18.

    Blackburn Discharged Sailors' and Soldiers' Association.—That this meeting, representative of the discharged men of Blackburn, send their fraternal greetings to our comrades in France, and furthermore desire to place on record our admiration of the splendid efforts they are now making to stem the German hordes, and desire to extend to the Commander-in-Chief and his men our appreciation of their magnificent services to freedom that they are now rendering.

From FIELD-MARSHAL SIR DOUGLAS HAIG to THE BLACKBURN DISCHARGED SAILORS' AND SOLDIERS' ASSOCIATION.
26-3-18.

    Please convey to the Blackburn Discharged Sailors' and Soldiers' Association, on behalf of all their comrades in France, our grateful appreciation of their message of confidence and encouragement, which has greatly heartened us all.

D. Haig, F.M.
Commander-in-Chief,
British Armies in France.

General Headquarters,
27th March, 1918.

SPECIAL ORDER OF THE DAY
By FIELD-MARSHAL SIR DOUGLAS HAIG
K.T., G.C.B., G.C.V.O., K.C.I.E
Commander-in-Chief, British Armies in France.

The following telegrams are published for the information of all ranks:—

To FIELD-MARSHAL SIR DOUGLAS HAIG from PRESIDENT WILSON, WASHINGTON.

26-3-18.

    May I not express to you my warm admiration of the splendid steadfastness and valor with which your troops have withstood the German onslaught and the perfect confidence all Americans feel that you will win a secure and final victory?

From FIELD-MARSHAL SIR DOUGLAS HAIG to PRESIDENT WILSON.

26-3-18.

    Your message of generous appreciation of the steadfastness and valour of our soldiers in the great battle now raging has greatly touched us all. Please accept our heartfelt thanks. One and all believe in the justice of our cause, and are determined to fight on without counting the cost, until the freedom of mankind is safe.

D. Haig. F.M.

General Headquarters,
28th March, 1918.

Commander-in-Chief,
British Armies in France.

PRINTED IN FRANCE BY ARMY PRINTING AND STATIONERY SERVICES.

PRESS A—3/18.

SPECIAL ORDER OF THE DAY
By FIELD-MARSHAL SIR DOUGLAS HAIG
K.T., G.C.B., G.C.V.O., K.C.I.E
Commander-in-Chief, British Armies in France.

The following telegrams are published for the information of all ranks:—

From HIS MAJESTY THE KING, BUCKINGHAM PALACE, to FIELD-MARSHAL SIR DOUGLAS HAIG.
27-3-18.

I wish to express to General Salmond and all ranks of the Air Service of the British Empire in France my gratification at their splendid achievements during this great battle. I am proud to be their Colonel-in-Chief.

To HIS MAJESTY THE KING, BUCKINGHAM PALACE, from FIELD-MARSHAL SIR DOUGLAS HAIG.
27-3-18.

General Salmond and all ranks of the British Air Service in France desire to express their most loyal and heartfelt thanks for your Majesty's most gracious message. They are specially proud to think that they are rendering good service to their King and Empire at this critical period of the war, and the knowledge that they have won the appreciation of their Colonel-in-Chief inspires them to still greater efforts.

To FIELD-MARSHAL SIR DOUGLAS HAIG from THE COMMANDER-IN-CHIEF, INDIA.
26-3-18.

The Army in India is watching with sympathy and entire confidence your conduct of the present struggle, and your old subordinates are convinced that you and your brave troops will see this battle through to a successful issue.

From FIELD-MARSHAL SIR DOUGLAS HAIG to THE COMMANDER-IN-CHIEF, INDIA.
27-3-18.

All ranks of the British Army in France send grateful thanks for the message which you have been good enough to send us. We are all greatly touched and encouraged by the sympathy and confidence of our comrades in India.

To FIELD-MARSHAL SIR DOUGLAS HAIG from THE PRESIDENT, CHAMBER OF COMMERCE, CARDIFF.

26-3-18.

His Majesty the King having graciously and truly assured you that the people fully realise the valour of the heroic troops under your command, the Members of Cardiff Chamber of Commerce to-day at annual meeting assembled ask that you will accept their grateful appreciation of the magnificent defence the troops are making for the preservation of the freedom of mankind, wishing you God speed.

From FIELD-MARSHAL SIR DOUGLAS HAIG to THE PRESIDENT, CHAMBER OF COMMERCE, CARDIFF.

27-3-18.

Very many thanks for your message. All ranks are greatly cheered by the welcome appreciation of the efforts we are making in these anxious hours. It is truly encouraging to feel how fully we can rely on the manly spirit of the whole nation.

To FIELD-MARSHAL SIR DOUGLAS HAIG from THE MASTER, EDINBURGH MERCHANT COMPANY, EDINBURGH.

26-3-18.

With profound gratitude to, and with unbounded admiration for the splendid heroism of the British Army in France under your skilful leadership, the Company of Merchants of the City of Edinburgh send you warm greetings with full trust and confidence in the ultimate issue of your great endeavour. You and your brave officers and men are never absent from our thoughts and have our constant prayers.

From FIELD-MARSHAL SIR DOUGLAS HAIG to THE MASTER, EDINBURGH MERCHANT COMPANY, EDINBURGH.

27-3-18.

Please convey to the Company of Merchants of the City of Edinburgh on behalf of all ranks of the Army under my command our grateful thanks for your message. The knowledge that we possess the confidence of our countrymen at home is a great source of strength to us in this tremendous struggle for a free existence.

To FIELD-MARSHAL SIR DOUGLAS HAIG from THE LORD PROVOST, GLASGOW.

27-3-18.

The glorious valour and resistance of the troops under your command has excited the greatest admiration among the citizens of Glasgow, who await the result with calm confidence.

From FIELD-MARSHAL SIR DOUGLAS HAIG to THE LORD PROVOST, GLASGOW.

27-3-18.

Your message of generous appreciation of the valour of our soldiers has greatly encouraged us all. Please convey to the citizens of Glasgow our heartfelt thanks for this expression of their confidence.

To FIELD-MARSHAL SIR DOUGLAS HAIG FROM THE LORD PROVOST, EDINBURGH.

27-3-18.

The citizens of Edinburgh and the people of Scotland are watching with intense admiration and heartfelt sympathy the tremendous efforts and unconquerable resistance of the forces of all ranks under your command. Their valour, devotion, tenacity and endurance stir with profound emotion and thankfulness. Our hearts are with you and the Army, and with unflinching confidence in the sacred issue we express assurance of unwavering and whole-hearted support from all classes of the community.

FROM FIELD-MARSHAL SIR DOUGLAS HAIG TO THE LORD PROVOST, EDINBURGH.

27-3-18.

The whole British Army in France joins with me in sending our heartfelt thanks for the stirring message which you as Lord Provost of Scotland's illustrious capital have been good enough to send us. I beg you to express to my fellow citizens of Edinburgh and the people of Scotland our gratitude for their unflinching confidence in us and our resolute determination to show ourselves worthy of it whatever the future may have in store for us in this great battle for freedom.

D. Haig. F.M.

Commander-in-Chief,
British Armies in France.

General Headquarters,
28th March, 1918.

SPECIAL ORDER OF THE DAY
By FIELD-MARSHAL SIR DOUGLAS HAIG
K.T., G.C.B., G.C.V.O., K.C.I.E
Commander-in-Chief, British Armies in France.

The following telegrams are published for the information of all ranks:—

To FIELD-MARSHAL SIR DOUGLAS HAIG FROM GENERAL BOTHA, SOUTH AFRICA.
27-3-18.

    We are watching with appreciation strenuous efforts which you and your gallant men are making in this supreme struggle for the liberty of mankind, and we are earnestly praying that complete success may crown heroic noble stand which the Sons of Freedom are making under your able leadership.

FROM FIELD-MARSHAL SIR DOUGLAS HAIG TO GENERAL BOTHA, SOUTH AFRICA.
29-3-18.

    Please accept our hearty thanks for your message. All ranks of the British Armies in France are greatly cheered by your generous appreciation of their efforts in this great struggle, and are very proud of the confidence which the peoples of our great Empire place in their Army's ability to win.

To FIELD-MARSHAL SIR DOUGLAS HAIG FROM LORD DESBOROUGH, TAPLOW.
27-3-18.

    The British Imperial Council of Commerce representing the Chambers of Commerce of the British Empire desire to express their unbounded admiration of the heroism and devotion displayed by the troops in withstanding the German onslaught and their complete confidence that they, in conjunction with their brave Allies, will be successful in their fight for the maintenance of freedom and justice in the world.

FROM FIELD-MARSHAL SIR DOUGLAS HAIG TO LORD DESBOROUGH, TAPLOW.
29-3-18.

    Please convey to the British Imperial Council of Commerce the heartfelt thanks of the whole British Army for their message. Their appreciation and confidence is a great encouragement to us in this stern fight.

To FIELD-MARSHAL SIR DOUGLAS HAIG FROM THE LORD MAYOR, MANCHESTER.
26-3-18.

    Manchester sends greetings to the brave officers and men under your command who are fighting so gallantly for their country, and expresses its unabated confidence in you and them.

FROM FIELD-MARSHAL SIR DOUGLAS HAIG TO THE LORD MAYOR, MANCHESTER.

29-3-18.

The whole British Army has been greatly encouraged by the message of confidence you have been good enough to send us from the citizens of Manchester. We send you our heartfelt thanks and are determined to see that our just cause shall prevail in this great fight for freedom.

TO FIELD-MARSHAL SIR DOUGLAS HAIG FROM THE NATIONAL SOCIALIST PARTY, LONDON.

26-3-18.

The National Socialist Party sends you and all soldiers and comrades under your command heartiest congratulations on the magnificent stand you are making for the independence of our country and the freedom of the civilized world against the most barbarous and inhuman enemies of modern times. The National Socialist Party is confident that you and your glorious Army, in concert with Petain and his splendid battalions, will achieve complete victory, and will secure for us and our Allies permanent peace for universal democracy and the co-operative commonwealth.

FROM FIELD-MARSHAL SIR DOUGLAS HAIG TO THE NATIONAL SOCIALIST PARTY, LONDON.

29-3-18.

Please convey to the National Socialist Party the best thanks of all ranks of the British Armies in France for their welcome message. It is truly encouraging to feel that we possess the confidence of the United Nation.

**General Headquarters,
29th March, 1918.**

*Commander-in-Chief,
British Armies in France.*

SPECIAL ORDER OF THE DAY
By FIELD-MARSHAL SIR DOUGLAS HAIG
K.T., G.C.B., G.C.V.O., K.C.I.E
Commander-in-Chief, British Armies in France.

The following messages are published for the information of all ranks. Messages of thanks have been sent in reply:—

To FIELD-MARSHAL SIR DOUGLAS HAIG from THE PREMIER, VICTORIA, BRITISH COLUMBIA.
27-3-18.
You and British Army have the thanks, confidence and prayers of British Columbia.

To FIELD-MARSHAL SIR DOUGLAS HAIG from THE MAYOR, RICHMOND, YORKSHIRE.
26-3-18.
Burgess borough of Richmond, Yorkshire, thank Army for splendid defence and are proud of brave troops in heroic resistance offered against great odds, confident that enemies' effort will be defeated. Our thoughts and prayers go out to you and your troops in this hour of trial.

To FIELD-MARSHAL SIR DOUGLAS HAIG from THE MAYOR, WEST HAM, LONDON.
28-3-18.
The Citizens of the County Borough of West Ham are watching with admiration and calm confidence the heroic defence of the troops under your command. They are satisfied that their gallantry will ultimately achieve the victory for democracy and liberty throughout Europe and send their heartfelt sympathies to all those who are now suffering in their country's cause.

To FIELD-MARSHAL SIR DOUGLAS HAIG from SECRETARY, ODDFELLOWS, M.U., PORTSMOUTH.
27-3-18.
The Portsmouth District of Oddfellows, Manchester Unity, sends hearty congratulations to British Army on the gallant fight you are putting up against such great odds, wishing you every success.

To FIELD-MARSHAL SIR DOUGLAS HAIG from MacGREGOR, TAIN, SCOTLAND.
28-3-18.
We, North Scotland, follow your peerless strategy and valour of your unconquerable Army with profound admiration. Britons never shall be slaves.

To FIELD-MARSHAL SIR DOUGLAS HAIG from BROOKS KING, TAUNTON.
28-3-18.
   Mothers of British Army watch with profound gratitude and perfect confidence the glorious stand made by their sons in France; God bless them.

To FIELD-MARSHAL SIR DOUGLAS HAIG from WOUNDED BOYS, RED CROSS HOSPITAL, CLEVEDON, SOMERSET.
26-3-18.
   Our heart and soul are with you to-day.

To FIELD-MARSHAL SIR DOUGLAS HAIG from STAFF, POST OFFICE, WIDNES.
27-3-18.
   Movements watched with keenest interest. Congratulations to self and men; cheero.

To FIELD-MARSHAL SIR DOUGLAS HAIG from CHAIRMAN, BARGOED AND GILFACH RECEPTION FUND, S. WALES.
27-3-18.
   The Committee of the Bargoed and Gilfach Reception Fund wish to convey to you and your glorious Army their warm admiration in your great fight for freedom and right. We have every confidence in your Generalship and the valour of your unconquerable men.

To FIELD-MARSHAL SIR DOUGLAS HAIG from THE SCOTTISH FEDERATION OF DISCHARGED AND DEMOBILIZED SAILORS AND SOLDIERS, DUNFERMLINE BRANCH.
27-3-18.
   Congratulations to you and troops under you on the magnificent stand you are making in this great battle.

To FIELD-MARSHAL SIR DOUGLAS HAIG from WORKMEN AND STAFF OF GREEN AND SILLEY WEIR, CENTRAL WORKS, ALBERT DOCKS.
28-3-18.
   To the bravest of the brave; carry on brave comrades, we are proud of you. Our thoughts and prayers are with you night and day. Don't worry about us; we will stick it to a man.

To FIELD-MARSHAL SIR DOUGLAS HAIG from THE MUNITION GIRLS OF THE NATIONAL FILLING FACTORY, HAYES, MIDDLESEX.
27-3-18.
   The Munition Girls of the National Filling Factory, Hayes, Middlesex, send greetings to the men at the front. Brave boys, stick it out and we'll back you up for all we're worth.

To FIELD-MARSHAL SIR DOUGLAS HAIG from THE SECRETARY, UNION JACK CLUB, PAISLEY.

28-3-18.

The Paisley Branch, Scottish Federation, Discharged and Demobilized Sailors and Soldiers wish to express our confidence in you and our brave comrades under your command and ask you to assure them that in their absence we who have been fortunate to come back are actively engaged in the work of securing greater recognition of the services they are presently rendering.

To FIELD-MARSHAL SIR DOUGLAS HAIG from THE MINISTER (CHAIRMAN) OF THE STANLEY ROAD BAPTIST CHURCH, BOOTLE, LIVERPOOL.

26-3-18.

The Church and Congregation of the Stanley Road Baptist Church, Bootle, desires to express its profound admiration of the magnificent courage and heroism of the British troops under the Command of Sir Douglas Haig, displayed in the battle now under progress, and wishes to assure Sir Douglas Haig, officers and men of the confidence we have that God will strengthen them all for all further sacrifices until Victory for the cause of the Allies is secured.

To FIELD-MARSHAL SIR DOUGLAS HAIG from SECRETARY, WEST HAM BRANCH, NATIONAL FEDERATION OF DISCHARGED AND DEMOBILIZED SAILORS AND SOLDIERS.

29-3-18.

The West Ham Branch of the National Federation of Discharged and Demobilized Sailors and Soldiers are proud of the heroic stand made by the troops under your command, and are confident that British courage will triumph.

To FIELD-MARSHAL SIR DOUGLAS HAIG from THE SECRETARY, EMPLOYMENT BUREAU, DUBLIN.

29-3-18.

The Irish Disabled Soldiers and Sailors at the Soldiers' and Sailors' Help Society Employment Bureau, 30, Molesworth Street, Dublin, send to their gallant comrades in France their admiration for the splendid fight they are putting up, and wish they could lend a hand.

General Headquarters,
30th March, 1918.

Commander-in-Chief,
British Armies in France.

SPECIAL ORDER OF THE DAY
By FIELD-MARSHAL SIR DOUGLAS HAIG
K.T., G.C.B., G.C.V.O., K.C.I.E
Commander-in-Chief, British Armies in France.

The following telegrams are published for the information of all ranks:—

To FIELD-MARSHAL SIR DOUGLAS HAIG FROM PRIME MINISTER, SOUTH AFRICA.

29-3-18.

Am requested to transmit following resolution:—That we, the Members of the Parliament of the Union of South Africa in Parliament assembled, desire to express to Field-Marshal Haig and the Forces under his command our deep sense of the valour and tenacity shown by them in the great Battle now in progress. We are proud to think that our brother South Africans have quit themselves like men in that desperate struggle. We fervently pray that the Almighty may grant complete success to the Arms of Britain and her brave Allies, and we earnestly hope that the issue may lead to the establishment of a general and lasting peace among the nations of the world.

FROM FIELD-MARSHAL SIR DOUGLAS HAIG TO PRIME MINISTER, SOUTH AFRICA.

29-3-18.

On behalf of myself and the whole Army under my command in France I beg to convey to you and to the Members of the Parliament of the Union of South Africa our heartfelt thanks for your inspiring message. The fine part already played by South Africans in this great battle is a symbol of the strength and unity of purpose that binds together all parts of the British Empire. No effort will be spared on our part in order to secure a lasting peace.

General Headquarters,
30th March, 1918.

Commander-in-Chief,
British Armies in France.

PRINTED IN FRANCE BY ARMY PRINTING AND STATIONERY SERVICES.   PRESS A—3/18.

SPECIAL ORDER OF THE DAY
By FIELD-MARSHAL SIR DOUGLAS HAIG
K.T., G.C.B., G.C.V.O., K.C.I.E
Commander-in-Chief, British Armies in France.

The following messages are published for the information of all ranks. Messages of thanks have been sent in reply:—

To FIELD-MARSHAL SIR DOUGLAS HAIG FROM THE PRESIDENT, BRITISH WORKERS' LEAGUE, GLASGOW.

29-3-18.

Glasgow Branch, British Workers' League, expresses admiration and gratitude to you and heroic troops whose dauntless bravery is making the world safe for democracy.

To FIELD-MARSHAL SIR DOUGLAS HAIG FROM THE GENERAL MANAGER, SHELL WORKS, PONDERS END, MIDDLESEX.

29-3-18.

We the workers of the Ponders End Shell Works, Ponders End, Middlesex, realising the urgent and vital demands for both shells and guns at the front, wish our soldiers to know that we are fighting with them every inch of the way with the fixed resolve to give them our greatest possible output. Good Friday, 1918.

D. Haig. F.M.

Commander-in-Chief,
British Armies in France.

General Headquarters,
31st March, 1918.

PRINTED IN FRANCE BY ARMY PRINTING AND STATIONERY SERVICES.   PRESS A—4/18.

SPECIAL ORDER OF THE DAY
By FIELD-MARSHAL SIR DOUGLAS HAIG
K.T., G.C.B., G.C.V.O., K.C.I.E
Commander-in-Chief, British Armies in France

The following telegrams are published for the information of all ranks:—

To FIELD-MARSHAL SIR DOUGLAS HAIG FROM ADMIRAL SIR DAVID BEATTY, GRAND FLEET.
29-3-18.

The Grand Fleet are following with greatest admiration and sympathy the magnificent efforts of their comrades of the British Armies in France. We are confident that the near future will bring with it the reward of their endurance and great sacrifice.

FROM FIELD-MARSHAL SIR DOUGLAS HAIG TO ADMIRAL SIR DAVID BEATTY.
30-3-18.

All ranks of the British Armies in France return their heartiest thanks to their comrades of the Grand Fleet for their most encouraging message.

To FIELD-MARSHAL SIR DOUGLAS HAIG FROM GENERAL DIAZ, ITALIAN GENERAL HEADQUARTERS.
29-3-18.

To you and to the glorious Armies which through the formidable shock of the enemy give luminous proof that no power on earth can weaken British strength and determination, I send my greeting and that of the Italian Army, which, with brotherly spirit, follow with confidence the fortunes of the tremendous struggle, and with admiration looks forward to the final victory.

FROM FIELD-MARSHAL SIR DOUGLAS HAIG TO GENERAL DIAZ.
30-3-18.

Please accept on my behalf and on that of all ranks of the British Army our heartfelt thanks for the greeting you have been good enough to send us from yourself and the glorious Italian Army. At this critical time your expression of confidence and generous praise has greatly encouraged us.

To FIELD-MARSHAL SIR DOUGLAS HAIG FROM THE ARCHBISHOP OF CANTERBURY, LONDON.

29-3-18.

You know how the whole people is united in thankful and proud recognition of the tireless valour of our soldiers in this supreme trial of their endurance. At this great moment Easter brings its welcome message, "Out of sacrifice and death comes the renewal of life."

FROM FIELD-MARSHAL SIR DOUGLAS HAIG TO THE ARCHBISHOP OF CANTERBURY.

30-3-18.

Your Easter message of comfort and encouragement is greatly appreciated by the whole Army. We send you our most grateful thanks.

General Headquarters,
31st March, 1918.

D. Haig. F.M.

Commander-in-Chief,
British Armies in France.

SECRET   COPY No 2

OPERATION ORDERS No 20
9th (Northumberland Hussars) Bn. Northumberland Fusiliers.

1. RELIEF
The 103rd Infantry Brigade will relieve the 102nd Infantry Brigade in the RIGHT SECTOR (34th Divisional Front) tomorrow the 7th inst. The 9th (Northd. Hussars) Batt. Northd Fusiliers will relieve the 25th Batt. Northumberland Fusiliers in the LEFT SUB SECTOR.

2. ORDER OF RELIEF
"C" Coy of 9th Battn. will relieve LEFT Coy of 25th Battn.
"B"   "   "   "   "   "   CENTRE Coy   "   "   "
"A"   "   "   "   "   "   RIGHT Coy   "   "   "
"D"   "   "   "   "   "   SUPPORT Coy "   "   "

3. TIME OF DEPARTURE
"C" Coy - 5.30 p.m. "B" "A" and "D" Companies and Battalion Hd. Qrs. at 10 minutes interval between Companies.

4. GUIDES
At the rate of 1 per Company and 1 for Battn Hd Qrs. will be at MORTE HOMME B.17.a.8.7 at 7.30 p.m. and will guide Companies etc to Battn Hd Qr. (U.25.A.6.6) where further guides at the rate of 1 per platoon and 1 per Company Hd. Qrs. will be waiting.

5. INTERVALS
After reaching Battn HD. Qrs. Companies will move by platoons at 600 yards intervals.

6. TRANSPORT
Carrying Lewis Guns and rations for the 9th inst and Officers Mess Kit will accompany Companies as far as Battn Hd Qrs. when above will be man handled and transport return.
Limbers will report to Orderly Room at 6.0 p.m. for Orderly Room and Signal Stores and Headquarters Mess Kit.

7. ADVANCE PARTIES
As follows will proceed to their respective destinations tomorrow morning at 9.30 a.m.
1 Officer or Platoon Sergt. per platoon.
1 Lewis Gun N.C.O. per Company.
1 Lewis Gunner per Team.
Proportion of Signallers to be detailed by Signal Officer.
Proportion of Observers and Snipers to be detailed by Intelligence Officer.
Unexpended portion of the days rations will be carried and water bottles to be filled.

8. WATER BOTTLES
To be filled before Companies leave the Camp.

9. STORES
All defence and pursuit schemes, aeroplane photographs, working party details, details of work in hand and contemplated will be taken over on relief. Receipts for trench stores taken over will be rendered to Battn Hd Qrs. by 10.0 a.m. 8th inst.

OPERATION ORDERS No 20. (CONTINUED)

10 OFFICERS VALISES, MENS PACKS AND BLANKETS. will be collected under arrangements to be made by the Quartermaster.

11 WATER SUPPLY. Will be by watercart delivered to Battn. Hd. Qrs. under arrangements to be made by Transport Officer who will see that the tanks are filled tomorrow night.

12 COOKING Camp kettles will be taken. All cooking for "A" and "B" Companies will be done at Battn Hd Qrs. until further arrangements can be made.

13 RELIEF COMPLETE will be wired to Battn Hd Qrs. giving name of Company Commander.

ACKNOWLEDGE

Dated 6th March 1918

Copies To.
No 1. War Diary
2. Retained
3. Commanding Officer
4. 2d in Command.
5. OC "A" Coy
6. OC "B" Coy
7. OC "C" Coy
8. OC "D" Coy.
9. Transport Officer
10. Quartermaster
11. R.S.M.
12. Master Cook.
13. OC 23rd Bn. Northd Fusiliers.
14. Signal Officer
15. Intelligence Officer

Judson Craven
Captain and Adjutant
9th (Northd Hussars) Battn. Northd Fusiliers

SECRET **OPERATION ORDERS No 21** **Copy No 1**

9th (Northumberland Hussars) Battn Northumberland Fusiliers

1. RELIEF.
The 10th Lincolnshire Regt. will relieve the 9th (North'd Hussars) Battn North'd Fusiliers as Left Battalion in the 103rd Infty. Brigade Subsector.

2. ORDER OF RELIEF.
RIGHT FRONT Coy "B" Coy. 10th Lincolns will relieve "A" Coy. 9th (NH) Bn North'd Fus
LEFT FRONT Coy "A" " " " " " "C" " " " " "
SUPPORT Coy "D" " " " " " "D" " " " " "
RESERVE Coy. "C" " " " " " "B" " " " " "

3. NEW POSITION
The 9th (N.H) Bn North'd Fusiliers, relieve the 10th Lincolns as Battalion in Brigade Reserve in the following order.
Lincolns "C" Coy in Road in U.25.a by "C" Coy
  — "B" Coy behind Railway in T.24.d by "A" Coy
  — "A" Coy in sunken road T.23.d by "B" Coy
  — "D" Coy — — — T.29.B
                T.30.a and "D" Coy

Battn Hd Qrs — in cutting in U.25.B.

4. ADVANCE PARTIES.
Of 10th Lincolns.
A proportion of signallers, Lewis gunners, 1 Officer per Coy. and 1 N.C.O. per platoon from 10th Lincolns will report at respective Coy. Hd Qrs about 2 p.m. to take over trenches, Battle positions and stores.

5. ADVANCE PARTIES.
Of 9th (NH) North'd Fusiliers.
1 Officer or Senior N.C.O. and 1 man per Coy and 1 N.C.O. for Battn Hd Qrs. will report at Battn Hd Qrs 9th (NH) Bn North'd Fus. to proceed to take over shelters, battle positions and stores. Time 4.0 p.m.

6. STORES
All defence schemes, photographs, trench stores, flares, reserve water and rations will be handed over and the usual lists and receipts rendered and obtained.
The new maps CROISILLES Special sheet will not be handed over
Work in progress or contemplated will be handed over.

7. GUIDES.
For 10th Lincolns One per platoon from Coys. in the line will report to Battn Hd Qrs at 7.30 p.m. One guide per post will be waiting at Coy. Hd Qrs.
For 9th (N.H.) Bn North Fus. Coys. will arrange to find their own guides to lead platoons to their new positions.

8. INTERVALS
Platoons will leave at five minute intervals

9. PATROLS
Each Coy will send out a covering patrol similar to the usual dawn patrols:—
1 N.C.O. and 1 man of 10th Lincolns will be attached to each. Patrols will move out as soon as it is dark enough and remain out until relief is complete.

OPERATION ORDERS No 21 (Cont.)

10. TRANSPORT — Rations will be brought to CRUX dump U.25 Central or as may be arranged by the Transport Officer.

11. COOKING — All camp kettles will be brought out of trenches, also all petrol tins. Companies are responsible that they bring out the full number issued to them.

12. RELIEF COMPLETE — Will be wired to Battn Hd Qrs. by using the code word "FAIRLY" followed by name of Company Commander.
Companies will report arrival in new position by code word "SOLD" and name of Company Commander.

13. WATER SUPPLY — As by water cart; the Transport Officer will make necessary arrangements.

14. SIGNALS — The Signal Officer will ascertain what arrangements exist for communicating to all Companies in dugouts and battle positions.

ACKNOWLEDGE.

DATED 13 March 1918.

Copies To.
1. War Diary
2. Retained
3. Commanding Officer
4. 2° in Command
5-8. O/c Coys
9. Transport Officer
10. Quartermaster
11. R.S.M.
12. O.C. 10th Lincolnshire Regt.
13. Signal Officer
14. Intelligence Officer

M.W. Drysdale
2/Lieut & Adjt.
9th (North'd Hussars) Bn
North'd Fusiliers

SECRET.

OPERATION ORDERS. No 22.
9th (Northumberland Hussars) Battn. Northumberland Fusiliers

RELIEF. 1. The 103rd Infantry Brigade will be relieved in the line by the 102nd Infantry Brigade. tomorrow 19th March 1918. On relief the 103rd Infantry Brigade will move to positions at present occupied by 102 Infantry Brigade in third battle system and will be in Divisional Reserve.

The 9th (N.H.) Battn North'd Fusiliers will be relieved by the 25th Battn North'd Fusiliers and after relief the 9th (N.H.) Battn Nor.Thd. Fusiliers will take over positions vacated by the 25th Batt'n North'd. Fusiliers in T.20 central.

ORDER OF RELIEF. 2.
9th (N.H.) Bn North'd Fusiliers   25th Bn North'd Fusiliers
"A" Coy round railway in T.24.d will be relieved by   Coy.
"B" " in Sunken Road in T.30. a " " " " "
"C" " in road in U.25.a " " " " "
"D" " in Sunken Road in T.29 B. " " " " "
Battn. H.Q. in Cutting in U.25.B.

ROUTES 3. Direct to new positions. Companies will each send an Officer to reconnoitre the route tomorrow. All moves will be by platoon at 200 yards interval. Transport will move after dark.

GUIDES. 4. At the rate of 1 per Company and 1 for Battn H.Q. Dn. and 2 L/Cpl. Godfrey will report at 4.30 p.m. at Battn H.Q. Dn. and will proceed to T.29.a 55.80 where they will meet the incoming relief at 6.0 p.m.

ADVANCE PARTIES. 5. 9th (N.H.) Bn N.a.Th.d Fusiliers
The Battalion Lewis Gun Sergt. and 1 N.C.O. per Company will report to the Equalling Officer at Battn H.Q. Dn. at 1.30 p.m. and will proceed to take over shelters, battle positions, and stores.

TRANSPORT. 6. The Transport Officer will detail the necessary transport to convey Officers Mess Kit, Cooking utensils, Lewis Guns, Orderly Room and Signal Stores.
Companies will leave the necessary guards over these items; they will proceed with transport.

RATIONS AND WATER. 7. Will be delivered to Companies and Battn H.Q. Dn. at their respective new positions under arrangements to be made by Transport Officer.

COOKING. 8. All camp kettles and petrol tins will be brought out by Companies who are responsible that they bring out the full number issued to them.

War Diary

War Diary.

OPERATION ORDERS No 28 (CONT'D).

STORES. 9. All defence schemes, maps, air photographs, trench stores, reserve width, details of work in hand and contemplated and aircraft formations and gaps positions will be handed over and taken over on relief. Receipts for stores taken over and handed over and entries to of clear amm'n of guns etc will be forwarded to Orderly Room by 10.0 p.m.

GUARDS. 10. The following will be relieved by the Lt's for Right Sniper:
1 N.C.O and 4 men — M.H. AIRCRAFT GUNS — Bn H.Q. ST LEGER
2 men — BATHS — ST LEGER
1 N.C.O and 3 men — Coy H.Qrs & Stores — Gun Circus Dump.
4.15 a.m.

RELIEF COMPLETE 11. Nils to send 6 Batt. H.Q. Lrs using the code word "FRESH" followed by name of Company, commanders will report in turn position by code word "WIND" and name of Company commanders.

ACKNOWLEDGE

DATED 18th March 1918.

Copies to. No. 1 Own Army.
2 Retained.
3 Commanding Officer.
4 Second in Command.
5 Intelligence Officer.
6 Scout Officer.
7 H.Q. Company.
10 "
11 Trench Mortar Officer.
12 Lewis Gun
13 R.S.M.
14 Dr 2/5" Batt N & H Lincolns.

[signature] Lt/Col

2/4th and H'dy Lincolns

Operation Order N° R3

1. **Move**
   Battalion will move to GRAND RULLECOURT tomorrow.

2. **Route:** Laherliere - Saulty - Sombrin - Grand Rullecourt.

3. **Times for Parade:** Parade 8.45 am on main road thro' Laherliere in column of route in the following order H.Q. A Coy, Band B. C & D Coys. Transport will march in the rear of Battalion. Head of column opposite O.R. facing N.W.

4. **Routine:** Reveille 6 am.
   Kit Parade 6.30 am.
   Breakfast 7 am.
   Dinners en route

5. Officers valises
   Living Kit &c will be handed in to O.R. Stores by 8 am.

6. **Billeting Returns** will be handed in to O.R. by 8.30 am.

7. Billets will be left clean and tidy

8. Rear Parties: The Sanitary Corporal and 2 men per Coy will be left behind to see that all billets are left clean. They will assemble at 11 am at starting point, fork roads ~~Lakentine~~ at "J" in Station at Lakentine when they will march under the Senior Officer or NCO to destination.

9. Synchronization of Watches. Lieut Baker will report to Brigade Hdqrs. at Starting Point at 8.05 am for the synchronization of watches.

10. Advance Parties. 1 Senior NCO & 1 man per Coy, 1 NCO & 1 man from Batt. HQ & 1 NCO each from Transport & One Stores will parade at OR. at 6.40 am under Lt Wilkinson and Interpreter and proceed to destination to take over billets reporting to Billet Warden.

ACKNOWLEDGE.

SECRET.   OPERATION ORDERS No 24.   COPY No 2
                    9th (Northumberland Hussars) Bn Northumberland Fusiliers   0024

1. MOVE — The Battalion will proceed by route march to WAVANS and BEAUVOIR-RIVIERE to day

2. ROUTE — REBREUVIETE – FREVENT – VACQUERIE – LE BOUCQ.

3. TIME OF PARADE — Parade 7.50 a.m. in column of route on road outside Guard Room in following order:-
"C" Coy Bn HQ Dr, Band "B" Coy "A" Coy "D" Coy.
Transport will march in rear of the Battalion. Head of column to be opposite guard room facing N.W.

4. ROUTINE —
Reveille   5.0 a.m.
Sick Parade 5.30 a.m.
Breakfast   6.0 a.m.
Dinners   EN ROUTE. To be served at 12.50 p.m.

5. OFFICERS VALISES, MESS KIT etc — Will be packed ready for collection by 7.0 a.m.

6. BILLETS. — Will be left clean and tidy.

7. REAR PARTIES — The Sanitary Corporal and 2 men per Coy will be left behind to see that all billets are left clean. They will assemble at Starting point Cross Roads immediately North of N in WAMIN at 10.30 a.m. and march under the Senior Officer or N.C.O. to destination

8. MARCHING OUT STATES — To be rendered to Orderly Room by 7.0 a.m. prompt.

9. Synchronization of WATCHES. — 2/Lieut Baker will report at Starting Point at 8.15 a.m. to Brigade Major for the Synchronization of watches. He will also hand to Brigade Major the marching out state of the Battalion

10. ADVANCE PARTIES — 1 Senior N.C.O. and 1 man per Coy, 1 N.C.O. and 1 man from Battn HQ Dr and 1 N.C.O. each from Transport and Q.M. Stores will parade at O.R. at 6.0 a.m. under 2/Lieut Wilkinson and Interpreter and proceed to destination to take over billets reporting to Town Major

ACKNOWLEDGE.

Dated 26 March 1918.

                                                    [signed] Drysdale
Copies To
No 1. War Diary   13. Intelligence
  2. Retained   14. M.O.
  3. Commanding Officer
  4. 2nd in Command   2/Lieut Adjutant
  5-8 Companies   9th (Northd Hussars) Bn Northd Fus
  9. Q.M.
  10. T.O.
  11. R.S.M.
  12. Mess Cook

[SECRET]   MOVEMENT ORDER No. 25.   COPY No.   OOR5

1. MOVE
The 103rd Infantry Brigade will entrain at FREVENT on 28th inst:
The 9th (N.H) Bn Northd Fusiliers will proceed by No. 8 train leaving at 4.14 am and will march via VILLERS L'HOPITAL and BONNIERES to entraining station.

2. PARADE
Time 11.45 pm In column of route as follows:-
A Coy, Band, B Coy in the village on the WAVANS-BEAUVOIR RIVIERE road. Head of A Coy to be at cross roads on the main DOULLENS road.
Battalion H.Q. C and D Coys on their alarm posts by the Church.

3. TRANSPORT
3 Cookers, 1 Water Cart, 4 Lewis Gun limbers and the mess Cart and pack animals will leave at 10.30 pm and proceed to entraining station under the Quartermaster via NOEUX - VACQUERIE LE BOUCQ and LIGNY SUR CANCHE. They will proceed by No. 7 train leaving at 5.14 am.

4. OFFICERS CHARGERS
Will proceed with Battalion at 11.45 pm

5. RATIONS
For 28th will be carried on the man and on the Cookers. Rations for 29th have been dumped at the entraining station and will be loaded in bulk on No. 8 train under arrangements to be made by the Quartermaster who will report to the Adjutant when they are loaded up.
Water Carts to be filled before leaving billets

6. OFFICERS MESS KIT
To be dumped at R.Q.M Stores by 10 pm. It will be conveyed in the mess Cart.

[SECRET] OPERATION ORDER No. [COPY No]

DO 25A

1. MOVE. The 103rd Inf: Bde will move to-day. The 5/(NH) Bn: N.W.H. Inf: will move to ESTAIRES.

2. PARADE. Time 1.15 pm. In column of route as follows:
A Coy, Band, Bn HQ's, B Coy, C Coy, D Coy. Transport will march in rear of the Battn.
Head of column to be opposite the Estaminet at VERTE RUE near Battn HQ's.

3. ROUTE. VERTE RUE – LA COURONNE – NEUF BERQUIN – ESTAIRES.

4. OFFICERS MESS KIT. The mess C.R.A will call for Officers messkit commencing with D Coy at 12.30 pm prompt.

5. ADVANCE PARTY. 2nd Lt WILKINSON, 1 Senior N.C.O per Coy + 1 N.C.O from Bn HQ's + Transport will parade at Bn HQ's at noon + will proceed to destination + take over billets reporting on arrival to the Town Major.

6. RATIONS. The Refilling Point for rations for consumption on 30th inst. will be

(878) W1. W8811/M2754 (E. 1851) 25,000 Pads. 10/17. M. & B., Ltd.   Army Form **C348** (Pads)

MEMORANDUM.

From | To

Date..............................191 |

at Cross Roads, South of T in ESTAIRES
at 3 p.m.

MEALS   Teas will be served on arrival in
         billets.

BILLETS OC's Coys are responsible for seeing
         that their billets are left supremely
         clean & tidy.

BILLETING Will be rendered to OK by 6 p.m
RETURNS   tonight.

ACKNOWLEDGE   Date 29/3/18

COPIES TO:-

   1 War Diary
   2 Retained.
   3 CO.
   4 2nd in C
   5-8 Coys.
   9 QM + TO
   10 RSM.

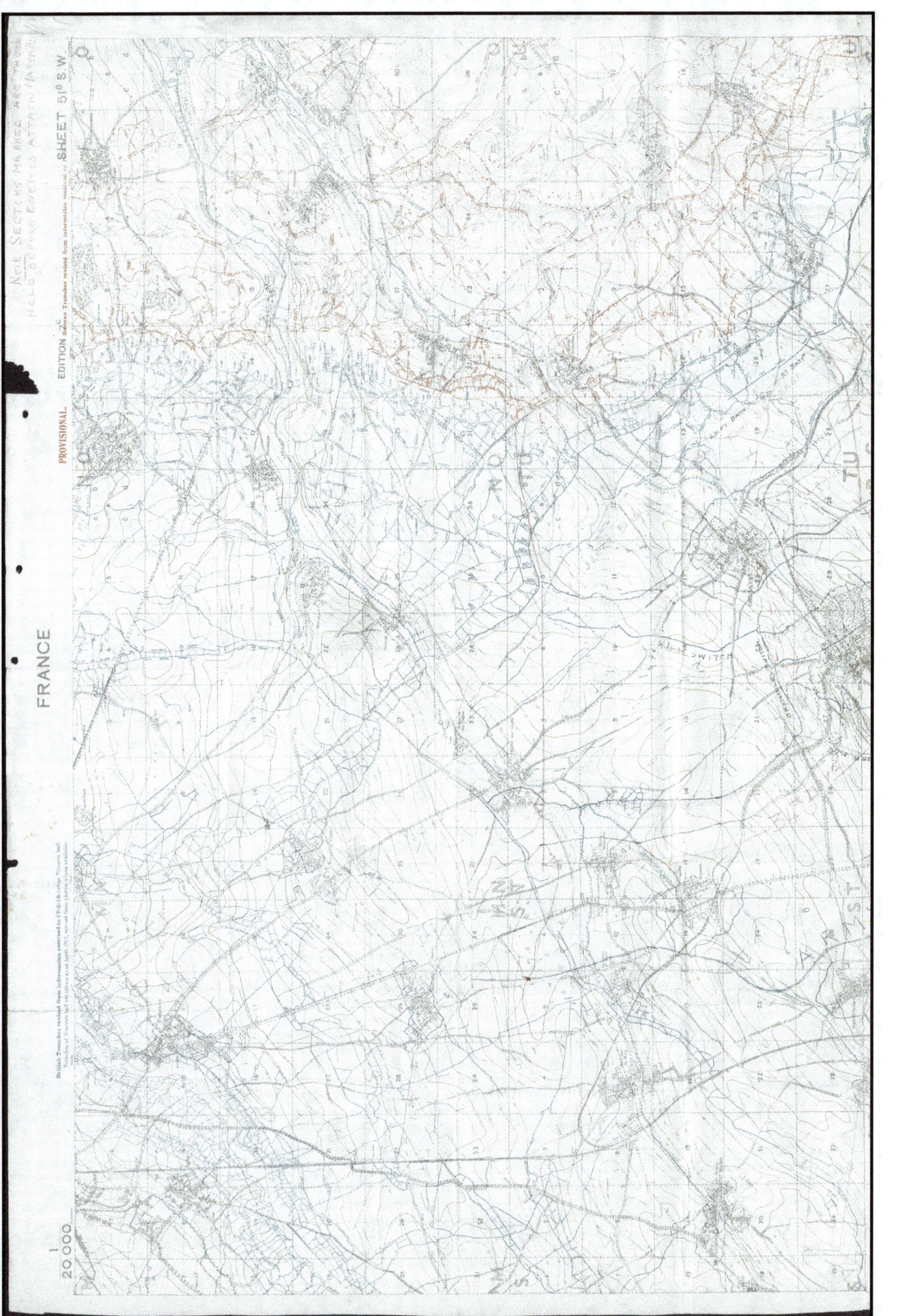